Praise for Lee Dunne

*Lee Dunne is witty and engaging,
he can stop you in your tracks*
The Sunday Times

One of the most unusually gifted artists I have ever met
Jose Quintero

Dunne writes in a wholly modern idiom, racy and vivid
Evening Standard

Most novelists waffle too much. Lee Dunne never does.
Alan Prior, The Stage

*His novels are a genuine contribution to
sociological literature.*
John Jordan, Hibernia

*He made a name for himself due to his characters' liberal use
of swear words and their raunchy encounters. No less than
seven of his books and two of his films were struck down by
the censor, earning him the dubious honour of being the most
banned author in Ireland*
Ireland on Sunday

*Dunne's virtue is that he writes in the absolutely authentic
voice of Dublin…and by God he can write*
Sheffield Morning Telegraph

D1150796

About the Author

Lee Dunne was born in Dublin in 1934. He has written twenty-two books, including the critically acclaimed novels *Goodbye to the Hill, Paddy Maguire is Dead* and *Does Your Mother*. Eight of his novels, along with two films, were banned in Ireland. An extraordinarily prolific writer, Lee has written an astonishing 2,000 radio and television scripts for shows such as *Harbour Hotel, Konvenience Korner, Callan, Troubleshooters, Fair City* and *Kennedys of Castleross*.

At the age of 69, Lee earned an honours Masters Degree from IADT.

My Middle Name is Lucky

Lee Dunne

Killynon HouseBooks

First published 2006 by Killynon House Books Ltd.

ISBN: 1-905706-04-9

ISBN: 978-1-905706-04-4

A CIP catalogue record for this book is available
from the British Library

Cover design and text layout by Agnieszka O'Toole

Printed and bound in Denmark by Nørhaven Paperback

KILLYNON HOUSE BOOKS
Killynon House, Turin, Mullingar, Co. Westmeath, Ireland
Website: www.killynonhousebooks.com
Email: khbooks@iol.ie

Acknowledgements

For my friend Bill Cullen for his encouragement and for launching this book, even though he'll do a roast on the night! Thanks pal!

I would like to thank Agnieszka O'Toole for her cover design which I love.

To my publisher, friend and devoted editor, Jason O'Toole, all my thanks for his loyalty to my work.

Dedications

Always for Maura.

And for Brigid Kelly, the first person ever to encourage me as a writer when I was thirteen-years-old.

Also for Vincent Smith the quintissential 'Harry Redmond' and for my God Daughter, Lee Smith.

For Ivan and Orla and Polly, close to our hearts.

And in memory of the late Constance(Connie) Smith, a "Hill Baby" like myself who starred in Hollywood movies and helped me keep my own dream alive. R.I.P

chapter one

A memory that stuck right up front in the mind was the moment in the musical 'Forty Second Street' when Warner Baxter, the director, tells Ruby Keeler, the chorus girl, who is going on last minute as understudy to the Leading Lady: 'You're going out there a nobody, come back a star!'

So you've worked it out for yourself that I was a born romantic coming into this world with my heart on my sleeve even though I was in the nude at the time.

It didn't take too long for the romantic, crazy part to show. Come on, you have a seven year old kid living with seven other people in two rooms who starts telling his family and anybody else who'll listen that he's going to be a writer – you can hardly be surprised he is regarded as not being *the full shilling*.

So there I was, a nutcase who didn't hear anything at school because he was writing stories in his head and starring in these movies in his head when he should have been listening to Irish and arithmetic in which he had no interest whatsoever. Like I didn't want to be a Civil Servant or work in a bank, and I resented the fact that our English classes were shorter than the Gaelic sessions. So I got nowhere at school and I didn't care because I was busily hooked into the dream as I stepped out along my barefoot way.

As a kid I heard the great Al Jolson singing 'There's A Broken Heart for Every Light on Broadway' and I loved that song. It was so romantic and nobody was better than Jolson when it came to ladling on the emotion. Little did I know that one day I'd remember that song while I was standing on Broadway thinking 'Yeh Al and one of them is mine!'

I can tell you now that the colour of my hair has changed, that these days I tend to wear shoes out of doors, but I go on being dedicated to the dream, the incredible unchanging fantasy that is the writer's life. This is where you exist between words and ideas, dreams and nightmares as you keep climbing towards the top of the mountain, your own personal Parnassus. This is where the gods go laughing for you because in your own way pal, you've never quit on the dream and you are wise enough not to give time or attention to wondering where the madness comes from in the first place.

And maybe, just maybe, they knew that even when you got to the age of seventy-one with a respectable professional writing career to your credit you would somehow have held onto the feeling that you are just starting out.

I happen to believe that when a kid's parents don't get along, he is bound to find somewhere to hide away from the angry silence that is so abusive to your hearing heart. This is what I did anyway – I found an escape hatch through dreaming of scribbling and being some kind of star.

My mother Katy Rogers and my father Mick Dunne were incompatible. In those days the private reasons for the battle of the sexes weren't talked about and parents seemed to be unaware that the oil spill of their shared intolerance wasn't in the least way conducive to what you could call a home life. In a nutshell there was no such thing as a home life in the house as we called the Dublin Corporation flat we were squeezed into at a complex called Mount Pleasant Buildings. Even though the two eldest brothers were gone to England there were still four of us plus my parents existing in a flat the size of a shoebox.

So, like most people at our level of society we shuffled along in a life that was not much fun for any of us. My father

– a decent skin – who never got over the gas that hurt his lungs and his heart during his teen-time soldiering in the First World War – and Katy had different ideas about what bed was for. Rose, my only sister, heard from Ma how he wanted to jump into bed all the time, while, she, mourning child, a baby girl who died as she was being born, had shut up shop.

No need to draw you a picture of the fireworks that were a part of the day to day. It's a tough way to live. Your people are at each others throats over something that has nothing to do with you. But you can end up cramping in fear as your father – a guy you love in the worst way – comes in the door, because you know that you can rely on the violent language of intolerance to start all over again within minutes. Like you can love your father yet wish that next time he goes out, that he won't come back. Of course your heart goes out to him – every penny coming in the door is through his kids. Rose delivered milk until Michael took over – twice a day before and after school. Then it was my turn, Ma desperately need-ed the *five shillings a week wages* while I kept the ten pence (at this time there were two hundred and forty pence in a pound or twenty shillings) which I got from a very good Catholic woman for whom I delivered papers while I was doing the milk. She thought this was a fair wage for deliver-ing a heap of newspapers – I disagreed and to balance things up I robbed magazines, cigarettes and anything I could get away with which I sold to somebody or other with a charge in it that had to come from my own anger.

So there was no home life, none, this claim backed up by the fact that I never once saw my parents go out the door in each other's company, and I mean not once. This had hurt me from my first noticing it – other kids parents went out together even if it was only once in a while to the Prinner or the Stella to see a film from the cheap seats. Some went to Mass together, but not from 162 Mount Pleasant Buildings they didn't.

It was like the people in our flat were never really together, like, we never did anything as a family. Even my first ever day at the seaside – myself and my kid brother, Brendan, were taken by John O'Toole's Ma along with him and his brothers Whacker and Gary who lived in Rugby Villas right by the flats. A few years later when I was drowning at that same spot, John O'Toole, a big kid who could swim like a fish, dived into the sea and dragged me out.

Twenty five years on he hailed me one night while I was driving my cab in London. He was barely friendly when I reminded him who I was – he dismissed my thanks for saving my life – he seemed bereft of the memory – and hurried away from me as though he was trying to get away from the past or something, and I never saw him again.

I've never forgotten that day at Williamstown because I had a great time. Mrs O'Toole bought boiling water from a dealer and she made tea that was the best I had ever tasted. My mother didn't like tea – she was addicted to the cuppa coffee as she called it and I went the same route.

When there is nothing much happening where you're at, I suppose you're bound to go somewhere else for a bit of action. I went into my head with the stories that never quit and I sang a fair bit while I was out working. We had a radio now at two shillings a week and I found I could remember any song once I heard it a couple of times. I didn't chant on the home front – you tried anything new at 162 and you usually got put down for it.

I was steeped in luck because I did a Mickey Mouse paper round in the mornings along with the milk delivery. This put me in the privileged position where I could nick a couple of comics a week without having to shell out any readies and I got into serious reading of The Hotspur and The Champion, gobbling up the stories of Wilson (where did he come from?) and Smith of the Lower Third (my first glimpse of life in a public school) and Rockfist Rogan, R.A.F. Not forgetting The Man Tamer from Muskrat (one hundred and eighty pounds of solid bone and muscle) and last but by no means least, Punch McPhee, The Fighting Sea Cook.

These stories were my *somewhere else*, each of them a place I could escape to and be learning something at the same time. And before long they led me to my first books which became highways to places and situations that fired my imagination and left me always wanting more and more of the same. Like, when I was in a plane with Biggles (by Captain W.E.Johns) there was no scent of the flats on my gansey because it was a flak jacket and I was too busy in the action to be thinking about where I lived. In the Battle of Britain I played my part, the furthest thing from my mind being the battlefield of the day to day life that I hated from my earliest moments of memory.

By the time I reached thirteen I had read short stories by Somerset Maugham and the Yukon tales of Jack London, and I was in love with the Reading Room in the Public Library sitting across from the Town Hall clock on Rathmines Road.

When I was twelve I got myself a job on Saturdays as a butcher's delivery boy, earning five shillings for a twelve hour day. This came with the *Butcher's Wrap-Up* – all the leftover bits of meat and fat and bones which provided great Sunday stew for the two years between the age of twelve until I got my proper job at fourteen and had to work the five and a half day week.

I was also a part-time gardener and *general chancer*, giving Ma most of what I earned and I was always on the lookout to make a few bob. I felt I had to help Katy who, for all her explosive ways, went on battling the odds to keep us from being evicted. The rent of our flat was only three shillings a week but she was always in arrears, always worried about money.

Somehow she fed us day to day on a diet of spuds, baked beans, porridge, and she made great rice pudding. This kind of grub along with *tuppence* worth of daily broken biscuits and the four pints of milk I stole and drank every day, while

I was working for Nellie Rafter, helped me become a tough and wiry kid even if I was about as broad across the chest as a kipper herring.

At this time I was very vain about my looks – Ma used to say I'd wash my face away because I hated to be dirty and was always at the cold tap cleaning my face and hands. One time she accused me of just doing it to look in the triangle of broken mirror that stood in the ledge in our scullery 'because you're so *'beauteeful'*. I just kept my mouth shut because there was more truth to her accusation that she was aware of.

This vanity thing was one of the reasons I hated fighting in the street. The kids around the place were always at it, the least thing and there'd be a punch-up, two street-arabs like myself trying to beat the crap out of each other. I managed to avoid a lot of fights because I didn't care if some kids thought me a coward. Whatever they thought meant nothing to me, but I could be goaded into a fight, some won, some lost, by any kid that called me Leo the Lion.

Around the age of twelve, I was so fed up fighting kids about my name that I changed it to Lee – an unofficial act, no papers were signed or statutes altered. Some years later I came to see it as a rejection of my parents' way of life, but at the time I just didn't want bruises and cut lips all the time which you were likely to get even if you won another stupid fight.

Needless to say everybody thought, once more with feeling, that I was nuts and it took a full two years before my family finally began calling me by my chosen name. I think all kids should be just given a number until they're old enough to choose the name they want for themselves.

At thirteen I was interested in girls and praise the Lord they were certainly interested in me. But the attraction they had for me was like nothing compared to my need to be in the library with my head bent over another book.

That Reading Room was a house of books, a home of all the books I couldn't afford to buy, and a place of escape and tranquillity that was beyond money or possessions. You could have taken a bite out of the silence which like meat and butter and any kind of cake was beyond scarce on the home front.

Presenting myself at the library the first time I got some funny looks, and when I was leaving after a few hours reading I could see the staff making sure I hadn't a book or two stuffed up my gansey.

At this time my family couldn't borrow a book from the Public Library. You had to be a householder, as in owning your own house to be allowed do that. Or your application for a library ticket had to be signed by a householder as a guarantee that you would bring the book back and Ma wouldn't let me ask anybody to do that.

So my father, a truly decent man who had also fought in the War of Independence and the Civil War and had been wounded in both, could not take a book out of the library. The soldier home from the pointless killing fields of Europe and Ireland – a bullet in his back that he would take with him to his grave – was being told by the powers that be you are not worthy pal.

Down all the years since that time I have had to forgive myself for the bile that from time to time arose in my throat over this monstrous treatment of those who had become the have-nots through no fault of their own.

Make no mistake about it the poor and the dispossessed, the underprivileged in our country were treated as second-class citizens. I used to gag with anger when I heard this crap about our country being *the Land of Saints and Scholars*. It might have appeared to be this paradise to the chosen few but a just society it most certainly was not. And as this angry teenager watched the rich get richer and the poor stay poor, I had my own name for Ireland – *the land of thieves and robbers*.

In the library I read 'War and Peace' by Count Leo Tolstoy – what an amazing book. All the long drawn out Russian names did cause me some problems so I called the important characters Ryan and Murphy and so on, because this was an almighty read for a young guy who had cut his teeth on Captain W.E. Johns' 'Biggles' and Jack London's 'Call of the Wild'.

Before long I came upon 'The Great Gatsby' by F. Scott Fitzgerald who was probably as well educated as Tolstoy but chose to write in the modern idiom. Not that he let you forget he had a classical mind and the kind of writing ability that made me read the book over and over. I loved the book so much I vowed I would always have a copy by my side wherever life took me and I've managed to keep that promise made to myself all those years ago, well mostly. Sometimes I'd give my latest copy to somebody who had never heard of Scott Fitzgerald believing their life would be the richer for having met him. But before long I'd go and buy another copy simply because it felt right to be in his company in that way.

While the Reading Room at the library was a very important place to me it was going to *the pictures* that saved my life. For four pence – 4D– in *The Prinner* – The Princess Cinema, you could see a double-bill, say a western and a thriller, while for 6D in The Stella you got adventure stories and musicals and of course love stories.

By the time I was twelve I was reading my name on the screen where it said *Written by* so you see I was fantasising about scribbling for a crust, before I ever wrote anything. This mad dreaming thing stemming from a fascination with the stars I loved – Edward G Robinson (Edward G to me) and Cagney and Bogart (we hadn't got around to calling him Bogey at that time) and my early wrist jobs flew on the images of Janet Blair and Lana Turner and dozens of other beauties

I was probably about thirteen when the only teacher I had ever respected encouraged me to go on writing but not before he had given me six of the best on each hand for doing it while he was trying to teach me Long Division.

Mr. Gallagher was a Corkman and the Headmaster at Tranquilla Boys National School which I attended for three and a half years after my mother – me having told her I would kill myself if she didn't get me away from St. Mary's on Richmond Hill where the brutality turned my stomach. Ma had slapped my face, recognising my drama queen act since she herself was no stranger to throwing shapes, but she did get me to the school on Upper Rathmines Road for which I will always be grateful.

Mr. Gallagher was standing over me before I realised it, so taken was I by the story that seemed to be flowing from my pencil. As I looked up to find him there I automatically turned over the copy book and put my two hands on it.

'What are you writing?'

I don't know where it came from but I heard myself say: 'It's private, sir.'

This kind of behaviour was unheard of then – we are talking about 1946-47 B.E. That means *before everything* which was a time when kids were told to shut up by parents, *little pigs should be seen and not heard* being a euphemism for *nobody has the slightest interest in what you have to say.* So for a kid of twelve going on thirteen it would have been a brave gesture but I had no sense of that as the Headmaster moved up the classroom beckoning for me to join him.

He indicated that I should hold out my hand and he gave me six of the best with a cane that was in the whole of its health. Then he motioned for me to produce the other hand which I did and he repeated the punishment. Then he told me this was for lack of respect and lack of attention and then he again asked me what I had been writing.

Even though my hands were stinging I felt no animosity to this man. He was very decent to the boys and I knew I was some kind of favourite with him. And having caught me red handed he was more than entitled to leave me in the same state after the caning.

'I'm writing a story, sir,' I said quietly, half hoping the

other kids wouldn't hear it.

'May I read it?' he asked.

'Yes sir,' I said and I went back to the desk and fetched back the copy book. I opened it and handed it to him and he motioned for me to go back and sit down which I did. Then he sat down and took a few minutes while he read what I'd been writing.

He kept me back after school and sat me down in a front desk so that he could talk to me from behind the table he used as a worktop. He told me then that he was very impressed with my story – an adventure story, about a boat taken by pirates, in which the hero – a boy of twelve – alerts the Coast Guard Officers – they have sailed close to check that all is in order – by hoisting the boats flag Upside Down. After which the capture of the pirates is practically a formality and the boy is a real hero.

Mr. Gallagher thought the story well told and was happy to see that I could write as well as I did. He encouraged me to keep on studying and writing, and above all to read the classics and the great novelists. And up to the day we broke up for the summer hols six months short of my fourteenth birthday – my last day there at Tranquilla – he never took a cane to me again though I might have deserved a good larruping on more than one occasion.

In January 1949, at the age of fourteen, I began working in a proper job as an office boy in a firm of insurance brokers at Commercial Buildings on Dame Street. I lied with impunity in the interview – adding two years to my age, knowing I could get away with that. Had I told the bald truth about my lack of education and had I given my own address as opposed to that of my friend, Brigid Kelly, I would not have got the job. Living in certain Dublin Corporation flat developments turned you into some kind of pariah in the minds of most *respectable* people so I did what I had to do to get to work on the understanding that if I was caught out later and got the hammer, well, fuck it, at least I had actually got the job. The truth was that the truth about me and my life would have made that impossible at that time in Ireland.

Lying was part of my life in those days and I can admit that I wasn't leading a just life since I was robbing food and milk, stealing books on almost a daily basis. I had no problem about being a book thief and I resented *the haves* to such a degree that I would willingly have robbed them and their houses. Except that I knew if I got caught it would trample on the only thing Ma seemed to have left, which was that none of her kids had ever been arrested or had even brought a Flatfoot to the door.

Although I started work in the office early in the new year, by which time all night school terms had started, I signed up for an English class in Rathmines Technical School, which was next door to my own personal reading room in the library.

I met some nice looking girls there, girls that weren't behind the door about coming forward. But I was intent on improving myself, wanting to know about grammar and syntax and all the other stuff you hadn't got to when you left Primary School at the age of thirteen and a half. By now I was convinced that I would be some kind of writer though truly I was ignorant of how to go the right way about anything connected with writing or with literature and all that stuff. But I knew that when I sat down with a pen or a pencil in my hand something started to happen and I felt very good about this.

I knew I was a bit odd, always had been, like, not that many kids start thinking they wrote the film they just paid 4D to see in the Prinner picture house on Rathmines Road. The thing is that I wasn't scared about being the way I was, which was just as well because the dreams were, if anything, getting bigger by the year. It had got to the stage where I'd sent off a few offerings to magazines and one to the national radio station. Then one Friday in that summer of '49 I got a sign that my being some kind of dreamer wasn't necessarily an incurable disease.

On what I call *that fateful lunchtime* – for a few minutes – I was over my own personal moon just from hearing my first poem read out on national radio. This was unusual around where we lived. People in *Corpo flats* only got their name on the wireless if they were the defendant in a court case.

My immortal words were heard on a Sponsored Programme – commercial radio having arrived on the Irish scene a few years earlier.

One of the first sponsored programmes at lunchtime was the Imco Show. For fifteen minutes every Friday, Imco Cleaners and Dyers advertised their services across the radio waves.

The show was compered by Eamon Andrews – at the start of a career that would take him to the top on television over in England – and a newspaperman called Terry O'Sullivan.

The two guys were called *Spotless* and *Stainless* and they made corny gags and played records, their gimmick being that they encouraged listeners to send in poems praising or, if the mood was on you, criticising the programme.

I wrote a poem giving the two guys a hard time. I can remember only the last couple of lines which – since the show went out on Friday, and this day has always been connected through rain with Sunday – might make sense – so here it goes:

Wet Friday, wet Sunday, so they say,
We wish that Imco would change their day
If they did they would have more friends
And we would have more fine weekends.

As the poem was read out my mother, hearing my name as we ate our fish and chips, slapped my face in reaction: 'What have you gone and done now?'

Sitting there in my first suit, bought for work – Burtons Best at two pounds ten shillings, am I a model for an Al

Capone of the future? Yeh, sure! But then Ma was nothing if not dramatic. My primary concern was to quieten her down so that we could hear my magic words being read out by Eamon Andrews, my prize for this opus being a voucher for a pounds worth of dry cleaning.

Magic words indeed! My mother would have put up quite an argument to contest this idea – she had her own dream, only it was for me. To make her life complete, all I had to do was stay in the nice, permanent office job, work hard, study, get promoted, *stay away from drink,* get a nice respectable girl, save up, get married, have children, and never look crooked. Not much when you say it quick. That was all that the Ma wanted.

Of course I couldn't tell her that I already hated working in an office even though I was well treated and I could handle the job. Mind you, I did have one problem in the shape of the general office manager, a guy called Murphy, who would never suffer from piles since to my mind he was the perfect arsehole.

It wasn't easy living up to the white collar bit since I had only the one shirt. Some mornings when I got in from doing the paper round – this paying the instalment on the bike – I had to wash my shirt collar with Sunlight soap (which had to be made from petrol or something) before riding into the office with the collar still damp around my neck.

On that special Friday you'd believe I was excited but so fed up with Ma for her mouth and her right hander that I actually couldn't finish my 'One and One. And this was the highlight meal of the week and came from the same chipper where I last spoke to Connie Smith just before she was scooped up to be a movie star.

That's right, my sister's school mate, Connie, who lived on the other side of *the buildings* had won *a Film Stars Double* beauty contest in Dublin. She had entered – on an application form she found in a girls magazine – as Hedy Lamarr – and part of her winner's prize was a film test in London. And she would go on to play the maid servant that finds *The Mudlark*, played by Andrew Ray under the dining table at Windsor Castle just before Queen Victoria is to sit down to dinner in the film of that name. From there she would become Constance Smith and go on to star in the movie *Taxi* with Hollywood legend Dan Dailey and later with Larry Parks in a story called *Tiger By The Tail*.

That such a miracle could happen in the life of our own. Connie Smith had made me more than ever determined not to settle for what I called the ordinary life. I knew I had to go out there and claim fame and fortune and anything else that was going for a guy with some kind of writing talent wrapped around an imagination that never quit, the same fella having a neck like a jockey's ballocks.

And no matter how Ma felt about me and my dreams I knew I wouldn't let anything stop me, not now. My God, Connie had gone from living in a flat exactly the size of ours – her father dead from Tuberculosis – to a career as a movie star. Well, you better believe I was more determined than ever to do whatever it took to follow in her golden footsteps.

Anyway, to make a long story interminable, I sold my prize – the dry cleaning voucher – for fifteen shillings to Mrs. McInerney who lived across the concrete hall in the concrete flat block we lived in with iron bars in place of windows on the landing above the open hallway in from the street. If I mention the open rubbish bin in the entrance to the flats I do so only in fairness to the genius who probably won a prize of his own for coming up with such a brilliant, life enriching idea.

Mrs. Mac, the neighbour across the hall was okay, and as I hit my teens I had a lot of respect for her. She was a Catholic like just about everybody else in Mount Pleasant Buildings, but she'd had just two kids whereas everybody else around was banging them out like loaves of bread.

Even Ma, who shut up shop as much as she could, delivered seven, while a neighbour overhead had ten, and a woman on the top floor had eighteen.

I know, the mind boggles, but it's true. Incidentally, there was an age gap of fifteen years between Mrs Mac's sons so she had either found a miraculous cure for pregnancy or her husband had taken a long time to recover from their first adventure into conjugal rights. Either way, the lovely darling bought my voucher for fifteen shillings thereby becoming the first person I had ever known who actually paid money to have their clothes cleaned.

In reality that poem on the radio was no big deal but when I remember how many people congratulated me just for getting my name on the radio and for being able to write a poem and have the cop-on to get it into the radio station, I felt like some kind of writer, and I loved the feeling which – along with the growing belief that I was going to leave the job and Ireland before long – kept my spirits up and ready for action when the right moment presented itself.

My second reason for feeling I was a writer was the sale of an article of five hundred words to the *Times Pictorial* – this was published by the *Irish Times* – which paid me the princely sum of fifteen shillings. Not a lot you might well think but when you consider I'd been earning *five shillings a week* for doing a twice-daily milk round, you might see why I was delighted with the fee from the paper.

The idea for the article had come to me while I was having a bottle of cider in a pub on the corner of Stephen's Green and South King Street. In the upstairs lounge where you got some tasty looking women who were *gamey* just by being in the room, there was a mirror behind the bar. The barman, Eddie, a decent skin who'd had most of the women that were regulars in the lounge, asked any foreigner that came in to leave him a note or a coin which he glued to the glass, giving them a drink on the house to cement the fair exchange. And to his credit, the money in the mirror never ceased to be a talking point, each new note causing a response and some kind of exchange about the country it came from and an interest in finding out where the hell was the newest one most people had never heard of.

Without giving the story that much thought, I found myself writing that the root of all evil comes in all shapes and sizes, and from every corner of the world. I can't remember the exact text but the angle was, in my opinion, what sold it.

I wasn't surprised that I was handy with the words – after all, I'd been addicted to reading from the time I was seven years old. So, leaving out the movies and books and comics and newspapers – not forgetting music and song – words were my main interest in life. And though I was penniless, stone-flat broke come every Monday morning – those times can seem like halcyon days thanks to the burning dream inside me. That is until I remember how the hormones woke up to take the best laid dreams of youth and turn them into sexual fantasies that I would try to turn into reality on almost a full time basis during the next twenty or thirty years.

Before long I was to discover that most scribblers didn't make any money but instead of depressing me this made me feel that I was pretty gifted to have sold my first two pieces.

I have no idea where this penchant to opting for the positive came from but I can't deny that the minute a negative thought arose, I seemed to get the other side of the coin, the positive slant, somehow smart enough not to second guess the bonus this was.

This didn't mean that the situation changed just because you were in a positive frame of mind, but it helped me feel better generally and I retain the habit to this day. Looking back at all the sure opportunities that dissolved into thin air, I feel lucky that I was some kind of cockeyed optimist.

At that time in my life I seemed to be surrounded by people who were down in themselves at every given opportunity, of which there is no scarcity when you are living below the bottom rung of the success ladder. I'd have to say that my parents were entitled to be pessimistic and the same thing goes for most of the neighbours but what bothered me was that a lot of guys of my own age had no expectation that life was going to change in any way for the better.

I didn't go on about the way my own situation had taken a turn for the better and within two years of starting the office job I had quit hanging around with anybody from the flats. I was making new friends at dances in a couple of tennis clubs and up on Rathmines Road which a lot of guys like myself had come to regard as our personal strip. We hung out in a confectionery shop facing the library and next door to Campions great boozer where I could get a bottle of cider in the snug. I did this by handing the money in through a box hole while I stood off to one side. This manoeuvre gave the barman, who knew me well, the excuse that he couldn't see your face if anybody asked were you old enough to be drinking there.

Most of the other guys drank stout but I couldn't stand the taste of it. I liked cider because it tasted like apples and it made your head buzz faster than Guinness did. As time went on and I was still milling the scrumpy, one of the older customers gave me a warning about drinking that *madman's soup*. Others were there to back him up saying that it stole your mind. I acted like I was interested but as far as I was concerned they made it sound even better than I thought it was and I never quit drinking the stuff until I quit drinking period, a long, long time later.

In Rathmines I knew guys you could talk to about books and films and one of them, Michael Cunningham is a mate of mine to this day and we are still in constant touch through the beauty of Email. And still remembering many of those old movies we saw together as teenagers back in Dublin and later when we shared a flat in London.

To Mike Cunningham – Cunnyer – and me, films were electric. Certainly they had captured me and my imagination while I was still in short trousers. From Roy Rogers and Buck Jones to James Cagney, Edward G, and the main man Humphrey Bogart, I was with them all the way, from the sad-

dles to the limos, from the six gun duels to the spraying
Tommy-guns of the gangsters in the Prohibition stories that
filled the cinema screens for many years. And the actresses
that came across our eyes to fuel fantasies that remained firm
even after some of those beautiful women were dead and
gone.

Janet Blair was my first photo turn-on and I was only thirteen at the time. She was wearing a swimsuit on the front of
a motion pic magazine which I nicked from a shop. I had that
cover, folded over and held together with the sticky paper
from postage stamps until somebody nicked it on me.

She was just one in a long line that included Lana Turner,
the Sweater Girl, all the way to Jane Russell who increased
the masturbation rate in Rathmines to the point where it
went off the graph.

Fortunately there were Irish girls coming along who were
more than fetching and I always made sure I could buy a girl
a glass of cider when I was out and about looking for a bit of
action.

I also left the 'Mines and went into the city centre where
you could get a woman for five shillings. Crilly's on the quays
and another pub in Talbot Street were hangouts for what we
called semi-professionals, women who subsidised their
drinking by throwing the leg for a few bob. It's fair to say that
this was probably where most of us had what we would call
the first real ride on our journey to sexual experience.

I really liked those women and even though it was hard
finding five bob every week, I rarely missed and more than
once I got one *on the house* when I just couldn't raise the
money. I was so interested in my sex life that I never questioned my growing dependency on the cider to give me
whatever I needed to be brash and bold, which I had learned
made me attractive to the opposite sex. I was good looking
too, which helped a lot, and, yes I did think I was God's gift
to the females. A lot of women and girls went for me and I
got into the pants of those who wanted what I did. I thought

it was the most natural thing in the world, the thing for a young guy with flair to be doing. It never occurred to me that most of it was my way of trying to escape from the flats and overall dark and grey city of Dublin which seemed to me to be some kind of graveyard with lights.

chapter 2

At the risk of being immodest, I believe it was my looks that helped me get away from the flats and I was very happy that this was the case. Like, I had to go, and to get a job on the stage was like a dream come true.

This got under way in 1953 while I was touring Northern Ireland with *Showtime Parade*, part of the small company that took entertainment into the sticks – hence my novel *A Bed in the Sticks* which would present itself in 1968.

We were playing in a small town called Strabane, in County Tyrone, which had been an American army base during the Second World War and I saw black children for the first time in my life. The women were right out front about what they did and didn't want, bolder than many I'd come across even in Dublin.

Anyway, in Strabane, I sang in the first half of the nightly show just as I did everywhere else and like all the performers I wore stage make-up. I was dressed up in a white jacket and black pants and a kind of glittery shirt. This got me a lot of attention but I often felt I wasn't making it as a crooner because I hadn't yet got around to singing Irish songs which went well no matter what town you played.

The pop songs of the day were my bag but country people, many of them still living without electricity – rural Ireland was not *fully turned on* until 1956 – didn't have radios so they weren't familiar with much of the material I was presenting. Nonetheless the females in our audience were very good to me and George Quinn, the great guy running the show, smilingly told me not to burst my heart in the saddle.

It was summer and we were playing in a wooden booth with a canvas roof which we had erected in a few hours to seat two hundred or more people. The audience were gone by now but outside the booth I hear some female voices making a bit of a commotion by calling my name again and again and I see Mae and George exchange a glance that suggests something very unusual is going on.

Moments later there is a loud banging on the wooden wall of the booth and we hear a repeated chanting of 'We Want Lee' which causes me to burst out laughing, without recognising that I'm scared, until later that night.

Not really knowing what else to do we just sat it out until the girls went away home and we were able to make our way out of there. Next day the company was buzzing with what we all regarded as a phenomenal bit of carry-on and from that night on George asked me to go and stand just inside the entrance to our mobile theatre, welcoming all females young and old, and encouraging me to 'smile at every one of them as though you can't wait to get her into bed' which I did as part of the job. I didn't get paid anything more for the effort but there was no night after that when I didn't end up with some willing female, provided I had the energy.

I was working on the touring show because I felt I had something to give as Actor/Singer/Compere while my good looks were no draw-back at all. Having not forgotten what had happened for Connie Smith, I was putting myself out there in a small way, more than willing to take any break that might come my way. The idea of being a movie actor sat there on my left shoulder because I considered acting a cushy way of buying time to write though I knew even then there was no such thing as a free ride.

This truism was never far from my mind during the next five to ten years any more than the belief that I was meant to be a writer. No matter what happened to me, the urge to write never left me. And each and every week, even during the year I gave to The Knowledge to get my cab badge, I sent out my stories and articles religiously, willingly spending the money on stamps and envelopes. And I never despaired even though, despite all my efforts, I failed totally to sell anything for eleven years from the time my article had been printed in the Times Pictorial.

During three years on the road, I worked hard as a Touring Player, singing and acting. I also erected stages and whatever else needed doing on Showtime Parade as we travelled the length and breadth of Ireland.

I'd been very promiscuous since leaving home to go to work on Showtime Parade, never long without a sexual partner for a night or a week or so. My flings never lasted more than that because even if I was in a job I was always moving on in my head and I never kidded any woman that I was anything more than a passing fancy.

My drinking was consistent but up to this time I never lost a job or got in a fight over it. And I can say hand on heart that whatever job I took on I did my best to give value for my wages. Somewhere back in my family on my mother's side there was a Protestant clergyman and I seemed to have been injected with that work ethic that Prods are famous for. And I sent some money home to my mother every week of my life right up to the time I would get married. After that it was not so regular but I was never tight where Katy was concerned and I didn't give a damn if she was putting it on horses or whatever.

My parents were somewhat better off by then since my father finally got work shovelling coal at the Pigeon House power station at the end of Dublin's East Wall where the city limit meets the sea head-on. And I have just remembered that I also worked as a dishwasher, cocktail bartender, Stand-

Up-Comic, Merchant Navy steward, garage attendant and London Taxi Driver.

In all this time it was a rare day that I did not get some words down on paper while my reading continued voraciously even while I was studying for my taxi licence eight and ten hours a day while on The Knowledge of London.

My drinking was now sporadic – I had very little money and I needed a clear head – but when I got a few into me I always ended up by getting drunk. I was also getting laid with every willing female I came across in my pursuit of sexual sensation. I did this with the appetite of somebody that really believed the coupling of male and female had to come from God. Like, it was so great when it worked between two people, surely no lesser deity could have created something so wonderful. And to say I couldn't get enough of it borders on understatement.

Right through the years of endless rejection slips, I went on reading as naturally as I went on taking the next breath. It was my joy to read and I never thought of it as a task or an effort to learn something. I simply read for the sheer joy of soaking up the printed words of those I honoured as worthy scribblers.

I've already mentioned Tolstoy and other greats such as Dostoyevsky, Maxim Gorki whose books I found in a junk shop at Kentish Town while I was riding my bike as I studied The Knowledge. This was not far from Highgate Cemetery where I used to sit and eat a sandwich sometimes by the grave of Karl Marx who actually wrote *Des Kapital* in the British Museum in London.

I was devoted to Somerset Maugham, loved *Cakes and Ale* and *Of Human Bondage*. Maugham took me down the streets and alleyways of South London to the hovels and the grovels of the kind of people you'd only meet in Impressionist paintings.

How I remember *The Keys of the Kingdom* by A.J.Cronin – that man had my heart in his hand from the opening pages of that wonderful novel. The priest in that story was a great man and I believed in him all the way, glad to meet him, a Christian soldier so unlike the priests of my childhood.

I found Ernest Hemingway much to my liking though snobs here and there along my journey put him down as though he was a phoney. They tried to shoot down a man that wrote twelve major novels at a time when there was no television to help him sell books with its *personality chat shows*. A writer who would win the Nobel Prize for *The Old Man and the Sea* and you found critics – people that couldn't write home for money – dismissing him out of hand. It made me laugh while I shook my head in wonder at the gall of some people.

John Steinbeck was high on my list and when I found the work of Thomas Wolfe I fell in love with *Look Homeward Angel*, thinking my god, imagine being able to write like that.

But always I found myself returning to *The Great Gatsby*, maybe the greatest American novel of them all. I've never forgotten *where ashes grow like wheat into ridges and hills and grotesque gardens* and the tragic waste of Jay and Daisy's chapter of the American Dream.

Meanwhile, my own dream was like a bright light shining in my mind and I never for a second lost sight of what I wanted out of my life. Even as I spent a couple of summers in Jersey in the Channel Islands working as a cocktail bartender and even a Singing Bartender – still heavily into casual sex – I made sure I was writing for a couple of hours each day.

Speaking of the casual sex, I never ceased to be amazed by the way female holidaymakers went for the staff in the hotels I worked in. In my case, I served drinks till two maybe three in the morning. This didn't stop some lovely young women sitting waiting for me to close the bar so that we could go to bed together. I'm not complaining even though *the night work* meant that after a quick swim in the afternoons I had to sleep for two or three hours right there on the beach just to catch up.

Then came a girl who didn't go to bed with me because she was old fashioned and wanted to be a virgin on her wedding night. After the summer ended I saw her in London a few times before I sailed for New Zealand. Try though I did, I couldn't get her out of my head and a couple of years later – I was now a registered London Cabby – Jean Allison and I got engaged and we were married in March 1959.

We had a good honeymoon in Cornwall and we came back to our own terraced house in Gowan Avenue, off the Fulham Palace Road between Hammersmith and Putney. And waiting for me in the hallway was another pile of rejection slips.

I took the latest disappointment in my stride, determined that sooner or later I would get something published. I backed up the dream each evening after my days work on the cab by going to work for three or four hours in the kitchen of our home on the portable typewriter I'd bought for just twenty-four pounds.

When I bought the typewriter in Boots I also got a copy of Pitman's Teach Yourself Typing book and I learned to touch type in one marathon sitting of ten hours. Many years later a mate, John Boorman the film director, told me he had learned in the same way and we had a chuckle about that.

I felt very lucky to be a London Cab Driver. Having passed through *The Knowledge* I had my own badge, mine for life, once I didn't tarnish it through bad or criminal behaviour, and that bit of security allowed me to enjoy my writing without the pressure of it having to earn money to help me and my family stay alive.

About a year and a half after my marriage to Jean we were waiting for our first child to be born and I was more excited than I would have thought possible. The very idea of being a father filled me with good cheer, while I vowed to be the very best Da that ever lived.

At this time I saw a letter in the *New Statesman* from a guy called Maurice Girodias who ran a publishing company called Olympia Press in Paris. He claimed to be interested in receiving manuscripts from English writers, 'preferably tending towards the risqué'. I didn't even have to think about it. I was so full of sex – I loved it, I loved thinking about it, and talking about it, and I had always enjoyed reading sexy books. I also believed that it was the reason for just about everything that happened in life, and I knew I could write a horny book, no problem.

I took ten days off the cab to knock out a book called *Hell is Filling Up*, which, as a Roman Catholic, I actually believed even though I had rejected all religion years before and when drunk made no bones about claiming to be an agnostic.

It was about a good looking guy (like me!) arriving at a house in a place called Tatinua, an imaginary city based on Panama where I had been while going to and coming from New Zealand). The guy is after a job ghost-writing a book about a sexy landowner who has a couple of man-eating daughters – not too intellectually demanding, you understand. The romance of it appealed to me, wishful thinking clearly the genesis of what turned out an entertaining sexy thriller.

This was the first book I ever finished and I sent it off to Girodias in Paris, not knowing he had published Brendan Behan and God knows who else under pen-names since his company name was synonymous with pornography.

About six weeks after this I have a leaking gas pipe in the front hall of my house. An engineer from the gas company arrives and rolls back the lino inside the front door to raise the floorboards and deal with the leaky pipe. He does the job, puts the lino back into place and takes off. Next morning the smell is still there. The guy comes back, I decide to hang around, my presence designed to help the soft prick do the job properly this time. So I'm standing right there when he pulls the lino back and I see an oblong envelope lying there on the floorboards. As I bent to pick it up I realised it had come through the letter box the previous day, the guy hadn't noticed it and just put the lino down over it. And it might be there yet if I hadn't felt snotty about his attitude to his job.

The letter was from Maurice Girodias accepting *Hell Is Filling Up* and asking me if I could write him another one straight away. He would pay me $600 advance against royalties on both books and he enclosed a contract which seemed extremely generous to my innocent eye. It didn't matter. I'd have signed my life away to get a book published – even one I wasn't willing to put my name on. Thinking about this I told myself I was keeping my own name for my First Novel if you don't mind. But really, I just didn't think it was a good idea to put my name on what the Americans would call *A Hot Book*, maybe even *A Dirty Book*. So for that first story I used the name Peter O'Neill.

My wife Jean was very impressed, my mates were very impressed, and *let's face it,* I was very impressed. I mean the first book I'd put together, in ten days at that, and the guy was willing to publish it and pay an advance. And he wanted more. Believe me I didn't think it was the sequel to *The Book of Kells* or *Ulysses* or anything like that. It was *a Pot Boiler,* a plane ride, train ride book, all action and sex and violence with the kind of snappy dialogue you got in some of the old movies with Cagney and George Raft and Bogart. What was important about it was the fact that a professional, someone who made his bread by publishing books, was saying *You Can Write.*

I called the second book *The Corpse Wore Grey*, the big twist being that the dead guy was stuffed into a suit of armour which stood there while everybody was running around like blue-arsed flies until inevitably the hallway began to smell like a Gorgonzola factory. Anyway, Girodias bought the book and asked me for another one.

Meanwhile Jean had produced a miracle of her own, our first born child, Sarah, a girl who to this day warms my heart by saying, 'Hi Dad!'

Sarah landed on my heart on July 31st 1961. I held her in my arms in a beautiful kind of joy but awestruck and just a little scared at the same time. Jean was pretty wiped out, she didn't even want to talk about the labour, telling me in a whisper that she didn't think she'd ever be able to have sex again. I let that go by, thrilled more and more by every second of holding our daughter, and without trying I managed to move Jean to tears when I said, 'Thank you for our baby girl.'

Moments later she snorted down her nose at me like a horse as I asked, 'Can we call her Cassidy for Sean O'Casey?'

'No we fucking can't,' Jean warned me. 'We're calling her Sarah. Cassidy Dunne! Jesus!' You could have bottled her derision. 'Who'd do that to a little girl?'

In my own demonic way I was determined to be involved with Sarah from day one. I shared the caring, the night feeds, nappy changing, the lot, leaving out the breastfeeding. I just wanted my daughter to know that her father was there for her too. I thought that would be good for a child. As usual my intentions were the best once I wasn't out of the house, out there in the streets starring as Jack the Lad.

About a year after Sarah was born Jean took an evening job to get some time out of the house and I suspected to get away from me for a few hours. The money she earned took some of the responsibility off my shoulders but I was still driving the cab and writing most evenings. Now I willingly looked after Sarah while Jean went off to the El Cubano, a trendy restaurant in Knightsbridge. I loved feeding and changing my daughter and generally seeing that she was comfortable at all times. Those evenings with just the two of us were among the best times of my life up to then but it would be many years later before I came to see that when I was with Sarah I wasn't looking for anything for me, all I wanted to do was be of service to a child I loved more than my own life.

Hell is Filling Up was produced in a plain cardboard cover with just the title and my pen name on there over the

Olympia Press logo and I got a terrific buzz when I sat reading it. I gave a copy – I was given six complimentary copies – to a mate of mine Jack Connell who ran Finch's pub on the Fulham Road. He didn't put it down and when I told him I had banged it out in ten days he was impressed and expected me to go on to better things. My meeting Connell and becoming a regular in that wonderful pub probably changed the course of my life, and not always for the better.

Through Connell I met writers and painters and sculptors, musicians too, seriously bohemian people who worked hard and played hard and thought the rules were for children of a lesser god. So you might say I landed on my feet.

When *The Corpse Wore Grey* arrived from Olympia Press, it bore the same motif as the first one. With it Girodias sent me a letter enclosing a chapter from a book he was publishing, asking me to study it so that I could get some more heavy breathing into my third.

The pages were designed to raise any guy's blood pressure – a book like this would probably be a big hit among guys who were spending a year on a whaler. I wasn't sure about getting into this. It wasn't part of the route I had dreamed of. In that moment, while I was dithering, Sarah began to whimper in her cot.

In a flash I had her out of there, changed her wet nappy, making sure she was not in any need before I sat down to give her a cuddle. In moments I was overcome with gratitude for all I had. That was when I knew I wouldn't be going along the route that Girodias had mapped out for me, like no way was I going to beat out page after page of gratuitous sex, which is how the first leg of my writing career came to an end.

chapter 3

In the summer of 1964 I was minding Sarah and my son Peter who had been born a year earlier on July 3rd when I felt what I can only call an overwhelming urge to write down a story that somehow seemed to be demanding that I attend to it. I know this sounds a bit arty-farty but if you've come this far with me you will know that is not my way.

I knew right away that the story was bubbling up out of anger. I don't mean just the anger that I was going nowhere fast and drinking too much. Yes, bending the elbow to console myself which just lead to more promiscuous outings with women I picked up in the cab or in Finch's and the Queen's Elm.

The story had been cooking, so it seemed to me, in the anger of my early days. I kept it well hidden under the *Happy Jack* personality that I'd become but some stories didn't fade into the night because you bury them for a decade or two.

When the children were asleep, I called Jean who was still at the El Cubano, assuring her that all was well. She was off me at the minute but I tried to just let her be, not to expect warmth when my latest drinking bout had turned things chilly between us.

We had moved to a four bedroom house at East Sheen, a great place to bring up kids – you had Richmond Park on one side of you and the Thames on the other. And the added bonus that I now had my own room to work in, so with a strong cup of coffee inside me and another by my hand I sat down at my desk and started typing.

From the opening line the words just began to flow and I knew once we were under way that this story was in charge of me as opposed to the other way around.

It was based on my teenage mornings when for three and a half years I rode down the hill past McGrath's pub onto the Ranelagh Road going to work in the insurance office. The hundreds of times I'd said, choking on the vehemence I felt: 'Someday I am going to say goodbye to this fucking place!', wishing something would happen, something, anything that would help me get away from the flats and another Mount Pleasant Monday.

This seemed to be all I had to go on when I sat down but six weeks later, six weeks of evening writing after my days work on the cab, this nagging short story that wouldn't leave me alone had written itself as the novel *Goodbye to the Hill.*

This simple novel would change my life in more ways than one but before I had any inkling of all that would happen to the book I was delighted that my wife loved it.

Dedicating it to Jean might have been a bit of a stroke but it was right, the fair thing to do, after all she had put up with from me in the last year or so. And all in all I felt she was a bit proud of me.

I showed it to a couple of mates from Dublin, painters both, Joe and Kathy Magill. They said it was wonderful, maybe a bit horny for the Irish censor. I didn't care about that. I had no interest in Ireland. Whenever I thought of the place I could still taste the resentment I felt on the night the boat to Holyhead took me away from Dun Laoghaire: 'They should give this fucking country back to the Leprechauns, with apologies!'

The Magills said, 'Try Hutchinson, they published Brendan so maybe they'll go for this.' They were talking about Brendan Behan who was a big mate of theirs. I'd had jars with him a few times but I didn't like the way he put people down so he could raise a laugh from his cronies. But he was *a name* so I dropped the manuscript into Hutchinson Publishers in Great Portland Street, trying real hard to write it off for at least six months since some publishers could take forever to read your opus.

Three weeks later I'm drinking in the Queen's Elm on the Fulham Road wondering why it feels like a part of me is missing. I'm fairly jarred and I think maybe it's Jean, my better part, and my kids I'm thinking about here. Then Jean is there beside me and she hands me a piece of paper. 'A guy rang about your book. That's his phone number.' She is trying to be friendly but she is full of hurt, her face saying, 'What do pubs have that your wife and your kids and your own home can't give you!'

I call this guy Anthony Masters who has telephoned my home to tell me how much he has enjoyed reading my novel. He is so decent about it, praising it very highly and by the time I thank him and wish him all the best I am in fucking tears right there in the pub.

I get out of there and without a thought I get in behind the wheel of my cab and drive home, wanting Jean to be the first to know. She hangs up the phone as I come into the house and when I tell her the news she is civil but gets a cigarette going and tells me she's been talking to her best pal Betty Clarke. She has been asking her is this – the way we are – how marriage has to be? 'Because if it is,' Jean says, emptying her cup of coffee, 'then I don't expect to be married to you till death us do part. When we got married, that's what I wanted. So I'm just letting you know. I have been on your side, positive all the way, even with Dad. If you ever turn me off enough, that'll be positive too. You remember I said that.'

I promise her the sun, moon and stars, wanting to mean that I would never stray, that I would always be there. I say lots of things that it would have been good for a woman to hear if she could believe my words. Jean had only ever needed a halfway decent deal so she let the anger go enough that we made love that night even if we didn't melt into each other the way we used to. Afterwards Jean says with that sound that lets you know she is speaking despite herself, 'Congratulations you bastard!'

The guy at Hutchinson is called Giles Gordon and he tells me they will publish the book! I am totally knocked out. I mean this is not Olympia Press publishing Peter O'Neill. This is one of the world's largest mainstream publishers and they love *Goodbye to the Hill* by Lee Dunne. I swear if I hadn't been sitting down I'd have had to ask for a chair. Then Giles says to me: 'It's autobiography of course.' I tell him no, it's a novel. He's dead surprised. 'Surely it's your life story.'

'Are you serious?' Now I'm the one who's surprised. 'I couldn't write my life story. If I told everything my mother would skin me alive.'

He is not convinced and I ask him: 'What's the most auto-biographical part of the book?'

Without a seconds hesitation he replies: 'Where the younger brother, Larry dies of tuberculosis.'

'I never had a brother called Larry, never had a brother died from anything yet. If you don't believe me you can ask Ma.'

I could see he heard the ring of truth in my voice even before he asked me with real sincerity: 'But how on earth did you achieve that effect? I was deeply moved by the passage.'

'Thousands of kids died from TB in Forties Dublin. Larry was for them. I wrote him for them, the ones nobody knows about except their relations and pals. I cried when those words fell onto the page. I cried for the Poor little fuckers.'

I signed a contract after he agreed that the book would be published as a novel. Hutchinson gave me £50, the first third of my advance, and I walked out onto Great Portland Street floating on air. On the way home to Jean I found a shop that had a copying machine and copied the cheque, knowing the original wouldn't see the weekend. There was some serious boozing due to take place and I would be at home with Jean who was now pregnant with our third child. Just this once I wouldn't go astray.

Jonathan was born on 17 May 1965, an amazing little guy who would scarcely cease to be less. Within a few years he had fire in his belly and a touch of the mad laugh in his mind, he would light up all our lives and be much loved especially by Peter, the gentlest and nicest kid I ever met, and Sarah who had it in her to be a mother to the whole world.

Forgive me but I hold my hands up. I was knocked out by my wonderful kids, feeling such immense love for them and really wanting to be there to watch them grow and take on their part in the script of life. What a pity it wasn't enough to still the madness that could run rampant through me without asking my permission, all decencies cast aside when the moon inside me was full.

During that summer Ma phoned me to say that my father was in Jervis Street hospital and that he wasn't at all well. I was on the next plane home and when I saw Mick I feared the worst and my heart felt raped.

He was never demonstrative but he let me give him a gentle hug – he seemed even smaller than the eight stone tiger he had been in his life – and I learned that it was his heart that was keeping him down. The truth is there wasn't a lot to say to each other, there never had been, but for my part there seemed to be a box full of words that needed to come out, but didn't. He would have been embarrassed had I told him how I loved him, and how desperately sorry I was that my dream for him hadn't worked out.

This led me into a rerun of the scene with my mother in the flat at Mount Pleasant Buildings when I came home suddenly after eight months of factory night work in London. I returned to find that she had gambled away the money I'd sent home to Da in registered envelopes. She signed for it and then gambled it – she gambled the money for the dream, the confectionary shop that I wanted to get for him before he burst his heart shovelling coal for the Electricity Supply Board.

In fact, he was promoted from coal shovelling to a cushy Watchman's job but the damage which had begun in a trench during World War One was exacerbated to such a degree that the years of coal shovelling had put the tin hat on his chance of staying alive. So Da was going to die and that was that and there was nothing anybody could do about the injustice of it all.

As I stumbled out of the hospital determined to obliterate my feelings with booze, I hated Ma for what she had done and sneered at my stupidity that time I saw her heading into The Fun Palace on the quays, the fucking Fun Palace where she played Housey Housey at two pound a card with the money for my father.

When I came out of the alcoholic blitzkrieg on myself, I remembered him joking in his own acidulous way. 'What ever happened to the chicken farm?' This was his way of referring to the shop as I sat facing Ma who was dying with guilt, an hour after she had told me of gambling the money away.

I told him things were rough in London, work was scarce, money too, that the plan was on hold but just for the minute. I couldn't look at my mother as the stinking lie fell off my lips.

Then he said, 'Y'know somethin' – you never asked me if I'd like havin' a shop.'

My facial expression must have asked the question though I was speechless. He pulled a face and a smile lit up his mouth for a second. 'Can y'imagine me and some oul'one complain' about her Vienna Roll or somethin'. I'd have ended up hittin' her with it.' That was the one and only time we ever discussed the dream that Ma turned into a nightmare for me. Ah well.

A few days after I got back to London and my family, I got word Da had died and I was just too sick in my stomach to go back to Dublin for the funeral.

In my heart I was thanking some god somewhere that I'd seen him, held him for a few seconds in the hospital, but I cried bitter tears on and off for days before I was fit to be spoken to.

The novel was published on 4th October 1965 and I should have been at the launch but guess what? I didn't make it.

Hutchinson were pretty miffed with me over not turning up but I just did what I had to do to get some publicity that might help people remember me enough to go out and buy the book.

The truth is I'd gone on the tear to give me the Dutch courage to deliberately miss the launch at the Cheshire Cheese in Fleet Street. What actually happened was that I got lost in the booze, finally drinking my way into an alcoholic blackout.

This is a period of amnesia suffered by the drinker and in this instance – another one of hundreds to come – I didn't emerge from the blackout until the day after the launch.

In a moment, I found myself in Brighton with no idea of how the hell I got there and with the help of a very decent copper I got myself back to London by cab since I could barely walk.

Without giving it a thought, I shrugged off any concern about being *out of my mind* for two full days and needing three more days to recover by which time I could barely hold down a bowl of soup.

In about ten days I was elated by the book sales and glad to go on the television shows that wanted to know me because they welcome every lunatic and alcoholic arsehole that shows up from time to time as long as the guy keeps the audience awake while he is on the screen. It didn't occur to me that to want success so badly that you were willing to place your mental health in very serious jeopardy was a major kind of sadness, and surely a sin against yourself. I guess this was because it wasn't the first time I had lost touch with the present when I'd had too much booze.

Six weeks later Hutchinson would write me a letter in answer to my query as to how the book was doing in the shops. They said 'it has sold well in excess of what we would expect from a first novel – two thousand six hundred at this time with repeat orders almost daily.'

A few weeks after this the novel was bought by Arrow Paperbacks, which was owned by Hutchinson. Then Houghton Mifflin of New York came in for the rights to publish *Goodbye* in America. Days later I heard that Ballantyne had bought the US paperback rights and I thought I had died and gone to heaven.

Hutchinson soon asked me for another book, a sequel to *Goodbye* since they felt that my rogue hero, Paddy Maguire had stimulated enough interest for a quick follow-up.

I had already started the new novel, calling it *A Bed in the Sticks* which would be built around my time in the world of the touring player, where, in my case anyway, every girl seemed to have her own hayshed.

I hadn't said anything to Hutchinson who weren't taking any chances until they saw how my first book would sell. One thing you soon learn about publishers is that they rarely take chances and when they do it is not because you are a sweetheart or anything like that. Every move they make is motivated by one thing only, sales.

Paddy Maguire, the hero of *Goodbye to the Hill* was based on me and because I seemed to attract all kinds of people, some of them as odd as myself, and grab at every situation that held out the prospect of *sensation* I had stories to burn. So I gave Hutchinson an outline for the second book – a fictional account of my life which had somehow been as busy a switchback ride as any story I might have made up about Maguire.

But first I had to make a trip to Dublin to do the publicity round for my first novel. *Goodbye* had caused a sensation in

Ireland, saved from being banned by just one vote cast by the wife of a prominent politician. This lady would later tell me she thought it a wonderful book that would be recognised in time as the seminal novel of Dublin in the Fifties.

Taking me to the airport for that plane ride home was my pal, Johnnie McCusker – we'd gone to New Zealand together on the SS Ruahine, having the odd punch-up when we went a bit stir crazy – thirty-one days at sea is a long time for a first tripper – all of it just part of sensation seeking.

We got to talking about my boozing while we drank coffee at Heathrow – my plane being late coming in, so what else was new. I'd been hitting the juice pretty badly and McCusker was trying to say don't kill yourself over in Dublin. You know what the boozing can be like.

I told Johnnie I wasn't going to drink on the trip and he threw me a fish eyed look that spelled *scorn*. Stupid as it sounds I made him a promise that I wouldn't drink in Dublin and he said, 'Can I tell Jean you said that?'

I told him to go ahead and before I left him he actually said as a kind of soft apology, 'I believe you.' I gave him a hug and felt good about my decision not to drink on this trip.

When we were airborne a tasty hostess asked me would I like a drink and as though I was looking in through a window at Lee, I heard him say, ' I'd love some brandy, Miss, thanks.'

The way this could happen is something that amazes me even to this day. It is as though your mind simply flips over and your voice is working from a different script to what was there before your eyes just moments before. Remembering it like it was yesterday I can promise you that the guy ordering the booze is in a totally different place to the one that had promised his best mate that he would not be drinking this trip. And there is no evident shift, like you don't have to consider the situation, there is no guilt, no shame, no anything, just a violently strong desire to drink that you will do almost anything to get what you want.

While I was going home to get publicity for the book, I

would have preferred that there were no photographers at the airport. Thanks to the publicity people in Dublin several press guys were waiting to meet me and take my picture as I came through customs, one of them, who had read the novel, thanking me for the laughs the novel had given him, at the same time expressing his surprise and his delight that it had not been banned.

Within days I was on this and that radio show, pictures of me *three sheets to the wind* had appeared in several papers and I was being greeted in the streets of Dublin by all kinds of people who wished me well. And by the Saturday night I had been booked to appear on *The Late Late Show* which was the top rated show in Ireland and a must if you wanted to sell books.

As I went on television I was fairly jarred but, with a mean amphetamine edge to my mind due to dropping a handful of speed in the early part of the evening.

In other words I was not the usual all smiling, ever grateful kid from the slums who was being feted on the country's premier television show by the most famous man in the country, Gay Byrne.

Gay and I got along fine and I managed to give him a few laughs while I touched up the ordinary happenings surrounding my non-appearance at the book launch with lines like 'I went out for a drink and went out of my mind!'

After we got through plugging the novel Gay Byrne asked me if I'd stay on and meet some of his other guests. Afterwards, I realised I should have left the drink alone in the commercial break. Had I done the smart thing I wouldn't have offended the comedian Hal Roach, a funny guy who didn't speak to me for two years afterwards.

As the show went on, I tried to keep a rein on my angry streak but I was touchy and argumentative without even trying, finally tearing a strip off this American clergyman, a sort of benign racist, who finally admitted under my relentless questioning that he had no black members in his congregation.

I knew this before the guy owned up – he was too good to be wholesome, so clean cut he squeaked, and I when I reminded him that Jesus was probably coloured since he was born in Bethlehem, a couple of racists in the audience yelled their objections of my behaviour.

I hadn't set out to be offensive – my anger exploded in the face of the sky pilot's hypocrisy and of course, Gay Byrne (the best chat show host in television history) just let me do my thing – you could fry yourself on Gay's show any time – while he, genius that he was – managed to hide his gratitude to you for ensuring that his viewers countrywide were staying awake.

I got some stick from some of the audience after the show but the other half told me I was right to have a go. Another example that no matter what you say, fifty per cent of your audience will agree with you and if you say the opposite, fifty per cent will agree with you, too.

chapter 4

My sojourn to New York in 1966 was to be a ten-day publicity trip for the American edition of *Goodbye to the Hill*.

It didn't quite work out that way and though I accept I was responsible for what happened, I would have needed to be made of cast iron not to succumb to the temptations that *The Big Apple* had to offer.

Enough to say that I was lionised to a degree I'd never known, everybody I met wanting to shake my hand and tell me they wanted to write a novel. Others were, within minutes, talking about how they had met Brendan Behan and Dylan Thomas and envying me though they were clearly an awful lot better off than I was in the financial department.

This didn't seem to matter to the New Yorker, decent to a fault and more than generous about buying drink and food – there is something about *writing* that attracts people of every size shape and colour. Of course they see the end of a journey when a book is published – a trip that began with a blank sheet of paper staring the scribbler in the face – pictures in the paper or the guy on television hustling his book. They seldom consider the work that is involved to take a story and spin it so that the reader doesn't want to put it down until he has finished reading it.

Let me admit that I could not resist the New York females that were there for me at every hands turn. Within a week or ten days I had keys to four or five apartments – all I had to do was call first, make sure the lady didn't have company already and I had a bed and a body for the night. One of those beautiful warm bodies belonged to a lady who was the first ever to say to me: 'Your place or mine?' which was one of the most mind-blowing lines I had ever heard.

A good guy in England, a journalist called Logan Gourlay had given me a letter of introduction to the world famous film producer who was decent enough to have me go meet him at his penthouse office on Fifth Avenue.

Otto Preminger told me he had read my book but since he was already up to his brains in two and a half movies he was not even considering it as a possible production piece.

In the moment I didn't care because I was like a thirsty dog in need of a water bowl as I gaped at the most stunning young woman I had ever seen up close. I can't remember her name though her face and her astonishing body were burned indelibly into my mind for years to come. And during those years I could not think of that lovely creature without going red in the face at the memory of my own culpability. In all honesty, I was so dumb that day – I made pass after pass at this lovely young woman without it ever occurring to me that she was most likely his girl friend – he had that kind of reputation and well I knew it. But I had no right to be so bloody discourteous to a man who had proved his worth on the silver screen and who had been decent enough to meet me at the request of an old friend. As I saw it later, he would have been entitled to have turfed me out of his office since I was bereft of even the common courtesy we all have the right to expect from each other.

When I left Otto Preminger's office I was limping mentally, so very ashamed of myself, heading for the nearest bar to get the hits I needed to help me wipe out the awful memory of what had just gone down. I didn't stop to think I was choosing not to remember the few quick belts of Jack Daniels before going to see the man. Had I not needed the *Dutch Courage* I might not have behaved like arsehole of the year.

When I had first arrived in New York I met a man in Downey's bar on Eight Avenue who produced musical shows for one of the world's most successful song-writing teams and he was a real friend to me from day one. He told me later it was to do with my hair – I had this blue-black thatch back then while he, like my poor departed father, hadn't a hair between him and heaven.

He took me to his club for lunch, introduced me to his friends in show business and put me in touch with some press people who wrote up me and my novel. Then he announced that he was giving a dinner party in my honour at Sardi's East which is where the rich go on Sunday night since the sister restaurant on the West Side is closed on the Sabbath.

My friend tells me this is no big deal, just a gesture to say glad to meet you and hope we'll always be friends. At Sardi's he introduces me to two beautiful women, one named Jenny who is about thirty eight, a natural blonde who is somewhat reserved but friendly enough. As we shake hands I'm working hard to try and keep my eyes off her stupendous breasts.

There are twelve of us at the oval dinner table, including the lady wife of my friend, a woman for whom I feel instant warmth. She responds to my openness telling me then that her husband thinks I am extremely talented and is envious of my hair. We have a laugh and when I turn to the person on my right hand side I find I am sitting next to the lovely Jenny who is drinking wine and looking at me over the rim of her glass as she does so.

There are waiters buzzing about but I pour a glass for Jenny and as she sips it she regards me with candour that has turned me on in an instant. She starts to talk about my friend whom I will call Eddie since I wouldn't want to embarrass his family.

'Eddie tells me you're written a wonderful novel, Lee. Do you have more or are you a one-book wonder?' Her accent is Ivy League and her overall demeanour suggests to me that she wakes up bathed in confidence and well-being on most days.

'The sequel is finished, Jenny. And I have several more on the list of work to do.' I'm telling her the truth and I try hard not to look like I want to gobble her up.

'Any way your novel would make a movie?'

'Everyway,' I say, my inner ear pricking up.

She drinks her wine and I take a belt from my brandy and soda, wishing we were alone somewhere.

Eddie calls to me from across the table and we engage in some happy go lucky small talk and I make a gag that gets a laugh and we are then eating and drinking and making merry. I am taking things easy with the brandy which I love, and can't help noticing that Jenny is putting the wine away with a sort of quiet industry that is impressive.

By the time we get to dessert she is rubbing the back of my neck and she is whispering into my ear that if I were to lose twenty pounds I would be an Adonis and she could take me to Hollywood casting director friends.

'I can also get people that matter to read your book as a possible movie.' I'm giving her my eyes as she goes on in this vein and I confess I find her more attractive by the minute.

Then a big guy Lou something calls to her from across the table, 'Jenny am I hearing it right – you want to buy the Beverly Hills Hotel?'

Need I tell you that I might well have fallen off my chair had Jenny not been holding my hand. As it was I couldn't look at her for fear of drooling. God forgive me but the permutations that were running through my mind almost made me ashamed of myself. Would I lose twenty pounds? Would I walk, run, ride a bike? She needs Adonis she can have him. I have to shake my head to stop from having a brainstorm.

Jenny squeezes my hand as she answers Big Lou. 'It looks a good deal on paper. My guys are looking at it very seriously but no decision before Thursday.' She raised her glass and went on, 'I'd like to toast our Irish writer, Lee. May all his dreams come true.'

The response to this was warm but I couldn't help seeing

that Eddie was having something of a hard time. Meanwhile, Jenny comes right out with it.

'Make some time and let me take you out to the Coast, Lee. I have a home there, you could even do some work if you had a mind. And I promise you, I really can get you to the people that matter.' She is looking right at me, her eyes shining at the prospect and I say, 'That's very decent of you.'

She smiles and squeezes my hand on the table and by sheer chance I see Eddie react to the moment.

'You and I could be real friends, unless, unless you think I'm too old for you.' As she says this she knows fucking well she is perfect, perfect for me or any other guy with a hard-on for the sex and all the possibilities she is dangling like a carrot before me.

'You're perfect,' I say, really in need of a cold towel to press into my groin. 'I'd love to come with you to the Coast.'

A little later that evening I go to the washroom and am throwing cold water onto my face when Eddie comes in. He takes the trouble to check that there is nobody else in the place and then he comes to stand beside me. When he speaks we are looking at each other in the wall mirrors behind the wash basins.

'My young friend, I need a big favour from you here.' His naturally gregarious manner is not present, he is subdued and in some discomfort so that I immediately ask what can I do.

'You've met my lady wife, the best friend any man ever had. And you are having your hand held by the only woman I have ever loved, Jenny.' He paused and I just stood there not knowing what to say.

'Jenny is her own woman. We remain joined in some way but when she wants something she goes after it and tonight I see that she wants you in the worst way.' He stops speaking and is taking a deep breath and I can see that he is hurting in the worst way.

'I think she's just being friendly, Eddie. She's lovely and a real nice lady, it's not anything more than that.' I tried to sound like I meant what I was saying, having no idea whether I did or not.

'She can take you to the Coast, Lee. She can get you to the people – Jackie Lemmon is a close buddy of hers, she knows all the right people, and she has more money than God. And here I am asking you not to,' he shrugged until he found what he was looking for. 'I'm asking you not to accommodate her because I fear I will lose her for all time.'

As Eddie stood there deep breathing through his nose, I was remembering somebody in Downey's bar warning me 'just understand, kid, in this town, there ain't no such thing as a free lunch.'

During the next three days Jenny left six messages on the answering machine I shared with an actor called Paddy Bedford, another truly decent guy who had let me move in with him after my stint at the Algonquin Hotel paid for by my publisher ran out.

I have to admit I was sick to my stomach because I know I would have gone to California with Jenny, felt sure I would have grabbed the chance with both hands, and if sleeping with her was some kind of price, I wouldn't have been complaining. Being honest I would have slept with her had she been a waitress in Sardi's East, she was lovely and she was so into me that it could have been all kinds of fun bedding her, even if we're not talking about laughing.

On Wednesday night I was having a smoke before going in to see 'Philadelphia Here I Come' by Brian Friel, which was starring my buddy Paddy Bedford and another actor I knew, Donal Donnelly.

As I turned to put out my cigarette in an ashtray Jenny was standing a foot away from me. She had to see from my face that I was very sorry about not contacting her but she didn't give me a chance to explain anything, not that I'm sure I could have told her what Eddie has said to me in the washroom at Sardi's East.

'Who the fuck do you think you are!'

The words shot into my face like bullets and before I could respond in any way she turned and stalked away across the foyer. I left the theatre knowing I couldn't sit through the play that night. I was sick to my stomach and I went around to Downey's to tie-one-on.

I started drinking Jack Daniels and soon found myself wondering how it might have been had I decided to ignore Eddie's *request* that I stay away from the lovely Jenny, the lovely, very rich Jenny who went after what she wanted and when she didn't get it showed you that the lady was no lady.

It was all very attractive and I let the thoughts make me dive in head first, trying at the same time to blot out the nagging finger reminding me I was a married man and a father. I was very torn between what I wanted, which Jenny vowed she could provide, Eddie confirming this during his plea. I shook myself out of the fantasy, willing to do the right thing, having no idea that within a few weeks I would jump out of a plane without a parachute by falling in love.

At the risk of making you chuckle – I mean, what sort of gobshite in my position – married, a father, living off an overdraft – hustling to try and get a serious money break, which so far had not happened with *Goodbye* – so that I could pay my way without sweating about where the next thousand quid was to come from – would go all Hollywood and *fall in lurve?*

I practically shudder in disbelief when I think about it now. Of course I mean no disrespect to the lady, who really was a lady, but we were a pair of kids in search of an adult when there wasn't one to be found in the immediate vicinity. At that time though I felt I would die if I could not stay with her while inside my head sat my family, my wonderful wife waiting for me to come home and behave like a husband. I had been fobbing Jean off with lies about meeting Hollywood producers adding that some other publishers were head-hunting me, sweating under guilt's pressure, my life ripped right down the middle with me waiting for some miracle to take place that would sort out the mess I had got myself into.

Nothing happened and finally I knew I had to go, I had to leave my lady and head back to my family. For years after this time in New York I used to entertain guys I was boozing with, telling them in my *Jack the Lad* role how 'I missed the plane home by eleven weeks!'

As a direct result of having a novel published to good reviews I got into writing scripts for television and radio. But, being a kind of odd-man-out the breaks didn't come my way by the accepted route, as in getting good paying work through your agent. The reason for this may have had something to do with *not having an agent* but the way I saw it, things happened and you picked up the ball or not. And up to this time I just hadn't found an agent worth having. I'd had two guys who should not have been let out of the house without a minder, but we'll let that one go.

Had I not been steeped in luck so that the novel had been chosen by Richard Lister for his *London Evening Standard Book of the Week* slot, I mightn't have attracted the interest of the people that helped me get into scripting for TV and the wireless.

My mate Jack Connell who ran Finch's pub on the Fulham Road introduced me to a young woman who worked as a Floor Manager on a popular television thriller series and I asked her if she could get me a script.

I'd seen the show she worked on – it was called *No Hiding Place* and while I might have watched it the odd time I wouldn't have been holding my breath for it to show up. This may be a roundabout way of saying I knew I could write better scripts than I'd seen on the show and when Penny brought me one to read I was positive that I could produce better material.

First of all I studied the script layout so that I would produce something that looked right. Then I checked out the length of each scene. I had already worked out for myself that on television each segment should move the story forward or sideways – like something had to happen in each sliver of a few minutes duration to help the police – in this show embodied in the persona of Chief Superintendent Lockhart and his team – get closer to the truth or be sidetracked by a plot twist that must ultimately be untangled by the great crime stopper himself.

This may seem obvious now but at that time television was relatively new in my life and studying how a drama show or a cop show worked was very necessary for me if I was going to become part of the freelance team of scriptwriters that service the various television shows that make it to the screen.

Within days I was writing a script. I called it *Who Killed Cock Robin?* I thought this a great title because it tells you right away that there's been a murder, ergo another case for Lockhart to solve.

Cock Robin was, of course, a bad man, a gangster, and he is shot coming out of a night club in London. And away you go. I gave the script to this girl Penny so that she could put it into the right hands and I agreed to pay her half of whatever fee came along. She thought the script was good, but felt it would have more chance of being accepted if I put her name beside mine as co-writer. Since I was keen to sell the script I agreed and within a week we got word the script had been accepted. When it was shown it was favourably reviewed in the papers which surprised the producers since the show had been running for years without too many mentions. Next day they asked for another script.

By this time Penny was telling people that we were co-writers even though I had written every word of the script, only adding her name as a political move. When she came to me about the second script I suggested she go away, develop an outline giving me the basic plot. From this three page guide I would write a script. Unless, I suggested with my tongue in my cheek, she wanted to write a *first draft* which I would rewrite before we submitted it. As far as I know she never put a word on paper because that was the end of my interest in that particular show and in that young lady. I had no objection to sharing the money the script earned but I bitterly resented to co-writer bit because it wasn't true. And I had enough baggage of my own without picking up a young woman who talked about writing when she was on a coffee break from her well paid, well-in job in television. I had given eleven, twelve years of my life to the writing before I touched for Olympia Press and I wasn't into playing games – to me writing was a very serious business and for better or for worse I was going to ride the range alone.

After this experience with the cop show I sent my novel to Story Editors at the various television companies and soon I was meeting story editors, all of them to a man, frustrated novelists. All of those guys had graduated BA, at least and you got the instant impression that the university connection did you no harm when you were looking for a job in the media.

In fairness to most of the story editors I met, they were decent guys and they were open enough in their appreciation of having a real live novelist on the team, and one guy, a Welsh wizard of a scriptwriter called Kenneth Ware became a friend as well as a mentor in the art of writing for television.

Within a very short time I had written for *Troubleshooters, a fifty minute weekly series starring Robert Hardy and Ray Barrett.* I also wrote for *Vendetta,* starring Neil McCallum who would tell me years later that the first part I had written for him earned him so much work that he had bought his farm from the proceeds.

I wrote a script for *Taxi* the *Sid James* series. Somebody had nicked this idea from an outline of mine called '*Morrie's Clock*' (The Taxi Meter) – which a dope of an agent of mine had been trying to peddle to that same network. Never mind, these things happen and I was glad to be on the script writer's list – writing for Sid James was a good looking credit on any-body's CV. I wrote for many more series including some scripts for Irish television and then I had the good fortune to meet a guy called Mark Grantham. And where did I meet this gifted American writer? Why in Finch's pub, where else!

In Finch's at around the same time I'm with a guy called Mark Grantham, a genial American writer who sips on a pint of Guinness and sucks an old fashioned pipe. I'm having a few whiskies and sipping cider while Mark tells me he knows about my novel which had gone into paperback in England and Ireland shortly before I went to New York to do public-ity for the American edition.

That night Mark told me he had come to Dublin to study at Trinity and while he was wining and dining and discovering the wonder of Irish girls, he came up with the idea for this radio soap.

I thought it was terrific, romantic like, that an American should arrive in Ireland, *the land of the writers*, and be the guy to create Ireland's first real radio soap opera which was called *'The Kennedy's of Castleross'*.

Mark had seemed almost shy when I congratulated him on his record running radio show over in Ireland which seemed to have been running a couple of times a week for about three hundred years. Mark told me he had actually written eight hundred episodes of *The Kennedys of Castleross* but that he was finished with the show, that he just couldn't face the idea of writing even one more script. When he told the people at the national radio station that he was quitting they asked him to try and find someone to take it on.

Because Mark knew that being published didn't necessari-ly mean being well-off he asked me right there in Finch's pub if I'd be interested in taking on the popular radio show.

I was so broke I didn't even have to think about it. I felt it would be fun to do, a challenge to work in radio and let's face it I needed money in the worst way. So I told Mark that I was very interested and he said he'd run my name past the guys at Radio Eireann the next day.

I'd only heard the show when I was on some flying visit home but I knew of its popularity through people talking about it whenever I got back to Dublin for a few days.

The show ran twice a week at lunchtime, and it was said that farmers took an alarm clock into the fields, set to give them enough time to walk back to the house before the show aired at lunchtime. And it was already the stuff of legend that when a character in the show died, Mass cards and wreaths would arrive at the studio. So you can judge for yourself what a smash the series had turned out to be.

When Mark told me the whole story of how he had come to the end of the road in his soap career – he had simply run out of the ability to plot – I thought you could hardly blame him – eight hundred episodes seemed like some kind of world record to me.

Just a week after that meeting with Mark in Finch's a *couple of suits* come over from Dublin to see me about taking on the role of scriptwriter on 'The Kennedy's of Castleross'. The fact that I was a published novelist, with some good reviews behind me, helped me get the offer to script the radio show but I felt it was the recommendation from Mark Grantham that swung the deal my way.

At the meeting, the producers, Donal Stanley and Billy Wall told me the show was to be aired three times a week in the new schedule, asking me would I be able to handle that volume of work. I said sure, knowing I could, and after I listened to four, maybe six of the taped shows they had brought with them I knew I could keep the shape and character of the series. I said I'd need character sketches and background facts about who had done what in the series, and so on, but those were just details. I also asked them to provide me with the last twenty scripts before my take over and I signed a contract soon after that.

I was surprised by the buzz I got from being hired by Radio

Eireann. The national radio station was a place where you needed second level education to get in the door and my dismal showing in the Primary Cert by one and a half points would have ruled me out even as a post room boy.

The money had something to do with the buzz too, but the idea of going down a new avenue of scribbling appealed to me. I was always open to learning something new, always loving the feeling you know when you're taking chances, flying in on a wing and a prayer, relishing the new challenge. All a bit *Boy's Own* maybe, but it made my heart swell just like it did when I saw *Frank Merriwell* in *a folly an' upper* in the *Fourpenny Rush* at The Prinner on Rathmines Road during my barefoot days,

chapter 5

So there you go. Within weeks of meeting Mark Grantham in Finch's boozer, I'd signed a contract to write one hundred and fifty episodes of a series – three shows a week for a year. I wasn't bothered that I'd never heard the programme on the radio – the tapes RTE provided gave me all I needed to make a start, so instead of being worried by what I'd taken on I felt very good about the idea of earning steady bread from the typewriter. And in a way I felt kind of honoured that for a year at any rate all the words of each episode of *The Kennedy's of Castleross* would carry my signature. It was no small achievement to be the writer of the programme that had already become a national treasure.

So I went to work on the show in good heart becoming more and more grateful for the forty five guineas a week it earned me. This took the pressure off both me and my good wife who had been working to keep the home fires burning. It also relieved me of the guilt I'd been feeling about not being the bread-winner and that was worth more than money to me.

The weekly fee also meant that I could give a bit more time to the books I was trying to write. Even churning out three shows a week I was free most of the time since I could write a script for the series in about two hours. This left me free to do the television work I was being offered on a semi-regular basis, earning great money – at least three hundred and fifty pounds for an episode in any of the popular series. This may not seem like much by today's standards but in the Sixties it was pretty good. I thought it was a godsend particularly as it helped support my need to write books and stage plays, which for all the time and work that went into them might never earn a writer a bob.

Writing novels is a wonderful thing to do. And it's even better when you get published. And better yet when your story is well reviewed and sells a lot of copies. But, unless you get really lucky with huge sales, or a movie deal, you're not going to get rich writing books. This won't stop you – if you've been bitten by the bug to write novels you are going to find, make, steal the time to be working on one, if only part time, because that's where your heart is.

The first thing I did on *The Kenno's* radio series was to knock out thirty episodes which put the show ten weeks ahead. Then I decided to go over to Dublin and meet the cast, soak up some atmosphere, have a few jars, go and see Ma, maybe walk around the old neighbourhood, do some silent novenas for help to be some kind of halfway decently behaved husband while I'm alone in Dublin's unfair city.

Before this happens I'm in the studio bar at the BBC in Wood Lane, London, when I'm approached at lunch time by an actor I've never met who greets me with the words: 'How'ya Head! Thought I'd say hello – I happen to be working for you at the minute.'

This guy is a leading man if ever you've seen one. Tall dark and handsome with a strong jaw and eyes designed to melt many a female heart. A big well-built guy yet sensitive and even vulnerable, you know – the kind women want to eat without salt. He tells me his name is Donal McCann and we hit it off right away.

As it turns out, he plays Brian Kennedy in the series I'm now writing for Irish Radio and we are destined to become great mates. He tells me he's at the BBC to record a play by another mate of mine, Tom Murphy, who is a hell of a writer.

As Donal leaves the bar to go back to work, we agree to have a night out when I got over to Dublin. Little did I know that this guy – his father had been the Lord Mayor of Dublin for a while – would turn out to be one of Ireland's most gifted stage actors.

So I'm writing *The Kennos*, doing quite a bit of television scripting, working on a new novel and drafting a stage play. I am also trying to be a good husband and happily spending a fair bit of time with my children as I've done whenever I was home from the time they first arrived into my life.

I had taught Sarah to read at two years of age. In the very week we brought her home from St. Beatrice's hospital I had bought Encyclopaedia Brittanica and twelve albums of the great classical favourites by Mozart and all those other guys. From then on the music played softly in the background most of the time. When I opened the encyclopaedia I began reading it with the intention of reading all the way to the end down the early years of our life together. It didn't matter to me that my daughter slept through most of it – I felt it would be good for her just to hear her father's voice as well as that of her mother. I wanted this kid to know she had two of us rooting for her. Jean and I had made a deal not to shout or row with Sarah in the room – my own early memories were shredded by the vocal violence, sometimes turned physical, that my parents dumped on us without giving it a thought. I also made a vow to myself that I would never say *no* to any of my children. I stuck to this decision and would say years later, 'Can we talk about this?' as opposed to the *no* word that shuts down all communication between parents and their kids.

I always had an old guitar in the house and I would sing to Sarah and Peter who arrived when my daughter was two years old – the songs I had learned as a child and sometimes I'd make up songs using their names.

Sometimes there was a problem when Sarah would say 'Sing that again Daddy', unable to understand what I was talking about when I said I couldn't do that because it was gone, it had passed by forever. The truth being that I couldn't hold onto something that passed through fast while I was singing the words to my kids. Anyway, I was doing my best on all fronts knowing that my marriage would most likely never recover from my admission to Jean that I had fallen in love in New York. This, of all the mistakes I had made as a husband, had to be the dumbest statement ever to drop from my lips. She had taken me by surprise as she drove me home from Heathrow after my trip to the States, asking me point blank, 'Did you have an affair?'

I was so torn, off balance with guilt and self-pity and you name it, that I couldn't find the wild heart that would have lied with impunity, automatically convinced that it was to save my wife the pain of such pointless knowing.

Any wonder that Jean clearly needed me to leave her alone? Which I did out of respect for all that she was – a very good woman, a wonderful mother who had come close to the end of her tether with me. So I spent most of my time working and the rest of it went to my children, when I wasn't out drinking.

The booze was now a very solid fixture in my life and I was so hooked that I failed to listen to well meaning mates who said I had some kind of problem and ought to talk to somebody about my drinking. I actually punched one guy who was big enough and tough enough to take me apart – he has long since forgiven me, for which I'm grateful to this day.

By August '67 I knew I was heading deeper and deeper into trouble with the booze. Then in a moment of madness I just quit drinking, having set myself a target of making it dry all the way to Christmas.

Some weeks after this Jean told me she thought I was doing terrific and things improved between us though I couldn't tell her I was going stir crazy by being in the house all the time.

I realised that I needed a job, a movie job that would take

me away from the house, give Jean some space. So I lay down on the couch and visualised myself working on a film I had written. This visualisation trick had been suggested to me by a Hypno-therapist in Clontarf called Sean Bourke and I was giving it a run around the block for the first time.

Within a week I got a phone call from a film producer called Bob Gallico who wanted to make a small movie of my short story *The Pale Faced Girl*. He asked me if I would write the screenplay – they wanted to shoot the film in Ireland as soon as possible. Bob was so enthusiastic about the story, for which I had a soft spot myself, that I agreed to have a meeting and kick the idea around. And I can't help thinking that, sure, it might have been coincidence, but it made me wonder, like, the offer had come in right behind my request to a god unknown.

I meet Bob Gallico and his director Francis Searle and I'm taken their enthusiasm for the story. We agree on money while Francis pours tiny drops of whiskey from a half bottle into his tea right there in the office. This was all the more surprising since Bob Gallico was a real straight guy.

I write the forty five minute script in a couple of weeks and I get paid, and the guys are pleased when I tell them I will be over in Dublin while they are shooting in April/May which is just months away. Not that I had any reason to be in Dublin at that time but I saw it as an opportunity to get away for a few weeks. The guys were bound to need some rewrites so I could work on the film unit, learn something and maybe meet an interesting woman or two.

I felt good about myself that I didn't need to go and drink to celebrate selling the story and writing the script for *The Pale Faced Girl*. Somehow I'd stayed dry through Christmas which my wife Jean regarded as an event that ranked alongside the opening of the Red Sea.

I had been building up to the idea of a lot of drinking over the holiday – I'd had my thirty-third birthday on December 21 – but, when I got to the boozer my mates were so sure that

I would get stinking drunk that I got the hump. I rebelled against my own predictability by sticking with coke right through the New Year. And I'm talking Coca Cola as opposed to sniffing nose candy.

We are barely into the New Year of '68 when a kind of miracle occurs that causes me to give serious respect to the notion of *visualising*.

Remember I am and always have been a dreamer, like I was fantasising in Technicolor while Hollywood was using that new process to make Esther Williams look even more delectable in her swim suit.

What happened on this February morning was something I could not have dreamed up even when I was dropping LSD. I think this is some admission from a guy who would in time earn the questionable compliment of being *Ireland's Soap King* – this on account of his going on to write over two thousand episodes of radio serial.

The fact that this miracle happened just days after I had delivered the polished rewritten script for *The Pale Faced Girl*' made it all the crazier, all the more unbelievable.

And again, it was a phone call, a phone call from a man I didn't know. It would turn out to be a good, positive call that romantically came out of the blue and I grabbed with both hands. How could I have known that it would alter my life to the extent that my dearest and most precious possessions would be taken from me in the not too distant future?

It was about nine on a cold February morning when the phone goes and I pick it up. I'm answering a call from a total stranger who tells me he is ringing from Los Angeles.

Right away, I suspect it is one of my mates taking the piss – Phil Connolly or Johnnie McCusker playing games after an all night piss up while I am still on the dry six months after I swore off the booze until Christmas.

But, just in case this call is for real, I play along as I try to work out which of my mates is doing the American accent. If it's a piss take it has to be Johnnie doing the talking. You'd have to pump lead into Connolly to kill his Clones accent.

Really, I need this like a sore anus but, I don't want to look foolish, so I wax cool, asking your man his name. He tells me his name is Daniel Haller. He claims he is a film director out in Los Angeles and that he has just read my novel *Goodbye to the Hill* and that he wants to make a movie of it.

'I'm glad you liked it,' I say playing Charlie Cool, at the same time vowing to myself that I am going to punch the shit out of whoever it is pulling my string on the other end of the line.

Can you blame me being sceptical? Like, was it possible I was getting another feedback to my bout of visualising? It can't be yells the awkward little fuck that lives in my head. What is going on here is like a weak strand in one of those old black and white movies that Hollywood churned out over a weekend with actors they dug up every few months. Like, this can't be happening, not for real.

But?

Oh yes. There is a But!

And it exists because I am not a normal person. How could I be called normal when I peddle my dreams for a living and want to go on writing for as long as I live?

To guys like me, a happening, no matter how crazy it seems to be, can always rely on a tiny part of me for support. This occurs automatically, just in case there's a pinpoint of possibility that the call, the chance, the merest sliver of the miraculous, is actually *the Real McCoy*.

My immediate problem is that I need to say something to keep my caller warm just in case he is for real, but not anything that is going to set me up for a shafting by someone who could well end up in traction if I am the victim of a fairly sophisticated piss-take.

So I say: 'Look, Mister Haller, I'm flattered by your call and your interest in my work but you have to understand, I couldn't possibly sell my book to a man I don't know.'

This is an outright lie. By this time, early 1968, two and a half years since *Goodbye to the Hill* was first published, I have not had any kind of tickle in relation to a film deal. This had brought me to a point that I was about ready to sell the book to *Lassie* if she had suddenly decided to abandon the dog's life for that of a shark, as in, Hollywood producer.

In response to my measured reply to his overture, Danny Haller asks me the name of my agent. I tell him I have signed up with Dina Lom. He knows her well, tells me he will call her. Should she agree to set up a meeting for tomorrow afternoon, he will fly around the Pole tonight to meet me. His last words on the call are: 'I believe you've written a truly great novel.'

I was nearly in tears and it was then I knew that the guy was for real because even McCusker couldn't have pulled off that last line without exploding into a storm of laughter.

Later that day, Dina calls me and tells me the meeting with Danny Haller is set for the next afternoon. She knows the guy well – 'He's a rarity in Hollywood, Lee, a really decent man.' Dina goes on to tell me he has directed mostly television shows like Kojak and the Dean Martin Show and has worked on many Roger Corman pictures, and he has a growing reputation, she assures me.

In other words, my agent believes the guy is for real and because she is a very professional lady who doesn't play games I agree to be at her office at the appointed time. Like, what have I got to lose except my sanity, right!

The next day, Danny Haller and I sign contracts in Dina Lom's office, she having made the deal for the film rights to the book, and another one for me to write the screenplay.

As I leave Dina's office, I have two separate cheques in my pocket. The reason for this is that I asked Haller to put the bulk of the overall monies down as the fee for the screenplay. This meant taking a smaller sum than he had offered for the rights to film the novel.

When Haller, out of sheer curiosity asked why, I told him straight that Hutchinson had screwed me by taking twenty five per cent of any film rights deal. The normal percentage, when the publisher was dealing with a writer that knew the score, was ten per cent. Because it had been my first time they had upped the ante by fifteen per cent. When you consider that they had given me the enormous sum of just a hundred and fifty pounds advance on the novel and would take at least twenty five per cent of the American publication deal, I felt they were crooks and I told them so. They didn't like it but all I could think was you can kiss my royal Irish arse.

When Haller and I left Dina Lom, I called Jean and told her the deals were done and that I had a pair of *Gregory Pecks* in my pocket and that I was going to buy her a new car the very next day. We had a chortle – she was genuinely pleased that I had got a break. Then I mentioned to her that Haller was taking me to dinner to talk about how I might approach the screenplay, and I was wondering what I should do about the booze situation.

At that time, neither Jean nor I knew anything about the disease of alcoholism, so she said go ahead and have a few jars. 'You've been off it since August, god knows you're entitled to drink today of all days.'

So with her blessing, I went to dinner with Danny Haller at the Carlton Towers Hotel. Days later I could remember a few shots of brandy before we went in to dinner. After that I had no recollection of anything we did or said but clearly I had imbibed enough booze to send me into an alcoholic blackout.

I did get a brief flash of what you might call the present moment. This was when I woke up with a good looking naked woman I didn't know, who is draped all over me. She's lovely enough to make not remembering what you have been doing to each other a criminal offence, but sadly my mind is a total blank.

Looking around I see that Haller had passed out on a couch fully dressed and it comes back to me that this flat belongs to the film company he was associated with in L.A.

Moving gingerly, not wanting to wake anybody up, I make it out of the flat, my body a mass of aches and pains so that I am like a guy walking on eggshells. This was just one in a long line of blackouts. This condition, this amnesia thing that can happen when you abuse your brain with the booze had been a frequent visitor in the months before I had gone on the wagon and I had been relieved that the blank episodes seemed to have passed on. So that I was assaulted by the shame I felt to have done it to myself again, even though the world and his wife would say sure you were entitled to have a drink and you after getting a real Hollywood deal.

I got myself away from Haller's flat, somehow making it down this spiral staircase from the top floor, my mind coming and going. Moments appeared and were gone with nothing showing up from the arrival of Haller and myself at the Carlton Towers Hotel off Sloane Street.

Even now I cannot be sure how I got from Chelsea to my home at East Sheen about three miles away. I imagine I called a cab but really have no idea. I fell in the bathroom at home and hurt my face badly and I went in shame to bed smelling myself and hating it even though I had scrubbed up like mad to get rid of the stink of booze and sex.

As I lay down beside Jean who was sleeping well, I knew I'd never before disliked myself this much. So despite the good deal that had been signed and paid for, and the ongoing exciting happening of writing my first Hollywood movie, I finally fell into a deep sleep not caring whether I woke up again or not.

Oh, how wonderful it is to be a macho man, a guy who takes his knocks and comes up smiling even if he's quaking inside, a guy who after six or seven months off the booze goes for dinner and a drink to celebrate the biggest deal of his life and gets wrecked beyond belief. A guy who turned into some kind of spiritual hobo when he drank, a guy who when booze said jump, only asked *how high.*

A guy who married a good woman who deserved better than he was producing in the husband department, a father who had not yet managed to grow up and who, after celebrating his first Hollywood film deal, would not be sober again until he quit drinking alcohol while he was attending his very first meeting of Alcoholics Anonymous in London.

This didn't happen the day after his celebration drinkies with his *Harry Hollywood* film producer. And it didn't happen the next week either. It took place twenty months later during which time the scribbler would turn his marriage into a car wreck, throw away the home life he had yearned for since he was a kid hiding from his life in the reading room of the public library on Rathmines Road in Dublin.

As I left Dublin originally, I vowed to myself that I would never come back to it. I yelled to the night by the mail boats rail that it should be *given back to the fucking Leprechauns with apologies.*

This was just the kid in me crying out in the anger that deprivation breeds but at that time I was sure it was set as cement. In the meantime, I had been back for short visits to see my parents and I'd written letters to my mother at least once a fortnight, sending some money in each envelope.

While I was in Dublin I just drank and picked up women and was always glad to be back on the boat and once more away from all that invaded my mind when I was back there. Which, I guess speaks for itself.

chapter 6

Now it's 1968 and I'm back in Dublin to write the movie screenplay of my novel. I also want to get to know the cast of *The Kenno's* and see if I can get in touch with my roots again.

What really surprises me is that, without any reservation, I am glad to be back, something I had never expected to feel again about my home town. At the same time I'm much aware that I am missing my children more than I miss my wife.

I know that Jean is not missing me – she is more than happy to have quit working, wanting nothing more than to be able to afford to stay home to look after our three children without the fourth one, me, fucking things up. I only know this because Jean was right out front when it came to expressing her feelings. This would change in time but by then she felt entitled to keep areas of her life private from me, and I don't blame her.

I was feeling okay about where I was at – for a change I had left her with plenty of money which had relieved me of all kinds of guilt and left me free to go sleeping around.

You might wonder how I could be so blasé about drinking again – my face still bore a scar from my bathroom accident at home on the night of the Hollywood contract celebration.

This is one of the amazing things about alcoholism – you can swear that you will never drink again -- you can promise this to your wife and your mother and your God, and even to your children – and you will be so vehement in your declaration of intended sobriety, that even though you have failed in the past, your loved ones will believe you, and you can, within an hour be drinking without a pinpoint of conflict in relation to what you're doing. It's like your mind flips over, like a coin, heads and tails, the one blotting out even the memory of the other. And, once more with feeling, that was me during those new days in Dublin in the early part of 1968.

Though I lived in delusion a lot of the time, I felt free about the writing because I had never felt that I was doing it, that I was the man, that I am the writer here. Mates of mine, a lot of them talented people, both male and female, who were into the writing, many of them thought they were doing it, ergo, subconsciously claiming the genius that attached to some of their work. And they would be worried, angry, depressed that they were experiencing writer's block, they had run dry. I never bought into this. All I did was thank some laughing god and I accept that I was steeped to have come up myself with this daft notion that the scribbler – me – was just a channel for the ideas and the words coming through. So if I wasn't wet, as in, I do it, then how could I go dry, as in, I am not able to do it.

Look, I don't know anything, but I can swear to the fact that I haven't dried up simply because I never thought I was the man that was making it happen. And I feel the same way as these lines are pouring out – as far as I'm concerned, its all done by mirrors and all I have to do is show up, immerse myself in a zone where writing can happen, and then just say, as I always do to my imaginary writer in the sky, I'm here, what have you got for me today. And away we go.

As I said earlier I never doubted I could write *The Kenno's* for the reason stated above and as it turned out I was right. I was a real channel in the area of Soap. A fifteen minute radio show – the ongoing story kind with some sort of cliff hanger at the end of each episode – from start to finish an hour and a half to two hours. So each morning, during my early weeks back in Dublin, I knocked out a script and the outline for the next one.

And because I write what I'd like to read or listen to, I kept the radio stories full and dramatic, not forgetting funny. I like to write about characters that are alive and vital to the scripts, people you could spend a bit of time with even if you lived in different worlds.

You need a variety of colourful people – you want listeners to find a character that becomes their favourite. This is the key since ultimately it's the connection with someone in a serial that pull in the punters. But you have to remember that every series needs a *house bitch*, a *bore* and of course various romantic entanglements. And of course, the bitch is not all bad, while the bore has to be so boring that he comes over as funny, someone your audience laughs at as opposed to chuckling along with him.

I guess it's the same with a book. If you create characters that people can identify with, it seems to me you're on the way to building a readership. That's what happened with *Goodbye to the Hill* which really got me started on what would turn out to be a switchback career as a professional writer.

Another thing that comes in very handy if you want to write a book that will, hopefully, sell in large numbers is your anger. Anger in a writer can provide the juice to keep you going when the inclination might well be to throw your hat at it and go out on the piss. It certainly helped me get that lucky little novel written in such a short time.

This young guy, Paddy Maguire, woke up consistently to angry days. There is loads of anger about, everywhere he turns he sees hearts frothing with it. And he finds a pinpoint of light shining out of the gratitude that he's not feeling like that. Before going to work in the office he was delivering newspapers to pay the instalments on the bicycle he needed to get to and from his work in the city, just glad he loved riding the bike, feeling good that it was his machine once he kept up the payments.

He wasn't in love with having to get up so early but he totally hated the fact that his mother had to get up before that to make sure he got out of bed, and he double-hated living in the rabbit warren erected by Dublin Corporation to house some of Dublin's poor.

He no longer felt anger towards the father he loved to distraction because the guy had fallen down in the provision department where his wife and kids were concerned. At times he had to hide the pity he felt for a man who had, more than once, taken chances under enemy fire and come to nothing in terms of money or power or prestige.

He knew before too long that he was running to hide, to escape in his big dreams from the dismal reality that was his father's life, a Hollywood star in the making if you were to listen to the girls who never stopped telling him how good looking he was. This crazy young guy with a hunger to write books and films and god knows what else.

The dream never seemed to weaken or diminish — he'd been seeing his name in the credit list of the good movies he saw down the years and he could literally ache at times just to be out of the flats and away in England or America.

In London or New York or Los Angeles there was surely a chance for the things he dreamed about to happen, as they would never come to pass if he settled for the life that his parents lived, which to him, and again he felt shame, was some kind of living death.

He felt trapped — his mother needed both his wages and his emotional support as she battled to survive a life she would not have wished on anybody. He was devoted to her, loved her even when she was being hateful which she could be when the mood took her — but she was there to listen to his dreams and listen she did, often throwing some daft wish he had expressed back in his face when she thought he was getting too big for his boots.

With his brothers and his sister he had problems – to them he was a brat with a big mouth. Billy who was two and a half years older had nicknamed him Piggy Gabby and thought him stupid to have ideas so far above his station. The pair could still throw a punch at each other but he had quit answering his sister back because she could dish out a slap if he got lippy within range of her right hand. And, of course, you couldn't hit her back, she being a girl like.

This simple thread was the basis of a short story I was going to write simply because it nudged its way into my consciousness some fifteen years after I had broken contact with those around me who thought anger was a given. My tale started to arrive on the blackboard behind my eyes, all chalked up in some kind of understandable sequence while I was driving my cab around the twin cities of London and Westminster to make a living.

Not that long after that first taste of success with my novel, here I am in Dublin with money in the bank, a flat right in the city, and a Hollywood screenplay to write. An exciting time for me and with the home town full of available women, it was an easy place to be once I made enough contact by phone with my kids so that I didn't get crushed by another load of guilt.

For all my wishful thinking about doing everything right in terms of being professional and producing manuscripts that were impressive in themselves, I got a terrific run at the script for Danny Haller and found myself holding thirty pages that seemed to me to be good film material. During the last ten pages I had been sipping brandy and being honest, I needed to get out of the flat and get a drink or two. So breaking my golden rule about presentation I folded the pages and stuck them in an envelope which I mailed off to Haller from South Anne Street post office.

Within a week I got a telegram from the man in Los Angeles saying: 'Wonderful work, Lee, keep going,' which was a great relief to me because I felt I had let myself down by the shoddy way in which the work had been sent to the man who had put down his money. And I vowed that no matter what was going on I would never be that slapdash again. I had been given some kind of gift and it deserved more respect than I had shown on what was a very important deal in my Mickey Mouse career.

A couple of weeks later I *expressed* the rest of the script, clearly marked 'first draft' to Danny Haller and just days later he rang me to convey his excitement. He told me then that he would be sending over a story editor to work with me on the next draft and that he was going to shoot the picture in Dublin from June onwards.

I was very excited by the news and right away thought of having my children and, of course, Jean, if she wanted to come over, with me for some weeks in the summer.

While Jean was making up her mind about my offer, I moved to a house on the Southside of Dublin which had four bedrooms and was situated in the kind of middle class housing estate where the kids could play in complete safety. They could also be at the Eastern Seaboard which was only five to ten minutes from the house by car and I was looking forward to swimming with them once we got the weather for it, not something you can take for granted in Ireland.

While I waited for Haller's story editor to arrive from Los Angeles I doubled up on *Kenno's* scripts to put the show a full two months ahead. This would give me all the time in the world to do the next draft of the script, but it also helped the producers who had to deal with actors who needed a time out of the series.

Some of our cast would be going on holidays while another had touched for a part in a film and these situations had to be accommodated in the interest of continuity, since the trade mark of a characters in a long running serial is their voice, ergo you can't have replacements because it just doesn't sound like Peadar or Christy or whoever.

In truth, I could fill many chapters with the goings-on that are part and parcel of any long running soap opera. But since I have a lot of story between now and the magic words *The End* of this tale, I'm going to share just two snippets that stand out in my memory.

Remember that when I agreed to write the show I hadn't met any of the cast except Donal McCann. He had told me to meet him in *The Plough* which faced the Abbey Theatre and was home from home to the repertory company of actors in need of alcoholic sustenance. So I'm in there waiting for Donal to show up when I am, literally, accosted by an irate guy that I have never met before. His opening gambit went something like: "Well the cursa Jeyzuz on you anyway, Mister Fucking Dunne!" which has to be registered as one of the most original greetings I've ever been privileged to receive.

"Do I know you?" I say, offering this little rhetorical dance while I try to decide whether I should punch this guy out or just give him the Liverpool nod, to prevent his anger driving him to the point where he presents me with a knuckle sandwich.

"I'm Pat Laffan." This big, rangy guy informs me angrily as though it should mean something to me. Which, in the moment, it does not.

"Are you a fighter or a talker?' I ask him like someone who is genuinely interested in finding out.

"What?" He doesn't understand what I'm getting at. 'What the fuck is that supposed to mean? I'm Pat Laffan and you killed my fucking character in your first fucking script for The Kennos and me only after buying the Volkswagen on the fucking drip.'

I immediately lost the urge to punch this guy out. Shit and Damn. I had killed off the doctor in the soap opera because Mark Grantham had got himself into a plot bind he couldn't get out of.

I saw right away that if I wasted the doc the problem was

solved in an instant. Obviously, this would have occurred to a writer of Mark's experience but, being a truly decent guy, he didn't want to write the actor out of the series. Whereas, not knowing any of the cast except McCann, I had no qualms about killing a character, well, not until I was face-to-face with this very decent guy whom I had deprived of the three guineas he needed to make the payments on his second-hand car. It seems incredible as I read it – three pounds three shillings per episode – but that is exactly what Pat Laffan was earning for each appearance as *The Doctor* in *The Kennedys of Castleross* on national radio. I learned over time that this was the fee paid to most of the actors.

Marie Keane, who played *Mrs. Kennedy*, earned eight guineas per episode with a guarantee that she would be in every show – twenty four guineas for a mornings work which wasn't bad pay in those days. As far as I can remember, I received forty five guineas for the three shows each week which was pretty okay when you consider I was now renting a house in a decent suburb for eight pounds a week.

Of course I apologised to Pat Laffan – a fine actor and a talented theatre director – which was cold comfort really, but I did promise him that when the chance came my way I would make it up to him in some small way. Years later he was not behind the door in announcing that his role in my film *Wedding Night* launched his film career, which happily turned out to be a lot more worthwhile than all the episodes of *The Kennos* put together would have done.

The other story that stands out in my mind concerns an actor called Vincent Dowling, one of the most charming guys ever to grace the Abbey stage – he would go on to produce and direct theatre in America and perform personally for President Ronald Reagan in the White House. But back in those far off days of big dreams, endless erections and small earnings, he played the lead, Christy Kennedy in the radio show.

Vincent and I always got along and the odd time he would

ask me to drop him from a couple of shows so that he could do another more lucrative gig, his need for understanding always accompanied by the heartfelt wish: 'But for Jesus sake don't write me out or I'll have to take the Pioneer Pin.'

Being something of a drinker myself I understand his need to avoid sobriety or any of its relatives and we get along fine. Then one day he comes to me – he has the chance to go to New York with a show – can I write him out fast, but keep the door open. I do this with an open heart even though it means a lot of work since the soap is plot-driven.

Having started to move him *off mike* I get a speedy return from Vincent who is practically embarrassed, asking me to drop his dropping, if you see what I mean, since the gig that was taking him to America seems to have been cancelled. I don't share my sense of relief with him – he shouldn't be allowed to feel good here – and after I've himmed and hawed for about eight and a half seconds I tell him it's alright, he stays in the show.

Two days later the guy is in my face again telling me that this time the trip to the States is definitely on, and pleading with me to write him out, leaving the door open for him to come back in when he comes home. Obviously, an actor's life is a factory that manufactures insecurity like some people make phlegm. For example, an actor could leave Dublin in a show that is to open on Broadway and be home again in ten days because the critics didn't go for it. And when a show is labelled a *turkey* the cast are, once more with feeling, darling, out of work.

Without trying to be arty or anything, I foreshadowed the absence of the character Christy while Vincent was still with us by a series of angry outbursts – some to his mother, which was unheard of in the show. I also wrote a couple of scenes where he got mad at his girl friend, as I set him up for some degree of a nervous breakdown, the extent of this being contingent on how long Vincent was going to be away. All of it being contingent on his fucking American trip actually coming to pass.

So now, I'm writing soap, and I'm adding bubbles to keep this actor *in* or *out* depending on the guff that goes on behind the possible production of any play anywhere anytime. Until finally I have Christy acting like something is driving him crazy. This is the penultimate stage of the set-up, like if he goes on from here he will end up in some kind of psychiatric unit for a few weeks or more.

Then Vincent the actor comes to me and tells me the trip is definitely *off*. As he promises me that even if the producers come back to him again he will not ask me to write him out, I keep my hands in my pockets to stop me strangling him.

I give my predicament some thought and come up with precisely nothing. So I leave the work and I go to Jammet's on Nassau Street for lunch, where I meet a very fine Dublin woman who has a reputation as man hungry. I'm more than happy, delighted in fact, to tell you she was, and that we shared the first of many a great time in the feathers that same afternoon.

Over the next few months I was more than happy to be one of her paramours especially when she could get us both into the Shelbourne *after hours* simply by standing on her head in the foyer – she had legs that went all the way up to Belfast – and refusing to budge until the Night Porter finally opened a bottle of Kreug or whatever.

Back at the typewriter I was presented with a diabolical exit from my predicament with The Kenno's, a plot strand landing on me that was almost beyond heightened reality. I didn't care. I was up to my nose hairs in Vincent's problem and I decided that he had to pay for all the messing about I had endured while his producers messed him about before finally throwing in the towel on the US trip.

That same week I was doing *The Late Late Show* and having fun with Gay Byrne and when he asked about the difficulties that were stitched into the writing of a radio serial, I led him towards my story about Vincent Dowling and his trip to America.

I explained how I had set up the nervous breakdown – the metaphor for this being a new born calf that Christy had come to love.

'So finally,' I say to Gay, 'Christy is faced with the imminent death of the calf he loves so much – it has eaten fresh grass and could die from Blackleg, in fact it's unconscious, as he comes to examine it for the tenth time that day.'

Gay Byrne never forgot he was always on camera so that even if you were boring the arse off the man he would give you that look suggesting you made Einstein seem like a dummy and he was doing just that as I set up the punch-line of the story.

'If Christy doesn't do something, something that needs doing, something urgent, drastic even, the calf is going to go for its tea.'

And Gay, the perfect host, feeds me the perfect question: 'So, come on Lee, what does he do'?

'He gives the calf the kiss of life...'

Gay Byrne and the entire audience explode into laughter and it's some moments before things quieten down.

'You certainly got your own back on Vincent there alright.' Gay is looking at me as though I need psychiatric treatment.

'Half the letters we got, and there were plenty, came from people congratulating Christy on having the courage to give mouth to mouth to a calf,' I said, with a face on me like a funeral wreath. Like, setting up Gay was never an easy thing to do.

But this time I got him and Gay asked, 'And who did the other letters come from?'

'Unmarried farmers asking for the calf's name and address!' I said with a deadpan face.

This brought the house down and we went on to do a really good show that night.

One last thing that happened before the show ended – a

young guy came on carrying a guitar and combing his hair with an open knife. Gay introduced us on camera and I sat and listened to the singer laying out his stuff. He was mad as hell with just about everything but there was a feel to him that was good and honest so that when Gay asked me, as someone who had some kind of success story going, what I could say to the guy, what advice could I give him, I simply said: 'I just hope he finds the way to make his anger work for him.' The guy was this young Dubliner called Bob Geldof and it seems to me that my wish for him came true. A remarkable man, Bob Geldof.

From my opening script for The Kenno's I was having a good time and I soon had the show written well ahead – at times it was two months in advance of what we were recording – this meant that the producers could record all the scenes that included this actor who was going on his hols or that actress who was about to work in a movie – so it worked for the good of all concerned, and I had more time to indulge my favourite pastime.

My next door neighbour was a nice guy called George England who had a lovely lady wife and several children. George told me one day that his marriage bed was flush against the parting wall against which was the bed I slept in. And in which I stayed awake quite a lot of the time.

Lucky me, I was finding or being found by the most sensational women God could have sent my way and since he had given me the energy to accommodate so many during that summer there was no shortage of spring activity in the bedroom.

George sort of summed it up one day when he said to me: 'If the wife happens to get pregnant again it'll be your fault. We have a system that's worked exactly as we want it to work, but the activity night after night on the other side of the parting wall, well, times there's nothing for it but y'know!'

As I said he was a lovely guy and he and his wife would have nothing but my respect and my gratitude for putting up with me during the short time I lived beside them.

At that time, part of my problem was that I thought myself indestructible. I was also afflicted with a need to never turn out the light, wanting to keep the party going, sleep the very last thing on my mind.

Another problem was that with the publicity I was getting I was a target for some of the predatory females that every city produces, Dublin being no exception. Since I lived like a single guy I was fair game to them as they were to me, and having a place to take a lady is always a bonus, so it's not any kind of miracle that a guy could get laid around the clock. Even back then the women of Dublin were ripping their way out of the dark ages of sexual repression and I was only too happy to give them a hand to get beyond the clutches of the ten commandment mind-set.

My Hollywood producer, Danny Haller, sends a beautiful English lady, Francis Doel over to Dublin to work with me as my editor on the second draft of the film script.

Francis and I hit it off straight away, and within hours she is showing me the finer points of screenwriting. I was very happy about this arrangement, always keen to learn something, but she looked so lovely sitting across the work table from me, that there were times when I found it very hard, if you'll pardon the expression, to keep my mind on the script. But that lovely English rose and I were never more than good pals and I like to think we remain so to this day.

Francis was very impressed with my work rate, telling me that if she got a page a day from a Hollywood screen writer she was lucky. The way we worked, we discussed a scene or two and she made comments intended to be helpful, then she would go away and I would get on with the writing. She was surprised that I had a handful of pages ready for her at the end of the first working day and to my delight every day thereafter until we finally nailed the script down and put it to bed.

Danny Haller arrived a few days later and when Francis and I joined him at the Intercontinental Hotel in Ballsbridge he was handed a bound script with the title *PADDY* in bold lettering on the cardboard cover.

I hid my disappointment that the film wasn't being called *Goodbye to the Hill,* having learned during the shooting of *The Pale Faced Girl* that there's a lot of cutting and making it up as you go along in the filming of any story. Nothing is sacred, including the title that was even then burned into the collective consciousness of Dublin city.

To my chagrin the movie would be released as 'Paddy' two years later and there was nothing I could do about it. There were other things as well that left me wanting – I'll tell more as we go along.

Meanwhile, though working as an Associate Producer on movie and earning a decent salary for it, I continued writing my daily radio script before being driven to the film location. Many mornings I had sent a young woman away with passionate kisses and promises not always kept, before I got down to the series script, so as you can imagine I was not getting that much sleep. I came through the six-week shoot which proves you can go a long way on duck eggs and Dexedrine.

Right now I want to tell you that just days before we started shooting *Paddy* – by which time a lot of time and money had been spent on the movie – it was about to be called off because we had lost our leading man, Donal McCann.

When we began casting the picture I brought Donal along to meet Danny Haller and the man from LA had flipped out. He thought McCann a natural leading man who could go all the way in Hollywood, something I had felt since I first met him that time at the BBC in London.

Donal signed up for the role of Paddy but then backed out at the last minute – he had landed the lead in a two handed play called 'The Au Pair Man' by Hugh Leonard, one of

Ireland's best and most successful writers.

The play was going into London's West End and Donal would be playing opposite a legend, the wonderful Miss Joan Greenwood. He told me the news without a hint of concern that he was causing me a major problem, the extent of his non-involvement like a blow to my idea of what was fair and right.

In the moment I realised this was just how he was, that he would always be like that, he would always do what was right for him without giving a damn what people thought about him, whether you were a mate or not. I didn't like what he did but I didn't hold it against him.

When I broke the news to Danny Haller he threw the head completely and within half an hour he was ready to pack his bags and head for the airport and a plane ride home to L.A.

I hadn't said much up to that moment. Now I stepped in and told him to his face that he owed me another shot at getting him a new leading man.

He didn't seem to want to listen – he was shattered and acting like a kid whose favourite toy had been nicked. Then I heard him say that the movie was off but I stopped him leaving the room at the Intercon and told him I wasn't ready to lose my chance just because a self-centred actor was doing his own thing, regardless. I waxed very forcefully as I told this to Haller, going on to tell him he owed me a couple of hours to come up with a replacement for McCann.

Tamara Assayev, who was co-producing, took me aside and asked me did I really think I could find the right actor in a hurry. Without hesitation, I was telling her I already had somebody in mind and that I would go find him, talk him through the part, but that I needed two hours. Tamara told me to go ahead, that she would sit on Haller to get me the time I needed to pull the picture and my dream of a Hollywood movie credit out of the fire.

I left the hotel in Ballsbridge and took a cab into the city. I felt pissed off with Donal McCann, sorry for myself and very sorry for Danny Haller. I was remembering those moments after I told him the bad news and I realised how much of himself he had already invested in the film. Months of his time and heaps of emotional input along with his money and his desire to get the movie made, meant he had all kinds of stuff to handle if the movie went down the tube.

All this was jigging on my mind and it was good because it was stimulating my teeth gritting determination that I was not going to let this opportunity slip out of my hands. This was to the forefront of my mind as I went into the Abbey Theatre and sent in a message for an actor called Des Cave to come out and see me about something very important.

Des was an easy guy to like and a fine young actor who would go on to play leading roles in the national theatre. When I told him I wanted him for *Paddy* in *'Goodbye' the movie*, he jumped at the chance to meet Danny Haller.

I took him for a walk and tried to give him an insight into Paddy. Des had read the book but I was offering him stuff from inside myself that he wouldn't have been familiar with. He was a good listener which was why he was such a good actor and by the time I got him to the hotel to meet the man, he was as ready as he was ever going to be. With me hoping he was ready enough.

Just before I took him into the room to meet Danny Haller, I said to Des that he had to breeze in as if he owned the place and lay one of his million dollar smiles on whoever was there with the director. Des has no idea of how great that smile of his was but the minute he flashed it, I saw Tamara Assayev's eyes light up.

I made the introductions and gave Danny a run down on the kind of work Des had been doing in the national theatre. I just gave him the facts and I could see that both my director and the associate producer were very impressed that this young guy was a member of The Abbey repertory company.

A little while later after Des had read a couple of scenes with me playing Ma and one or two of the other characters against him, I saw Haller's rueful grin light up his face before he looked at me and said: 'You are one hell of a casting director.'

Haller offered Des the part, we all shook hands and while Tamara took the young actor away to talk salary and whatever, Danny and I got a couple of stiff drinks and touched glasses to toast the fact that the movie was back on.

We shot the film in six to eight weeks mostly on location in and around Dublin. It starred Milo O'Shea, a wonderfully talented actor who was, for my money, seriously miscast as Harry Redmond, being nothing like the street-arab who counsels the young Paddy in matters sexual and other things.

We had the great Peggy Cass, a stunningly talented New York actress and the brilliant Judy Cornwell who beds Paddy and enjoys a threesome romp with him and another character. We had Maureen Toal, a great Irish actress and Vincent Smith playing Paddy's older brother, Billy. Vincent would, in time, go on to play Harry Redmond as I had conceived him, more than a thousand times in the stage version of the *Goodbye* story.

We were blessed with the complement of a great crew led by an electrical wizard called Paddy O'Toole who was talented enough to be a lighting cameraman or a director.

This was a very good time career-wise for me and on a personal level a bit miraculous due to my meeting a man called Johnnie Dolan – he did the still photography on the film – who would become my mentor in 1969 when I finally put the plug in the jug and quit abusing myself with alcohol.

But lo and behold, when the movie 'Paddy' was released in 1970 it was banned by the Irish Film Censor on the grounds that it was indecent and obscene.

To my mind the banning of 'Paddy' was a sick joke that was due, probably, to a momentary flash of Maureen Toal's magnificent breasts. Whatever the reason, I thought our movie was about as obscene as the minutes of a Presbyterian Church meeting.

chapter 7

I was mad as hell when the Censorship Board banned my book *Paddy Maguire is Dead* in 1972. I had put my heart and my blood and my guts into telling the story of what happens to a drinking alcoholic if he does not manage to get free of the booze.

Or course, I had committed the cardinal sin in Ireland by talking about sex, about the sex life of an alcoholic called Paddy Maguire.

Obviously, the character was based on me – this was the third book in which the guy had featured, the other two being *Goodbye to the Hill* and *A Bed in the Sticks*.

It occurred to me later – long after the book had poured through my heart – that I had made the mistake of showing that it wasn't all bad. Surely, it had to be allowed that Paddy enjoyed a lot of the booze and the sex before he ran out of road and eventually, after a lot of hardship on his wife and himself, got lucky enough to put the plug in the jug.

Which he did by stumbling into an AA meeting in London and latching onto the idea *Stay Away From One Drink for One Day*.

I decided to try and do something about the situation and in company with my solicitor, the late Larry Murphy, I actually had a meeting with the barrister, Mary Robinson. But eventually I decided to take the matter into my own hands and this I did at the top of Grafton Street in 1972. What I did was this – I pinned a placard to my sweater which declared: PADDY MAGUIRE IS ALIVE AND WELL AND LIVING IN DUBLIN.

I then proceeded to give away a hundred copies of the banned book with the intention of being arrested and being taken to court where, hopefully, I could make a test case in the name of all writers.

I let it be known that I was going to do this – but not one writer turned up to give me moral support, though as always I had my pal Vincent Smith standing there beside me.

So, taking my time to sign each book, I began to break the law by giving a copy to anyone interested in having the book.

Within minutes of my arrival at the junction of Grafton and South King Street, two young Garda appeared and stood by as though monitoring the situation.

Since I am taking at least a minute to sign each book, things are moving slowly and I'm hoping that the press photographers I have lined up will soon get pictures of the cops taking me away.

My intention is that when they come to arrest me I will sit down so that they will have to lift me up to get me out of there. As they do so the press guys can bang off their pictures and we will have enough publicity the following day to begin building a platform against censorship.

After about twenty minutes I see one of the Garda being called over to the television shop on the corner of Grafton Street. In a minute he comes back across the street to me and tells me in a quiet voice, 'Mister Dunne, there's a phone call for you beyond in the television shop.'

I burst out laughing and say, 'Give me a break.'

As I look at the young Garda I register the respect in his demeanour which convinces me that he is being sincere.

'Are you kidding me?' I asked him defensively.

'No sir,' he tells me. 'It's genuine. There's a phone call.'

I indicate to Vincent to mind the books and I start to go over to the television shop with the young Garda by my side to help me get through the crowd that has gathered.

In the shop I pick up the phone and I say hello.

'Is that yourself, Lee?' The voice is familiar and I say, 'Yeh, Peadar, that's you, isn't it?'

'It is indeed. Are you in some kinda trouble there?'

'Not at the minute,' I assure him. 'How did you know I was here?'

'I was driving by on my way to Harcourt Terrace,' Garda Sergeant Peadar Casey tells me, 'and I wondered did you need any help.'

By this time a right few people have crowded around the window of the television shop as though they are making sure I'm not being smuggled out the back door and into a Black Maria.

Peadar Casey had tried to help me once before when a drunk drove into my parked car on Herbert Place. The night it happened, I was entertaining a young lady and didn't hear the bang going on outside. It was this decent copper who had taken the trouble to find out from a neighbour that it was my car that had been wrecked and he came to my door to break the news to me.

I invited him in, having left my lady friend in the bedroom, and thanked him for his decency. It was then he told me he owed me one: 'And maybe a lot more than one, Lee, for at times you saved my head when I was headin' for the kinda depression this job can bring on you.'

I gave him a cup of coffee and a doughnut and he munched away and sipped the hot drink while he told me the story.

'I read *Goodbye to the Hill* more times than you'd believe and there's one part in it that could lift me out of the deepest downer and that's no lie. D'ye remember,' he asks me, 'when Paddy comes up over the canal bridge and he notices that Noggler Green no longer has a three speed gear on his bike?'

'I do, Peadar, and Paddy's tongue hanging out for a three speed which he couldn't afford to buy.'

Peadar is nodding his head, about to explode with his huge

booming laugh. 'I took it off,' says Noggler, 'bloody thing slipped the other day an' I comin' up this bridge and I nearly broke me testicles.' Peader is already guffawing but he hasn't let rip yet.

'Nearly broke your what, Mister Green?' says the bad lad Paddy, getting' it up for poor Noggler.

'Me testicles, me ballocks,' says Noggler riding away with the moan 'only bitta pleasure we have left.'

Now I see and hear the power of Peadar's laughter and realise how much enjoyment he has been having every time he read this particular passage in the story.

'I carried the book around with me for years.' He said this as he got up to go. 'Don't need to since then 'cos I know it off by heart and as you can see, the picture still makes me laugh.'

Coming back to Peadar during my demo at the top of Grafton Street, I took his offer of help seriously. 'Can you help me get arrested, Peader?'

'What? What're you sayin' Lee? You're not back on the piss are you?'

'No way,' I tell him, 'but I need to get arrested so that I can take on the Censorship Board about banning my book.'

'What book have they banned on you?'

'*Paddy Maguire is Dead*'.

'I didn't know that. God what's wrong with them, are they craw-thumpers or what?'

'And I want to get the bastards into court,' I told him. 'I want to thrash this with them. I've got a smudge from every paper in town and some of the English ones too. You fix it for the two coppers standing outside to arrest me and I'll get front pages all over. Can you do that?'

'What's a smudge, Lee?'

'A photographer, Peader. I've a lot of press here. Now, can you get me arrested or not?'

'Oh Christ, Lee, I can't. As much as I'd like to help you, I'm sorry.'

In the heel of the hunt, I signed the hundred books and gave them away, the cops went off about their business and I remembered by pal John Dolan who had said to me beforehand, 'What happens if they don't arrest you, Sport?'

'They have to arrest me,' I insisted, 'I'll be breaking the law.'

John had not been impressed by this and he turned out to be right. And though there were pictures of me in the papers wearing my placard, the demonstration did nothing to alter the status quo in relation to book censorship in Ireland.

I suppose you could sum it up by saying, 'Oh yeh! Lee Dunne is a big deal. He's the head who couldn't even get arrested in Grafton Street'!

During the following six years I had seven more books banned and I even had a column cancelled. Rockin' the Boat! was the name of my column in the *Evening Herald* in the early 70's – the column that was going to change the face of Dublin and inject some much needed juice into the pages of the Dubs own paper.

The Editor of the paper, Aidan Pender, tendered this juicy description to me along with a real doozie: 'We are going to harness your talent for the benefit of the man in the street.'

I was delighted to be asked to write for *The Herald* and flattered that this guy responded to my need to write a column that would have a social conscience and not just be a heap of filler under a well-known name.

I told Aidan Pender I would go and stand at the bus stops in the rain with the people who were complaining about how long they had to wait – without any bus shelter. And I promised that I would write about the dangers of alcoholism and the drug culture that was riding high on our doorstep – you get the picture.

So, away we go – I write an introductory piece outlining my intention and I ask readers to send me their complaints and their gripes while I promised I would do all I could to help bring about some change for the better.

My second article was headlined in serious block capitals: I AM AN ALCOHOLIC.

At that time, a lot of people thought this a courageous step on my part but I didn't see it that way. I had been lucky enough to discover that alcoholism was a disease recognised by the World Health Organisation as being among the top three to five killers of mankind.

I wanted to say to the men and women who were still out there feeding their condition – you don't have to die from the booze. You can arrest it, ensure that you never drink again, if you just do what I did.

This wasn't a preachy article, it was a sharing of my experience my strength and my hope, and the added hope that it might reach even one person that thought – as I had done for too many years – they were some kind of sick creature for whom there was no hope.

The response to the piece was phenomenal and the papers editor was delighted with the way things were going.

The following week I was being minded by the Features Editor, Jack McGowan, a great guy, and when I presented my article *GOODBYE TO THE PILL!* Jack flipped out over it. I thought him a very brave guy since I eulogised the act of lovemaking and actually questioned the Pope's sanity for being against birth control.

On the day after the article appeared I got a telegram from the Editor himself telling me that due to an oversight he had forgotten he had an abundance of features and told me to hold my next column. He didn't go so far as to say and *The Next and The Next for like Forever* – but the message was loud and clear.

So the poor little guy had been on the receiving end of a blistering phone call from the Palace in Drumcondra though such a communication would probably travel circuitously, wouldn't you say.

I sought the Editor out, wanting the guy to tell me to my

face but he stuck to his guns 'an abundance of features' and I didn't bother to remind him about harnessing talent or whatever the jazz was that he laid on me before I offended the power that was as that time.

So ended the dream to help effect even a modicum of change in the lives of those lodged at the foothills of the system. I had allowed the column to live up to its name, *Rockin' the Boat*, and so it died young.

But I'm still here.

chapter 8

I just kept plugging away on the grounds that the only publicity you can call bad is your obituary. So in 1978, with several plays and endless radio scripts (that were not banned) behind me, I am about to direct the stage version of *Goodbye to the Hill*.

How did I come to write the story as a stage play? You can blame my pal Vincent Smith.

Late in 1968 he and I were walking along Drayton Gardens off the Fulham Road – I was in *The Big Smoke* to do publicity for my novel *A Bed in the Sticks* published by Hutchinson. As for Vincent, he had just finished taping a television role for Thames. As usual, we were talking about money, when out of the blue he says to me: 'Why don't you write a One-Man-Show-for yourself based on *Goodbye to the Hill*?'

This had never occurred to me though at times I'd been doing some Stand-Up and the odd cabaret gig to help keep the home fires burning. In the moment it seemed like a good idea and some weeks later I sat down of a Saturday evening to see what might happen in relation to a possible script. Within minutes the words started to come but they weren't for any One Man Show.

As a matter of fact, just over five days later I had a hundred pages of manuscript that had thrown themselves at me and the result was the stage play *Goodbye to the Hill*.

Plays had happened to me before, plays that were produced in The Gaiety and other theatres but none of them poured out the way this one did. For me it was more like a typing job than what you'd call a creative experience, and though it was turned down by producer Louis O'Sullivan – he couldn't see how it could be staged – I felt I had something very special on my hands. But with one thing and another, the script slipped onto the back burner and got stuck there for the guts of ten years.

Indirectly, I had Vincent Smith to thank for the play, but a decade after it had written itself out through me I had to very directly thank him for finding an angel willing to back the first ever production of *Goodbye*.

John Rushe was a laid back, laconic individual who shrugged *yes* when I asked him if he could afford to lose three or four grand. When you think of what it costs to stage any play in any venue today, three or four grand sounds like fiction but it was a lot of money to me at that time because I didn't have any of my own.

John Rushe hired the Eblana theatre for four weeks – not the most attractive theatre in town but the only one available. You pass the public lavatories on the way to the auditorium – we called it *The Only Toilet in Town with Its Own Theatre* – but the rent wasn't extortionate. It was also in the centre of town and well known to people from the suburbs since it was in the basement of the main bus station.

Because money was short enough, I brought my bag of tools from home – I had become pretty handy during the years since joining AA when I quit boozing in October '69. This was due to living in the countryside four miles out of Wicklow Town.

In the valley of Cullen Lower, my partner Nuala and I had rented an old house that we had turned into something a bit special. In fact it was beautiful enough for tourists to take pictures of it when they accidentally found themselves lost in our lane among the wheat fields of East Wicklow.

Living in the country is, overall, wonderful but when your home is off the beaten track you have to learn how to drive a nail and that – to get anybody to come to you and do any kind of repairs to an old house in what they consider to be the middle of nowhere will cost an arm and a leg.

I cast the play with help from Vincent who knew the scene better than I did. We did well, finding some very good players and we got very lucky when a small part actress named Dinky Heffernan came to meet me. To my mind she was the perfect 'Ma' and I cast her in a moment. I could see that some people doubted my judgment but Dinky was the rock around which the play flourished and before long this was generally accepted by those who'd had their doubts.

For me, the scenes between Ma and Paddy were wonderful and once again I'd been very fortunate in going with my gut when it came to casting *Paddy* the horniest teenager in Dublin.

Vincent had mentioned an actor called Frank Melia that I'd seen on television and I had chuckled as I remembered the guy's million dollar smile.

Frank was a very likeable guy and I reckoned he was a good enough actor for the emotional content of the role. Like me he had been born far from the silver spoon, so despite the ever-ready smile, there had to be a lot of anger in the guy. The edge that this gave the character coupled with his mischievous grin was bound to have girls falling over for him.

Bewley's Café on Grafton Street had always been very special to me – the mid morning cup of coffee, when I could afford it, during my time in the insurance office – a place where you could nick the odd bun without anybody calling the cops.

Frank Melia was waiting for me with his back to *the Harry Clarke's* and as I got to him he hit me with that sunburst smile. I shook his hand, more than ever convinced he was right for the role of *Paddy*. Of course, I'd have to dirty him up some – Frank had the face and the mind of a choirboy while Paddy was street-wise and somewhat street-worn. Right away I could see that I had a job on my hands – at this time, Frank Melia was so shy he blushed if somebody said *tits* in his company.

Anyway, I asked him right off if he knew the story of *Goodbye to the Hill* and he said of course, he'd read the book and loved it. Then I offered him the role of *Paddy*.

For a moment he seemed puzzled. Then he said with disarming ingenuousness: "You do know how old I am?"

I looked at him for a few seconds and I said in all seriousness: 'Probably twenty-four, five, but you don't look it.'

Frank burst out laughing and I chewed half a doughnut while he wrestled with a chortle that wouldn't quit. Finally, he found enough air to murmur, 'I'm thirty-four, Head. I've got a fourteen year old daughter.'

He tells me this with a face like a mass card so I know he is not kidding. I'm stunned but not for long. I tell him to smile and he does and my faith in my instinct is renewed. 'If you lose ten pounds you'll get away with it." He looks doubtful and I tell him to trust me. He nods though his eyes are not smiling. He's an actor – come on, he's not going to fight me to avoid taking the part.

After that we had more coffee and chewed the fat with him promising to cut down on the munchies and do some running. Before I left I gave him a copy of the script believing in my innards that he would make a wonderful *Paddy*.

From our first cast get together he was a wonderful tonic of a guy who seemed innocent enough that it was like he'd been under wraps for thirty four years. During rehearsals he'd frequently laugh like he was being paid for it. This would happen when the meaning of a certain line would land on him.

'Here!' he would cry out, his exclamation sounding the same every time. 'This is dirty!'

In moments the company would be doubled in laughter, while Melia at times on his back on the stage, his knees up to his chin, convulsed in the combination of amusement and enlightenment. Everybody just loved the guy – he was thirty-four, married, with kids and he looked like a teenager who had never even taken one off the wrist. No kidding, Frank acted like he'd been reared in a nunnery as opposed to the streets of dear old dirty Dublin.

After rehearsals each day, I built the set for the play with Vincent giving me a hand. I salvaged much of the material for the set from the basement of the theatre with the blessing of Phylis Ryan who held the lease. This same lady had produced another play of mine *The Full Shilling* at the Gaiety in Dublin back in 1972 and was one of the city's best known producers.

I found some black material in that same basement and turned it into masking curtain and I brought some huge scarves from home, hanging them to great effect in what was the bedroom of *Paddy's* mistress who at forty was twenty-two years older than our randy hero.

At the same time something else – something even more important than my stage play – began on that stage in the Eblana. Each day during lunchtime four women came to visit me and between us we launched what would become *Overeaters Anonymous* in Ireland. This came about when a friend of mine – let's call her Dymphna – took up my suggestion that we start something in Ireland to help people whose eating was out of control. I based the programme on the Big Book of Alcoholics Anonymous which had helped me quit drinking in October, 1969.

There was no magic involved – I simply took the word *alcohol* out of the equation and substituted the word *food*, telling the overweight ladies what I'd heard when I first joined AA – get ninety meetings in ninety days, and be willing to go to any lengths to get sober. In this context the word sober means 'not given to excessive indulgence'. In time the fellowship of OA would spread all over Ireland, so from a quiet home and a first beginning in our basement theatre a ray of hope for many came to life on the northern bank of the Liffey.

After the one and only preview of *Goodbye* I was happy with the cast, felt good about my script and just knew, in my water, that I had a hit on my hands. When you read the next line you might come to the conclusion that not everyone agreed with me.

'GOODBYE TO LEE DUNNE AT THE INTERVAL.'

My friends, you may read many theatrical reviews, but I doubt you're going to find another quite like this one.

This is the *Evening Press* headline over the review of *Goodbye to the Hill* by Con Houlihan which was published on the day after our opening night October 4 at Eblana in 1978.

Personally speaking, I had never seen anything like it and all those commenting to me about it thought it extraordinary.

Vincent Smith and John Rushe and I, differed from most of those commenting, since they were complaining, while we were jumping up and down with joy.

This is not a joke. As we three took turns reading out loud the banner over Con Houlihan's by-line we danced about like lottery winners since we knew bloody well you just couldn't buy that kind of publicity.

And when we saw the *Evening Herald* headline we nearly didn't bother reading the paper's review. This one said simply:

'OBSCENITIES IN LEE DUNNE PLAY.'

This was what the Dub's own newspaper said, while I thanked in my heart the sub-editor who had written the line. To get such a break – to have a complete stranger doing me such a favour by writing what can only be described as a money line – was more than anybody has the right to expect.

And what favours those two headlines turned out to be for the play, not forgetting the cast who would be working – and getting paid for some time to come. We could say this with certainty right away because we had queues already booking a week ahead, the second week looking like it would be a sell out by Thursday.

As I've said already, I wasn't surprised because of what happened at the single preview we did the night before we opened. It is no exaggeration to say that our invited preview audience ate up the play. A mixed bunch of people, some we knew – actors who were out of work – a bunch of plumbers and other tradesmen who had been working in the theatre during rehearsals – plus one female playwright who gave me such a hate filled look as she left the theatre, that I knew I had a hot one on my hands.

Having the tradesmen at the first ever showing of the play meant a lot to me – two of them had appeared in the Eblana during the second week of rehearsal, a couple of guys with a ladder and a bunch of tools who had come to fix the plumbing in the Gents at the rear of the theatre. I just happened to see them come in because the entrance was down front by the stage.

As they walked some way up the theatre with their backs to the stage, they heard *Maureen* (played by Madeline Erskine) say to *Paddy* (played by Frank Melia): 'I'm pregnant, Paddy.'

I saw the two guys stop and turn around, the next thing you know they ditch the ladder and the tool bags and slide into a couple of seats, while I restrained my hearty appreciation of such instant contact between the play and a couple of Dubs. And real Dubs they were, ordinary heads just like Vincent Smith and I, and precisely the kind of people I wanted to write for, without barring anybody from any level of society from buying a ticket for the show.

As it happened, one of the plumbers turned out to be a guy called Paddy Lynch who had lived upstairs in the same block as my family in Mount Pleasant Buildings where I was born and which I christened *The Hill* for my novel.

I only discovered who Paddy Lynch was when I went to welcome him and his mate during a break in rehearsal and of course I remembered him, a lovely guy whose mother was a very special woman.

We shared a smile when he reminded me that my kid brother, Brendan, who as a toddler could not pronounce the name Paddy, ended up calling this big guy *Foddy* which became our kid's handle until we outgrew nicknames.

There were a couple of other things, apart from those *amazing* review headlines, that, in my opinion, helped the play get such a huge response.

Firstly, a lot of people thought the novel *Goodbye to the Hill* had been banned. In fact, this had not happened. The book passed the Censorship Board by the skin of its teeth.

Some thought that *A Bed in the Sticks* had been banned in '68–this didn't happen either. And my third novel *Does Your Mother?* arrived in 1970 and passed without any problem

I happened to believe that a lot of people thought the play was based on the banned novel *Paddy Maguire is Dead* rather than *Goodbye to the Hill* – not that it really mattered.

The truth was that we had a real hit on our hands, which was entirely due to how Con Houlihan over-reacted to what he saw during the opening act on our first night in the Eblana.

Con Houlihan is, and always was a lovely guy, a huge Kerryman who can write about anything in his own unique style. His review for *Goodbye* was written in the heat of passion or porter, or both, after he stormed from the theatre and back to the *Evening Press* office. The headline told exactly how he felt about what he had seen on the *Eblana* stage and, lucky me, the play reaped the benefit of the big man's discontent.

To such an extent that after three weeks I had to phone Louis O'Sullivan, who had turned down the chance to produce the show – he couldn't see how I could stage it – to talk to him about hiring his theatre for a while.

Louis owned the *Oscar Theatre* in Ballsbridge, and I needed to hire it because we had only a four-week agreement at the *Eblana*. There was another show already booked to follow us in, so we had no chance of getting an extension.

When Louis hears my voice he gives me no time to talk business but goes into a rap something like this: 'Lee Dunne, what am I doing in this business? I turned down your play which you well know because I couldn't see how you would stage it. I turned it down and the other night in the *Eblana*, there were times when I was the only punter sitting in the seat he paid good money for, and why, you might well ask, I'll tell you why. I was the only one sitting because the rest of the punters were on the floor laughing at this play that I turned down.'

When Louis quit beating himself up we had a good laugh together and I asked him if I could rent the *Oscar* open ended since we were booking solid at least five weeks ahead. Louis was only too glad to accommodate us and we would run at his theatre for eleven weeks before going back to town to the *Eblana*.

In all we ran for twenty-six weeks on that first outing with the play that was going to be my One Man Show. And so began the story of that little play which has since become Ireland's longest running play, gathering a record that will never be beaten on the Emerald Isle.

Let me tell you now about an extraordinary happening that took place on opening night at the *Oscar* – an event that was quite unbelievable that got under way in the late afternoon.

By this time we had our lighting in place, the stage was set and dressed, my actors had done their run through, and we were all ready to go and get some grub before returning for seven thirty, the half before the starting time of eight o'clock.

As I'm about to leave the Oscar I notice that the lettering over the main door refers to last week's production which was George Bernard Shaw's *Arms and the Man*. I give the manager a serious pull to make sure he gets the strength of my need that the lettering be changed to read: Lee Dunne's *Goodbye to the Hill*.

Being Irish, the guy assures me that this will happen in a matter of minutes, he even swears to me on his mother's life that such will be the case. And like the old sweetheart that I am, I believe the little fucker!

There are many things that it took me a long time to learn on my journey so far, and one of them is this: 'Just because you are talking, and vehemently asserting a need, do not assume that the party you are addressing is listening to a single word that you are saying, particularly if he is nodding his head and perhaps even wearing a smile.'

Now, segue with me to the Shelbourne on St. Stephen's Green where a very rich American couple are eating an early dinner and talking about going to 'see a little Shaw' at some place called the *Oscar* which appears to be 'out of town'.

Ballsbridge is, of course, a very tidy suburb on the south side of Dublin city, which houses even now one of the last bastions of the British Empire, the Royal Dublin Society where the world famous Horse Show happens every year.

Are you by any chance ahead of me in this moment? Do you know what happens when this American couple, Ed Gifford and his lovely wife, Michael (yes that was her name) get out of their cab outside the *Oscar*? Are you picturing the words Lee Dunne's *Goodbye to the Hill* over the door? Of course you're not doing any such thing because unlike me you are not a gobshite! You, being bright as a button are picturing the words George Bernard Shaw's *Arms and the Man* over the door and you are hundred per cent right, since the little bollix of a house manager forgot about me and my pressing need once I had thanked him in advance for the thing that mattered most to me that he didn't get around to doing.

Anyway, the Giffords, the couple from Manhattan, take their seats. Ed hands his wife, Michael a programme and they discover – at the same time – that they are about to watch something other than the work of GBS who was born in Synge Street and was, by all accounts, a right crotchety oul' bollix.

'Something called *Goodbye to the Hill*', they say at the same time, thinking they will give it a shot until the interval. I know that this is how it happened and you'll see why if you read on a bit.

As the interval arrives to a rapturous reception from a full house, a large gentleman, a New Yorker, and his lovely wife seek me out. They have enquired of the usher if the author happens to be in the theatre, and having established that I am the guy they tell me there and then that 'we want to produce your wonderful play on Broadway'.

Are you asking yourself how many times this can happen to a guy? If you are, I don't blame you.

I thank the couple and suggest that if they feel the same way after they have seen the second act, I'd be only delighted to talk to them about the idea.

The play goes a storm, earning a standing ovation from the audience, the theatre buzzing with genuine enthusiasm. This is wonderful since it means more business because word of mouth is the best advertising any show can have going for it.

As the audience file out I find myself wondering will the New Yorkers be there when the numbers thin out.

Fair play to them, the Giffords are there shaking my hand and inviting me to join them for a late night supper and drinks at the Shelbourne.

An hour later, I'm having a snack – the Giffords are amazed to meet an Irish writer who no longer drinks booze – and Ed Gifford is showing me the publicity he earned for his production of *The Magic Show* which he turned into a box office hit despite the kind of notices that can kill a show on The Great White Way.

So he is a bona fide producer and no kidding, no himming and hawing, the guy says without prevarication – and clearly with the support of his lovely wife – that he wants to do my play right there on Broadway.

For someone who peddles dreams for a living, I never cease to be surprised that, even yet, I find it tough to believe that any big offer can actually happen for me. I've been fortunate that some things have come true, yet the possibility of one more real break remains a very tough nut for me to crack. And when a piece of my work, book or play or whatever, gets the kind of praise the Giffords were bestowing on *Goodbye* that night at the Shelbourne, I do my best to believe what they are saying. But I am also thinking, 'Dublin's one thing, Broadway is another ball game.'

Anyway, that night I promise to put a script in the post right away. They are leaving first thing the next morning – they understand that I need time to produce a clean and tidy manuscript. You should see the state of a play manuscript after weeks of rehearsal and early performances. It looks seriously diseased ergo I had to retype the whole thing, this being the days before word processors.

The days following are taken up with cashing in on the publicity that the amazing reviews had attracted so I had to put the typing of the play for the Giffords on the back burner.

I was also back to my script work on the Harbour Hotel radio series for which I had written the first seven hundred and fifty episodes right off the bat, still working with Noel Jones and Danny Riordan and getting a lot of help from another good guy producer Laurence Foster. Ultimately, I would scribble twelve hundred shows for HH, no mean feat, and to me a godsend because that job kept the home fires burning when things turned cold.

A week later I get a phone call from Ed Gifford. He's a bit miffed that he has not yet received the script. I promised to send him. Being honest, I am more than surprised he has called but I just dive into a rap that I've been ill with a bad flu and this time I will keep my promise to him.

And I do, sending him a completely retyped script which included the good changes we had come up with in rehearsal, express, within a week. Then I let that scenario move out of my head. Ed Gifford wouldn't be the first who wanted a script and then you never hear from the guy again.

You'll remember this is what happened with Mike McAloney. He had been to the play – jumping up and down with his over the top enthusiasm – and he had actually given me money for a twelve-month option and I hadn't heard a word from him since, and wouldn't have been amazed if I never heard from the fucker again.

This can happen because even though he has talked about Broadway to you, a producer can come across a story that turns him on even more than your production did the night he saw it on stage. Usually, a producer is throwing any number of balls in the air while doing novenas that one of them will land and make money for all concerned. If it happens to be your story that gets the *go* slot, you really have been touched by some kind of loving god.

So while I allowed for the possibility of the Giffords as possible producers, you'll guess I hadn't seriously thought of them like that. Nice people having an ego trip on a night out in Dublin, fair enough. I guess that had I really believed them I would have sent the script first thing. By finally doing so I was just putting another poker in the fire in the hope that it might just get red hot.

No matter what producers/publishers/movie makers tell you, you have no guarantee of anything until your book is in print, your play is on stage or your movie script is on screen. Like newspaper editors, the people who can make it happen for you, do so only when it is good for them. You don't really come into the equation unless they believe you can make money for them or make them look good in some way. And this is not offered in a critical sense. It's just how things are in the world of entertainment and information.

Out of the blue comes a lovely moment from that opening

night at the Eblana. A female friend of mine, married and not given to playing around, came gushing to me about Frank Melia.

You may recall that Frank is thirty-four years old with this in-built innocence that made him look like a teenager – well, get ready for this reaction from my pal, Penny. She comes to me eulogising about the play, ending her gush with: 'Honest to God, Lee, that young fella playing Paddy, I'd eat him without salt.' I gave her a hug containing all kinds of gratitude. Like she was right, Frank did look the part, and he played it to the hilt. But what my friend Penny didn't know was that even as she gushed about him and his good looks and the appetite he had engendered with her, he was actually three years older than she was.

chapter 9

It would be churlish to call Con Houlihan narrow minded, he is the most open minded guy imaginable, but some early lines in the play disturbed him *to the quick* and he overreacted in what you might call Todd-AO and Technicolor.

Let me explain that the first scene in any regular play is all about exposition – telling the audience what the score is for the characters at this time with bits of background thrown in. The trick is never write it like you are doling out information – it has to come from the characters as they share their feelings, spill their guts, react against something that has happened, and so on.

In this first scene, which I have edited here you get a lot of stuff very quickly but, it is accessible to any audience and I believe that the lines that bothered Con to distraction come at the end of this opening:

The young hero, seventeen year old Paddy Maguire comes into the broken down kitchen where his Ma is angrily recovering from a row with her departed husband – she has a secret that she is hiding too – Paddy slaps a coin onto the table to cheer Ma up.

Paddy

I got an extra shilling this morning. The Fabulous Fifties!
Isn't it great to be alive, Ma!

Ma
I thought said you got nothing extra.

Paddy
I got that from Missus Kaminsky. I did her a favour.

Ma
What sort of favour?

Paddy
*Made her a cup of coffee – She's very orthodox – I had to
pick up the shilling myself off the table. The Jews don't
even handle money on the Sabbath.*

Ma (Pockets coin)
*Thank Jesus, she's so religious. I hadn't a penny piece to
my name.*

Paddy
*Ma, will I nip down to the shop and get a couple of rash-
ers? Bacon sandwiches and sugary tea!*

Ma (Reacts)
*You can't go buying rashers with Mrs. Kaminsky's money
on a Saturday.*

Paddy
She'd never know.

Ma
I'd know.

Ma has turned quiet, retreated some. Paddy pours tea.

Paddy (Gently probing)
The row with Da, what was it about?

Larry (Off stage character) coughs. Paddy observes Ma
trying not to react to this. She fails.

Paddy
Is Larry any better this morning?

Ma (Hiding it)
Not much.

Paddy
That flu really has bleedin' muscles.

Ma
Coughing his lungs up – your da threatening to beat him.

Paddy
Ma, its not serious, is it?

Ma
*I've been keeping to myself, but God! Times I feel I'm just
going to burst wide open.*

Paddy
What is it, Ma? What's wrong with Larry?

Ma
He's got TB. Tuberculosis.

Paddy
Jesus Christ!

Ma
*God's going to take him on me. I've known it for weeks.
TB is killing children all over the country. Nothing any-
body can do.*

Paddy (Slams kettle down)
If we had money they'd do something

Ma
Hard at times to accept God's will.

Paddy (Bitter)
God's will! How could any God do this to you?
God in his almighty mercy! Jesus, help us all if
he ever loses his fucking temper!

There was a moment's pause as the shock of this line hit the first night audience which turned quickly into an explosion of laughter. This was exactly what I had expected since, even as Paddy's pain and his anger touched my heart, I had burst out laughing as the words landed on the paper during the writing of the play.

For a writer this is the perfect line – one where you deal with a character's pain, their inability to understand what's going on – something with which your audience can identify, while at the same time it evokes an amused, even startled response because it is clearly an outrageous thing to say.

I think that last sentence did it for Con – he couldn't handle the *fucking* word in the same sentence as God and Jesus. That's my opinion anyway, but whatever the cause, I agreed with Vincent Smith when he said that we would be jammed by Friday.

We both knew that the Dubs wouldn't wait to see what it was that drove Con Houlihan out of the Eblana. Dubs love the outlaw and that line was outlaw territory for the journalist from Cahirciveen. Dubs had never sided with Pat Garrett, the Sheriff – we were always rooting for Billy the Kid.

This was a genuine break for which I went on blessing Big Con and the sub-editor who used the word *obscenities* to highlight the Herald review, which could only help us to build an audience. This is just another example of the way life throws you a curve. I mean, here were words that were essentially critical in two newspaper reviews of the play and they turned out to be a gift from the gods gone laughing for the scribbler to whom a hint of outrageous is the bottom line.

So *Goodbye to the Hill* went on being a very lucky story, one that any scribbler would have been grateful for. Ever since the book was published thirteen years before we did the play at the Eblana I'd been lucky enough to earn a living as a professional writer. In all, I'd had fifteen books published – six of my plays had been on stage, some of them directed by me – and I'd seen many plays and scripts of mine of British television. I had also contributed numerous scripts to radio soap operas and I had seen three of my film scripts on the silver screen – just as I had dreamed it as a kid back in the Princess Cinema – *The Prinner* – and the Stella on Rathmines Road all those years before.

I had never thought of myself as a novelist or a playwright. I was simply being happy to be a professional writer, glad to have the ability to earn the daily crust, much of the time, by doing what I had done for nothing for the first eleven years of my writing life.

But in back of feeling lucky and grateful there was this niggling notion that I had stuff to write that was beyond any thing I had so far produced – so that I could end up resenting the fact that I was churning out radio and television scripts to buy the time to try and write a book. It was like I couldn't stay grateful for long. I believe now that ingratitude played a major role in the story of my tumble down into alcoholism. Most alkys are angry, ungrateful people even if they don't realise it.

How well I remember how my alcoholic anger affected my first trip to New York in 1966. Like, I should have been basking in gratitude as I stood looking into Doubleday's front window on Fifth Avenue, looking at the centrepiece which was the hardback edition of *Goodbye to the Hill*. The novel had just been published by Houghton Mifflin, one of the best houses in New York and Boston. And what was I doing? I was hissing under my breath, 'This should have happened years ago.' How sad it is to kill a great moment in a young life.

The truth is I got lost for a good while on that first trip to Manhattan, my standards slipped some. Thank God I wasn't out of tune when I turned down the offer of a trip to California with Jenny because my friend Eddie loved her. Sadly, I remained hanging around Manhattan, unaware that I had turned into a guy who would take drinks from strangers without ever buying one back. This was a total no-no on my charter for *Manly Behaviour* and I didn't even notice it until a Dublin born bartender, Teddy, pointed it out to me. On top of this my promiscuity just ran amok and then, to put the tin hat on the total imbalance of it all, I fell in love with a lovely girl who deserved a better shot than I gave her.

But, at the time, somehow you go on believing you're God's Gift to one and all. When you think that this kind of sad, reprehensible behaviour is fairly middle-of-the-road compared to where an alky can sink to, it gives you some idea of the power of the disease of alcoholism.

There were times like the odd moment of ordinariness when I sat down and wrote a list of all that I had going for me. And another list featuring all that was negative in my life. On the positive side I had good health, a good wife, a home, a family, a career and a pretty good way of life especially for someone born in a Dublin flat block that should have been pulled down a fortnight before they built it.

With half of the job done, I abandoned the exercise. In other words I had found a way to ignore what was written on the negative side of the page, another example of the blinding wilfulness of the mind that, if it does not get lucky enough to register Time To Quit, can find itself the minder of a brain destroyed by the Korsikov syndrome – The Wet Brain.

When this kind of thinking came anywhere near me, I got a drink into me fast and then another and before long my *Jack the Lad* persona slipped on like a mask and I got on with the day.

Given time, the day-to-day drinking would take its toll by becoming my grim reaper, the guy that harvested all the IOU's I had written to Some Day – this being the time when I would really get my act together. But, because Some Day would never come, he would finally dump all of my debits into my lap and tell me you better start dealing with your shit.

It's no lie to say that in the last five years of my drinking I damaged every area of my life but that was how it needed to play out for me to finally hear the words I needed to help me quit drinking alcohol and go about the business of trying to get sober.

It surprises me yet that the writing went on turning up, like in '68 there were the two movies I wrote and helped make in Ireland, and in September that year my second hardback novel *A Bed in the Sticks* was published in London by Hutchinson. And of course, the fact that stuff like this was still happening for you, gives you, as an alky, the power to get the alibi structure up again for another while. You can rationalise that *I can't be that bad if I'm doing this and I'm doing that*. You will grab onto anything that will allow you extend your drinking career.

Which I was still managing to do as we swept into the Spring or early Summer of 1969 when I did a major rewrite of a movie called *I Can't, I Can't* – which would be released in 1970 as *Wedding Night*.

This was for a Hollywood producer called Philip Krasne, the gig coming my way because a mate of mine, Mike Ruggins, had touched for the director's job.

Ruggins was a good guy I'd met while he was story editing at the BBC and he had commissioned a *Wednesday Play* from me while talking all the time about wanting to direct movies.

So I got involved with the film to rewrite of a script that had some good things in it but was very old fashioned. My main interest was in helping Mike have a decent screenplay to work with for his directorial debut. I also had a new book *Does Your Mother?* coming out later in the year so any publicity I could muster through writing the movie would be very welcome.

I go to work, staying and working at the Intercontinental Hotel in Ballsbridge and within a week I have Phil Krasne purring about my script. I feel it's going well but he makes it sound like it could win the Oscar. That was just Phil's way with any movie he was making – pity he wasn't as fast with the fee as he was with the compliments. But as I said I was doing it for Mike Ruggins and I was having a good time in Dublin.

When we are about to start shooting the picture Mike Ruggins tells me he is leaving, he can't take any more of Phil Krasne. It seems to me that Mike has got stage fright and I try to talk some sense into him.

Meanwhile, Krasne is complaining that Mike is trying to turn what is essentially *a bread and butter movie*, a story with a beginning, middle and end, in that order, into something like *Last Year at Marienbad*.

I point out to Mike that, if nothing else, he could earn real credibility by sticking with the movie to get his first screen credit as a director. But he won't be counselled and he takes a walk.

I'm packing up to head back to London when another director, Pierce Haggard calls me to tell me he is now going to do the movie. I'm pleased because it means my script can't be half bad – Pierce is an extremely talented man and one of the nicest guys around. He asks me for some rewrites and I have to tell him I'm going home since I have not been paid. He is embarrassed but we part friends and word has it that he did a very creditable job on the movie. Later on I did hear that he drove the crew crazy by insisting on shooting in sequence. Normally if you have a number of scenes in a certain bar or any particular location, you shoot all the scenes before moving on to the next location. That was bound to make for a heavy movie where the crew were concerned but thankfully it wasn't my problem.

As a footnote to this episode I can reveal that Phil Krasne never paid me for my work on that movie.

In 1974 a real nice man called Philip Evans came to see me from London. I was living in Ballyboden at the time and in the middle of mowing the lawn outside our cottage when he got out of a taxi and offered me a lot of money to write some 'funny, sexy books about London Cab Drivers'.

Since I like funny sexy books and London Cab Drivers, I said yes and he came into the cottage with me and talked while I made some real coffee for the pair of us. Normally, I make a cup of instant for myself but when a man is guaranteeing the rent and other things for a couple of years, you have to give him a cup of real java, right?

Philip told me he had just read *Paddy Maguire is Dead* which was banned in Ireland at that time. For those of you who have been living under a rock, I'm here to tell you that it has just been published by Killynon House Books after being *Off the Shelf* for thirty-four years. There is a brilliant and courageous defence of the book and an indictment of the Censorship Board by novelist, the late John Broderick that warms my heart and makes the book worth its money with the story thrown in to keep you from being bored on top of the bus.

In the time honoured tradition of writers – be they book writers, playwrights, poets, whatever – you put two of them together for five minutes or more – one of them will ask, invariably, or even invariably say, 'Are you making any money?'

Since I am talking with a publisher as opposed to a fellow scribbler, I have to use a more subtle approach, so I ask Philip

Evans, 'How soon do I see some bread?

Philip takes a contract from his pocket and tells me, 'If you can give me three titles, I'll write them on here and then I can give you a cheque for a third of the advance on each book. I have a blank cheque right here.'

Perhaps it's because I have always been a tad crazy but I'm hot at mental arithmetic and I have soon worked out that this is a tidy sum indeed and I say without thinking, 'First Title, *Midnight Cabby*.'

Philip chortles approvingly. 'Perfect old man, perfect,' and writes it down on the contract.

Now I venture forth with *The Day of the Cabby*.

Philip has another chuckle and writes this down. 'Nice play on Midnight Cowboy and The Day of the Jackel.'

Now I go: '*The Cabby Who Came in from the Cold.*'

Philip is clearly enjoying himself as he writes this down and then he remains silent while he goes about the serious business of writing the money words and numbers onto the cheque which he places in my hand, a big grin on his face.

'They capture the mood and the texture of exactly what I had in mind. We'll have fun with these books – directly into paperback under the Coronet banner.'

This being the paperback outlet of Hodder and Stoughton, one of the staunchest publishing houses in England, I was more than happy and Philip assured me they would put money behind the series.

An hour later he was gone, having asked me if I'd make myself available in London for pictures and stuff – expenses paid for by Coronet. I said sure, glad of a trip that was on the house and he said he'd be back to me within days.

Next thing I get a call from an American guy who directs television programmes for RTE. His name is Chris Darby and he has read an article of mine in *Cosmopolitan* about the fear of flying and wants me to be in a party of aerophobes flying to London as part of a documentary.

I immediately said yes even though I had quit being a white

knuckle flier from the moment I gave up the booze. Before this I had cramps in my hands every flight but, once I quit alcohol, I quit blaming the pilot for air pockets and turbulence, being able to reason it wasn't deliberate, and that he wanted to get home to his bacon and eggs too.

All the same I lied to Chris Darby and in due course would be on the plane with the always wonderful Maeve Binchy who really was an aerophobe. And Adrian Cronin who directed the *Late Late Show* and other things was even worse than dear Maeve whose hand I held, while trying to remind myself that I was supposed to look scared as well.

I'm in the Aer Lingus hotel in Kensington, my chore with Philip Evans over and done with, when I get a telephone call from a guy called Anthony Cheetham who tells me he runs a company called Futura. They publish books and he asks if I could come and see him as he has an offer to make to me that I might well be interested in.

That afternoon I meet this well established guy with Oxbridge written all over him. He is about thirty-years-old with the look of a man who had got his dinner every day of his life and I liked him though I'm not sure he felt the same way about me.

Anyway, even as I sit down, he tells me he has just read my novel *Paddy Maguire is Dead* and asks me if I would write him a series of funny, sexy books about London Cab Drivers.

I kid you not. Those were his exact words, syllable for syllable the same as those Philip Evans had laid on me in the garden at Ballyboden a very short time before.

I managed to hide the fact that I was dumbfounded and I told him I had just agreed to do a set of three Cabby books for Coronet. As I told him the titles he winced. 'Exactly what I had in mind, fun books with titillation, bordering on soft porn but not really dirty.'

I didn't say anything and he said, 'Do you by any chance have another series?'

Having played Draw and Five Card Stud with guys like

Connolly from Clones, McCusker from Terenure and Glasser from Kilrush, I had, at great expense, come to know the value of a poker face and I stuck it on rapidly for the benefit of this man who seemed desperate to be my publisher.

I nodded my head while taking a cigarette from my pocket. As I got the lighter going I said, 'As a matter of fact, I do have something might interest you.'

A good drag on a fag does wonders for the imagination and in a moment I had been presented with a beautiful idea that seemed perfect for the present situation.

Anthony Cheetham is sitting there with an expectant look on his face and I laid it on him with my best mass card face well and truly in place. This suggests sincerity which in this case meant I'd had this idea for a long time. 'How about a working class Forsythe saga, with tits'

His face lit up with satisfaction and he stood up, nodding his head emphatically. 'Yes, that will do very nicely.' He sits down again as though he had just thought of it, and asks me how long would it be before you could deliver the first manuscript?'

'If we can agree on the bread involved, not that long,' I said.

He sits down and makes like he is doing figures on paper and then he comes up with figures I thought very fair. And guess what, it was exactly the same offer as Philip Evans had made to me a short time before.

I avoided shaking my head in amazement – were these guys buying their approach to a days publishing from some guru who sold them the script, or what.

'I'd like to sign you up right away, would that be agreeable to you?' Anthony Cheetham said.

I told him it was fine and we agreed that I would go down the stairs and into the pub next door and sip a glass of orange juice while he had his secretary type the details into the contract.

My missus had gone off to Marks and Sparks to buy some underwear and stuff and by the time she got back I had signed up with Futura and been given my cheque and off we went to Ireland feeling quite flushed.

Nuala who knew nothing of the publishing world – *does anybody? I ask myself* – she suddenly thought that being a writer was like having a licence to print money. I gently disabused her of this notion, warning her that it was a peaks and valleys job – you had money one year and you could be broke the next, the drag being that you never knew what was going to go, to sell in numbers large enough to pay back your advances so that you could go on earning.

Anyway, I would write eight or nine books in all, most of them going to Futura, including two of the cabby stories which I called *The Virgin Cabbys* and my favourite title of them all, *The Cabfather.*

To finish this story, sadly Philip Evans was involved in a car accident caused by ice on the surface of a London street. He was a good writer himself, this lovely man destined to end up in a wheelchair.

The other man, Anthony Cheetham in recent times sold out his interest in Futura for something like fifty-six million pounds and became top buck cat at Random House.

In the Seventies I was back and forth to the UK on a fairly regular basis, accepting commissions to write television scripts, coming back to Dublin to write them, and then using the excuse of delivering them personally to have a few days in London and see my kids. I also had Sarah, Peter and Jonathan to visit me wherever I was living here at home.

I used to drive onto the boat and take my time motoring down to The Big Smoke, going different routes to see a bit more of the English countryside which is really very beautiful.

This story concerns a trip back home on the overnight boat and I get into the dining room in need of a large breakfast.

I'm sitting there giving my order to the steward when the Head Waiter appears and says to the steward: 'No charge for this man's breakfast.'

I'm amused and happy to meet such a warm hearted guy and as we shake hands I ask him why the freebee.

'Well, I'll tell you,' he says, sitting down to face me. 'First of all my name is Paddy Maguire.'

Here, he is mentioning the name of my hero in three of my novels and we shake hands again.

'So here's the story,' he informs me and tells me the following tale.

'I was reading *Goodbye to the Hill* in bed and I'm laughing and getting the odd turn on – you were a sexy bastard, weren't you.'

'Not so much of the "weren't' you",' I said in my warning voice. He has a knowing chuckle and presses on.

'My missus was going off to sleep and she said, "It must be some book, laughing like a drain and turning pages like I've never seen before", or words to that effect.

'I finished the book about two hours later and I closed it so hard – it was a hardback!' He laughed at his joke. 'I was so delighted with it, so moved, that I woke her up.

'Well, she couldn't believe I'd finished it and she sat up and said 'give me that here', and she started to read it as I went off to sleep the richer for having read your great book.

'An hour later she wakes me up and I'll tell you what, Lee, the missus gave me the best night we ever had in the Scratcher.'

He laughed, warm in the memory of their lovemaking and he stood up and shook my hand.

'Now you know why I can't charge you for your breakfast.'

And away he went about his business, still chuckling at a night to remember, thanks to the novel that pumped out of me in six weeks of evenings after I'd been driving my cab around London to earn the daily bread.

That's a very nice thing to happen to a guy who had to write because he had no choice in the matter and it had me feeling all the richer for having met a real life person called Paddy Maguire.

chapter 10

I finally got to a meeting of Alcoholics Anonymous and I heard enough that night and felt enough pain that I made the decision to put the plug in the jug.

It's a fact that I came out of that meeting knowing I didn't have to drink any more booze. As incredible as it may sound, especially after the crazy drinking or the last six years, I left Redcliffe Gardens to go home to East Sheen and my family, sure in my mind that I would never drink booze again.

The truth is that the AA message *Stay Away From One Drink for One Day* landed on me like a ton of bricks. I believed I could go without anything for a day and I thank God I never took another drink of alcohol from that day to this.

I've written before about this and I won't labour it again here. But it's worth saying that during that first meeting at Redcliffe Gardens in London, I heard a recovering alcoholic enumerate many of the symptoms of alcoholism.

There are at least forty seven symptoms of the disease named as one of the top five killers of mankind by the World Health Organisation.

I didn't know this statistic at my first meeting but I identified with the first seventeen symptoms mentioned by the guy who was leading the meeting and that was more enough for me.

That evening I didn't consciously surrender to the truth

about my drinking – it was more that *I was surrendered* by the state I was in. I sat there with my head down between my knees weeping like a scared kid with mucus running from my nose and I heard myself say to me: 'Jesus Christ! That's all that's wrong. I'm a fucking alcoholic.'

Afterwards when I remembered these words I was very taken by 'that's *all* that's wrong'. Like, right there was some kind of knowledge that things could be fixed, the disease could be managed, and I went back to AA for ten years to develop the necessary skills to ensure that I never drank alcohol again. This effort paid off – the plug stayed in the jug – but there would be one more fence for me to hurdle before I found what I call the regular sanity that forms the bedrock of the life I lead today.

I remember hurrying home to tell my wife 'that I have finally found a way to quit the booze'. Jean tells me she is glad I have got the message – of course, she has heard me swear off the sauce maybe a hundred times so you might understand that she is not jumping up and down to celebrate. And she asks me there and then if I will please just leave, her actual words being, 'Would you just give me a break and fuck off and stop screwing up my life. I can't take any more.'

I had nothing but respect for Jean and I was paying enough attention that I could hear the need in her for me to be out of her life. I expressed my sorrow and asked her to give me a couple of weeks to sort out my stuff, my immediate life, and I would leave.

We agreed there and then that she would tell the kids I had gone off working on another movie. We would then play it by ear with me having full visiting rights to see them so that I could go on being a part of their lives. When she asked me what about our house, I said my half is yours. She was a bit surprised but it was what I wanted and I gave her nine hundred quid out of my small stash, wishing it could have been ninety grand.

Jonathan was my youngest child but he was the only one

that quizzed me about the fact that I was going away again. He and Sarah and Peter knew that this wasn't a movie job that was taking me away and he told me with a lot of pain in his voice:'You're going to get divorced. I know it and I hate it and it's not fair,' while I sat beside him in the car with my heart in a sling and hating myself with a vengeance because my behaviour had brought us to a pass where the price was so desperately high for all concerned.

The remembered pain of those moments sitting with my youngest son in the car was another unforgiving dart to make me taste again the cost of my profligacy, but I didn't try to dismiss it. It had to be faced, allowed its time on the screen and I had to accept responsibility for playing the role of *Jack the Lad* with such unbridled enthusiasm.

This latest bout of guilt and self-pity was happening as I walked down the hill overlooking the valley of Cullen Lower on a day when the beauty of the Wicklow hills seemed to reach out to you in all its glory. I stayed with the pain of it, looking at it as opposed to looking for a positive image of myself. I paused for a while on the uneven hill to say the Serenity Prayer out loud. 'Grant me the serenity to accept the things I cannot change, Courage to change the things I can, And the Wisdom to know the difference.'

These simple words had never failed to release me from whatever was tarnishing my sense of well-being and moments later I was fit to get on with my walk towards home.

I rounded the lower corner of the walk and started on the uphill furlong to the old house, washed by a sense of acceptance about my wife and me. Like a fresh breath I was gifted with freedom from alarm or even disquiet as I considered that Nuala and I were very likely over and out.

This was the first time I had been capable of feeling this, hearing the words walk across my mind as I looked at them. It was in those moments that I could truly acknowledge the fact that when I'd entered the Rutland Centre for a seven week course in Reality Therapy, I'd done so, not to save my life, but to try and save my very rocky marriage.

Taken as I was by this sliver of invaluable hindsight right back to the treatment centre, I sighed at how ridiculous it now seemed, but I saw clearly that I had been in treatment for a couple of weeks before it actually dawned on me 'I REALLY AM AN ADDICT.'

As a recovering alcoholic, it surprises me now that it took me so long to realise this very self evident truth. But again, you have to understand the power of alcoholism. I mean, there I was in the centre, to get off the dope and stop sitting on my shit, but for ten years I'd been focussing on *I don't drink alcohol.*

In other words, I'd been giving myself a medal for staying away from booze and instead of facing up to this fact I was using dope as a substitute. Of course, I saw this as *a little present here and there*, like a joint. Soon this turned into the odd bout of serious dope smoking, and, then again dropping a few tabs of acid, popping Ritalin on the side, and not being beyond a sniff of nose candy when thing worked out that way. In a nutshell this meant I was steeped in delusion just like I'd been when I quit the booze a decade before.

My thinking would have run along the lines: 'Come on man – it's just a social thing. I mean, I'm not drinking, right!'

This is a perfect picture of how the addict can rationalize his behaviour no matter how destructive it is. And day by day, pain-filled minute by minute, I was learning the hard way just how much shit I had been sitting on all my life. What was even worse was the picture being painted for me by guys in the centre of what you had to go through for the treatment to work. From what I was hearing, it was going to be a very rough ride.

Luckily for me, God gave me fingernails strong enough to help me hang in regardless of how tough a situation turned out to be. None tougher in my experience than the seven weeks I spent in Rutland, where the counsellors – most of

ght - On my wedding day to my
st wife Jean in 1959. I am being
ngratulated by my best man,
chael Cunningham, a close
end to this day.

low - the actor Vincent Smith,
o is a great friend of mine, and
wife Nuala and my three chil-
n, Sarah, Peter and
nathan.This picture was taken on
cent's wedding day in 1973

My three beautiful children, Sarah, Peter and Jonathan, pictured in London.

Above - here I am signing a copy of a novel for the then Irish film censor, and good pal of mine, Seamus Smith. Circa 1990. I must add that Seamus was not the same film censor who banned my movies, Paddy and Wedding Night...that was before his time!

Below - Milo O'Shea, who starred in the film 'Paddy', and his wife Kitty pictured with me at Eamon Doran's Bar on 2nd Avenue, New York

José Quintero
~~35 Bethune Street~~
~~New York 10014~~

July 16, 1982

TO WHOM IT MAY CONCERN:

My first encounter with Mr. Lee Dunne was through his work
a play called "Casey", written with such beauty, humor, ten-
derness and a fierceness for survival, which after a first
reading, I committed myself to serve it, irregardless of
when or where it was produced   And when I met Mr. Lee Dunne,
quickly, for the openess and the gift of sharing is present on
the first handshake, I realised, that the play was as any
work of art is, a deep reflection of the man.

Mr. Dunne, and it gives me great joy to state it, is a
warm and generous friend, a god loving man, and one of the
most unusually gifted artist I have ever met

sincerely,

Jose Quintero
One West Sixty-Seventh St.
NYC., NY 10023

Abbeville

KINSALEY COUNTY DUBLIN

7th October, 1986.

Dear Lee,

Thank you very much for the inscribed
copy of your book.

I am very glad to learn that Nuala is
fully recovered and I hope I can get
an opportunity to come and see you both
soon.

With warmest personal regards and
good wishes,

Yours sincerely,

*The left hand letter is from the great Broadway director Jose Quintero who had wonderful
plans for my play and the letter of the right hand side is from Charles Haughey.*

*I wrote over 2,000 radio scripts, including episodes for Harbour Hotel, Kennedys of
Castleross and Konvenience Corner*

Above - Relaxing in bed with a good book in The Old House in County Wicklow. Circa 1979

Here I am with some very talented writers, Mary Lavin, Desmond Hogan, Francis Stuart and his wife Madeline Stuart, in Huston Station, Dublin, 28 November 1985

Me at 71 years young!
Photo by Michael Ryan

whom I hated for most of my time there – helped me save my life.

There were times during the treatment when I thought I would expire simply from the pain of being me, but I would go through the course ten times over to touch for the breakthrough that Mary Ellen McCann and Mary T Walsh and so many others helped me find in Reality Therapy.

Though it took me a while to know it in my feelings, I came out of the Rutland Centre *open to change*. We're not talking Wide Open to Change or anything like it but the tiny crack in the tight circle of my delusion was a genuine start, a real beginning to a life that in time could be delusion free. By staying clean and dry and by attending After Care and making changes in my lifestyle I could go on widening that circle as the natural process of *growing up* kicked in.

Ending my walk, excited about the possible deal for my play, saddened and paradoxically, relieved that the woman I'd married *till death us do part* was into being parted from me, I allowed the mixed feelings and focussed on feeling better about myself than I did as I was going into the centre like a blubbering idiot, not all that long ago.

So I wasn't into beating myself up that my wife needed a trial separation. She had her own reasons for wanting away and it's not for me to talk about what she was into but, let's face it, she was no Mother Theresa.

As this thought got a hold on my mind, I was disappointed at feeling blue about the wife being gone. It should have been easier since she had been so totally horrible to me for three years before she left. I can't claim that her behaviour – off the wall much of the time – was deliberate – I can't believe she would have wilfully set out to be so hurtful and destructive, but my God, she was so crazy at times that I feared for her sanity, and maybe mine too.

I'd been down this *get out of my life* road before with my first wife, Jean, who really was entitled to ask me to *leave and stop fucking up my life*. And leave I did, without argument, or anger, accepting Jean's right to be finished with this alcoholic, even though he really believed he had found the answer to his drink problem in that first meeting of Alcoholics Anonymous.

I accepted Jean's wishes that time though I had a wound like a bloody river running through me at having to leave my home and my family. Jean was a good woman – she would allow me see our children whenever I could manage it, as she said, 'As much for the kids as for you.' This was fair enough and I left her my share of our considerable house and what money I had, hoping that somehow my kids and I would come through whatever lay ahead without them hating me beyond repair.

So it should have been easier second time around but how often does the heart heed the logic proposed by a tortured head. As I had gone into Rutland, I felt like my heart was in a sling, so bruised by the knowledge that I had screwed myself, and worse, *I had screwed myself again*. Like, fucking up is a bad thing to happen to a guy, but *fucking up again* is beyond reasonable description. But I stayed grateful that I had the will to go on, to try again with never a thought of giving up thanks to my mad Irish heart.

I guess the heart went on pumping fiercely because I was a scrapper, and wanted to get well in every respect by using the spiritual juice that I had denied for so long.

Finally, through the course in Reality Therapy, I learned the hard way how to quit sitting on my shit. In the centre I got lucky enough to hear the truth about where I'd really been during the years I thought I was God's gift to the planet earth.

chapter 11

In my case, due to an amazing cathartic experience in the Rutland Centre, the blindness of my delusion was ripped from my eyes with enough tears to fill a bucket while I'm in a room with *my recovery group* and a whole bunch of people I don't know. My ship came in for me that day when a loving god sent my older brother Michael into the group to say what he had to say about me during *Confrontation Day*.

Confrontation Day is the Tuesday group, an all day affair which includes the staff, your fellow addicts and *the concerned people*: parents, spouses and even teenage children who are there to help you come to know what a total fuck-up you are. And luckily for me, it can also include your brother.

I am not being dramatic or romantic when I tell you that this Confrontation Day is the toughest day of your life on earth up to now. This is the day when the unfortunate people who have put up with your sickness, your addiction of booze and drugs and delusion, get the chance to tell you face to face – without any assaulted – just what a major arsehole you have been. And boy! Do some of them go for it!

This is the day when everybody gets to take a shot at you – even total strangers, people you have never even seen before can chip in with their tuppence worth to illustrate your total fucked-up-ness.

Of course you want to punch the fuckers out but, that's not

allowed. No matter what shit is dumped on you you've got to take it. Why you might well ask. Well since they are all *concerned persons* these people who dump crap all over you only do it because they care about you and they are only tearing you apart to help you quit being arsehole of the year. This, or any other year.

During what is truly a fucking torturous experience, there are a great many moments when you don't give a fuck that they are trying to help you. At times your main concern is with not burning up or just disappearing in a scream of steam. Man, I swear you are on fire all over – your temperature has to be off the chart and there's fuck all you can do about that either. There is nothing you can do about anything since you're such a total fuck-up and anyway – and this really is the clincher – No Matter What Anybody Says to You, about you – no matter what the fuck they call you – they can paint you as seven different colours of shit – *You Are Not Allowed to Answer Back.*

Did you get that?

You are not allowed to object or argue. You are not allowed to say one word throughout the entire ordeal.

That's it. You have to keep your mouth shut and take it right up the ass – the fact that you want to kill several people in the fucking room being something else you have to sit on.

At one stage I tried to say to Nuala – 'You smoked joint for joint with me, you popped barbs like they were fucking jelly babies, so the fuck-up wasn't all down to me.'

A great woman called Mary Ellen McCann almost came out of her chair to get at me, she a counsellor who put her life on the line for you. 'Just for once, Lee, shut your mouth and try to hear what is being said to you.'

So you had to sit and allow your partner, wife, whatever, to speak about what you did, what a loser you were, you had to take it even though your fucking head seemed about to blow right off your fucking shoulders.

It was total torture, no other name for it. You feel so hard done by that it's like being ignored by the guys in the Life Boat even though you're drowning and yelling your fucking head off.

That's how I felt anyway. Like my wife and I, we did it all together, and there she was like Lady Fucking Muck telling me what a prize prick I had turned out to be.

A guy in the whole of his health might have heard what was really going on – that this woman that loved you enough to marry you was pulling out shit she might have been ashamed of and she was doing it, not to get her rocks off, but to help you get off the shit that had been fucking up your life for far too long. You might have heard it that way if you weren't going out of your fucking mind with the pain of just being me.

So you don't think straight, you don't hear caring in your partner's voice. Of course you don't. You feel like you are in a big fucking pot with the water getting hotter by the minute and you are heading for boiling point and you are totally impotent when it comes to getting yourself out of there.

But some guys did get themselves out of there. Old-fashioned husbands who thought a woman's place was in the kitchen and the maternity ward – they wouldn't take it and I watched several of them as they stormed out of the hot seat and slammed the door going out like they wanted to alter the shape of the building.

Not me. I was in a bad spot, a place nobody would plan to visit, let alone live in, and I wanted out of it. And half crazy though I was from the sheer grief of being in that fucking situation, I knew that running from the room and the Rutland Centre wasn't the answer. I was in pain and unable to any longer deny that I had been deluded for years so even in my awful state I could still see that this would be jumping back into the shit that never left town and was just waiting around for you to come back to Mama. This was a total no-no. Somehow, I had come far enough towards recovery to know that I was lucky, even blessed to be able see this, maybe for the very first time.

Wanting desperately to be well and halfway whole didn't stop me hating what I was going through. Much as I revolted against being dictated to, I heard the kid inside screaming for the help to be well, well enough that he was no longer scared of his own fucking shadow. Very dramatic, sure, but that group room that day was like a sweat box with the need of the kid inside me so strong, so powerful that I believed finally that I would stay where I was for as long as it took to get well for once and for all.

I will never forget the pain and the sweats and the way your bowel became a bag of hot brown water during the Tuesday gig in the centre. Those first couple of Tuesday All Day Groups were like living in a nightmare. The apparent injustice of it all to your ignorant, shattered susceptibilities – it was all so diabolical, every nerve end screaming like a stuck pig.

Fortunately, into your third week you begin to allow deep down that this Confrontation Day is the main way they get into you. You get it together that unless you've lost your marbles completely you have to put up with the shit being dumped all over you. You just come to see that it's a case of take it, or take a hike. And all the hike will guarantee you, at best, is a half-life, something that you know, from experience, is not worth turning up for.

Tuesday is the time when the counsellors, with the help of your loved ones, the concerned relatives and friends, stir you up like soup in a pot. You get so scared so quickly on *Your Tuesday* that you seem to lose the ability to think. This really presses in on you as everybody in the room gangs up to push and push and push you all the way to boiling point. When it works, when they turn the heat up so that you quit fighting, there is an explosion inside you and the next thing you are doing is going crazy.

For starters you find yourself drenched in sweat. No kidding it's as though you have just stepped out of the shower and in moments you are listening to this terror filled voice yelling at each and every one of them about how you wish that they were all fucking dead.

In these moments, you're so crazy you can't see the eye contact between the counsellors, the invisible nod if you like, as they agree silently that they have got you ready to cough, to spill the beans, to take the first step towards the change you have to undergo if there is to be any real hope for you back out there in the madhouse we call life.

What triggered my cathartic long-awaited-for-outburst was surely caused by all the weeks of Reality Therapy leading up to that memorable Tuesday.

During your weeks of treatment you go through daily agony in your group – *you hurt when the group has chosen you as the target* – even the guys you get friendly with, and that's always a case of liking some more than others – those guys go for your jugular as though they want to leave you dead. And guess what – when you are in the pack as opposed to being the poor fucker in the hot seat you can be just as savage to a guy that you really like.

It just happens. You get caught up in the group energy which guarantees you are fear filled, you and everybody else present, the room feeling like it's about to explode.

After a few weeks of this torment you are actually getting to spots deep down inside that you didn't know about. It's a pain wracked discovery as you stumble upon the drawer you've been dumping your shit into forever and ever.

You might think you'd be grateful for this, that you would want to cough up the stuff causing you ongoing pain and shame and the consequent aggravation this dumps onto your day-to-day living. But something can happen that cuts across this intelligent response. It certainly happened to me so that in a moment you become this obstinate six year old who will die before co-operating, a sick brat who would sooner choke to death on the lie.

You get no brownie points for this. Like, the group may

have been working on you for an hour, with the encourage-ment of the counsellors who know that you desperately need to spill the bile you're drowning in. They know this for a fact just like they know that you can actually find a core of recal-citrance, a stubborn streak of such force that you turn into a power crazy obnoxious little shit.

These people are so aware of every move the addict can make that they almost scream in frustration as they watch you find that forbidden gear that will give you the power to drive away from them and their willingness to help you, and you so close to catharsis. They suffer in frustration when they see you won't share, you won't cough, you won't budge a fucking inch, the power of your delusion so obvious to them while you just grind your teeth and cling onto your shit.

For a time, they keep at you, quitting only when they accept that there is no way you are going to cooperate. While you are yelling inside that there's no way you will give these mother-fuckers anything, even though to a heartbeat they are fighting you for your life. You are so sick at this time that you can't even get your head around the fact that these are the good guys.

On my Tuesday they allowed me suffer a short time in the hot seat before they announced to me that they had been very fortunate to get the co-operation of somebody who was more than willing to help me by confronting me about the way I had lived my life. At that moment Michael appeared and I opened up like a can of peas when my brother sat in front of me and told me how it was.

Later, when I tried to remember all that went down between us that day, I couldn't do it. It was like it was all too painful to visit again.

Years after this I was sort of captured by a need to put words down relating to that time in Rutland, the story unfolded itself as a stage play. As it played itself onto the page, Michael had become Billy, as in the book and the play of *Goodbye* and Billy did what he did, said what he said, and I had no problem remembering every detail. I can't explain this but that's what happened and I share it with you now with a short lead in to set up the scene that would help me change my life.

Light: Group Room – Rutland Centre – Day.
The room is fairly crowded – about eight Group Members who reside in the centre for the seven-week course in Reality Therapy.
There are three Counsellors, two women and one man who is a psychologist.
Billy Maguire moves to a chair facing Paddy, both sitting so that they are slanted towards the audience. It is very clear that this is quite an ordeal for the brothers.
Note: It has been established in previous scenes that the audience are the Concerned Persons – one of two actors planted up front to make comments when it is appropriate.

Counsellor
In your own time, Billy.

Billy
He didn't have a chance, that none of us did.

Counsellor
Billy, hold it. This won't help Paddy one bit.
Tell him how you saw him without making any excuses.
Don't talk about him to us. Just give it to him straight, tell him to his face. That's the only way to help him get well.'

Billy takes a few moments to settle down. Tears hover and the entire group feels the emotion underneath the calm exterior.
Billy
You were always a gabby smart-arse, even as a kid, and

*you knew everything and nobody else knew anything. And
as you grew up your opinions got bigger and louder and you
were going to set the world on fire because you were going
to write books and films and be a film star and the rest of us
were just ordinary Joe Soaps. Only you made ordinary seem
like a title for a gobshite.'*

Billy stops for a moment, moved by the vehemence that
has caught hold of him.
Paddy is weeping, trying hard not to I burst into tears. He
fails to hide or control the sobbing noise.
Billy sniffs, hauling back his own tears and he hesitantly
presses on with his confrontation.

Billy
*'You helped me more than I can say when I first went to
London. Thanks to you I became a London Cabbie and
made a lot of money but you never let me forget what you
had done for me. And though I tried to be social, do things
with you, you never once invited me or my wife to your
house for dinner, it was like we weren't smart enough to
meet your arty friends from the world of publishing and
films and all that, like we weren't good enough for you.
'But there was worse than that to come that had   nothing
to do with my resentment to you or maybe a bit of jealousy
because you were going somewhere.
The times I dropped by your house to say hello and Jean
would tell me she hadn't seen you for a week or ten days
after you had gone out for just one drink, the mythical one
drink that seemed to take your mind away.
'I vividly remember one Sunday morning I dropped by
your house at about half eleven. I was going out to work the
cab. Sunday the traffic wasn't so bad, the work was easier.
You buttonholed me the moment you opened the door,
asked me to drop you down to the Sun Inn at Barnes. You
were shaking, like a bum needing a drink so badly, nothing*

else mattered. You didn't care what Jean thought of you, it was of no consequence that you were leaving your kids for maybe another week, who could tell.

'I gave you the lift down to Barnes and as we got there I tried to get you to come for a cup of coffee with me, maybe eat something but your mind was on the drink, you didn't even acknowledge my offer. What you did do? You asked me for the loan of a pound so that you could buy a drink.

'I was shocked, and even more so by the fact that you didn't seem to care what I thought. Like, this was the kid brother who fought for me, who sometimes annoyed me by looking after me sometimes, and me the older brother, but a guy who was always there for me, who put me right about many things though I didn't always listen. Here he was this amazing young fella from the slum we grew up in, an uneducated kid who had genuine talent as a writer and he was putting the bite on me for the price of a drink.

'I was sick to my stomach as I handed over the pound note. You had earned money I could only dream about and there you were like a bum and this was my brother, the pound note your entry fee, you knowing that in a minute you'd have people in the palm of your hand with your wit and your stories. Sure, the pub was full of blokes who would buy you drink just to be in the company of the local author they saw on television.'

Billy has to stop and recover, wipe his tears, blow his nose, and take some deep breaths. The group members are visibly affected. A couple of the women clients weeping and trying to keep it quiet. Paddy is in bits, weeping and wiping and sniffing and blowing his nose.

Counsellor
What do you think? How do you feel, Billy, When you see Paddy in this state? Tell him, tell him exactly how you feel.

Billy
Pathetic Paddy, that's the word that comes to mind first.
But it's more than that, worse than that. It's like, well God,
its like criminal to throw your life away, to maybe kill
yourself with drink and drugs.
You threw away the finest woman I ever knew. Your wife
was a lady and loyal to you beyond the cause of duty and
you threw her away, lost your children except for visits.
What do you think that did to them?
Surely to God you can see that too many have paid too
high a price for your galavanting and drinking and the sin-
ful, yes, bloody sinful destruction of a talent that had all the
potential in the world. I'm sorry for being so cruel but
Paddy, Jesus, can't you see that all the suffering, all the
pain, all the bloody destruction – God, surely, its time to
stop. And I'm not ignoring your own suffering. To look at
you right now, see what you're going through, God, I think
I'd just expire on the spot if I was in your seat. I love you,
brother, so many love you only you can't see it. God help
you, god help you, that's all I have to say.

Without another word Billy stands and Paddy and he,
blindly, come into each other's arms and they stand weeping both of them reiterating their words of love for the
other.

Counsellor
Our thanks to Billy Maguire. Sit down now, Paddy. We
need to hear from you.

Paddy sits, almost falling back onto his chair. While a
Counsellor accompanies Billy as he leaves the room,

In the Tuesday room, with Billy gone out, they let me stew
for some moments, nobody saying a word, all eyes on me as
though I am the Leprechaun and they were after the pot of

gold. The moments dragged on, moments where I felt I was like a pot of hot water bubbling as it got hotter and hotter and then I was spewing out the pain, suddenly locked into a cathartic diatribe that was not only involuntary but unmerciful and unstoppable.

I can't remember anything Michael/Billy said after this but he had already done well the work the counsellors had set out for him. In moments, moments where I felt I was like a pot of hot water bubbling as it got hotter and hotter and then I was spewing out the pain, suddenly locked into a cathartic diatribe that was not only involuntary but unmerciful and unstoppable until it ran out of gas.

In this condition the power of your self-pity is so far beyond belief that it is unrecognisable, non-existent really, since there is no recognition of it or anything else. What happens is sort of volcanic, one staggering eruption that goes on – the stuttering rendition as to how you really didn't have a chance, you never had anything and nobody ever understood you. This is the usual crap that has to be spewed out before you get to the shit you've been sitting on forever – which is the reason the counsellors let you get away with it.

Then comes the stuff that has been buried deep – the shame at being so poor, the resentment to your parents, the hatred of their ongoing uncivil fucking war, the lust you felt for your mother, your resentment to your father when you heard him getting his way while she urged him to hurry up and leave her alone.

There was more – the envy of others that corroded so much of your thinking, the shame you visited again and again as you cheated again and again on your marriage vows to a decent woman whom you had married in good faith, believing you would never cheat.

The way you have habitually minimised your shameful behaviour, burying guilt by focussing on the wages you gave the wife while ignoring the fact that you were drinking five times as much and actually seeking approbation for the fact that you never spent money on other women only laying those that wanted to screw and expected nothing else.

Unbelievable shit like this poured like coloured water. You can't find the power to rationalise because you have finally lost touch with your old alibi structure – the weeks of pain in your daily group sessions nudging you to the moment when you are broken down by the guts and caring of others, particularly your brother, to the crumbling, snot dripping mess that I became on that Tuesday afternoon.

I was lucky to vomit up enough, get off the shit I'd been sitting on forever to the extent that I had been opened like a can of peas. If this happened and I believe it did, it did so only because I'd had no choice in the matter. The stuff comes up just like vomit until you've cleared out enough to bring relief, the beginning taste of freedom that takes you beyond the fear of what the world and his wife now know about you, even though they have heard you accept that pride, stupid stinking pride, was your besetting sin.

I was so taken by the overall power of the eruption that I couldn't even try to stop the flow of shit and shame and sadness, sadness bursting with self-pity that stunned the gathering to silence for what seemed ages though I couldn't have guessed how long the outburst took.

I do remember that I was locked physically into the position I was in when the catharsis took off. My arms were folded and my right leg was across my left and there was no way to break out of that until I just collapsed in a semi-faint, oblivious to the tears and the gasps and the sobs of the people there to confront their own addict.

Not forgetting Michael/Billy who gained the praise of the entire group for the support he had shown me when he relentlessly went after me to help me get off my shit for once and for all. I still don't

Days later, I was surprised to remember his exact words but they are always handy to me through the character Billy that

I based on him.

I was surprised to discover how much I had hated my early life and that I had developed my *Happy Jack* routine to cover up my true feelings and this inherent sense of my own inadequacy. Any wonder a kid got into a dream as early as he could? The fantasy to be a writer was a place to hide in a home without a home life that never housed a book except those I stole from the shops all over town. Even today there are still bits and pieces of the shrapnel showing up from my earliest beginnings, thank to the Rutland staff that tore away at me to save me from self-destruction.

When you spend a lot of time on your own while you're trying to blot out anger at your missus and her separation – when you're in that spot where you see her good and bad and its got nothing to do with her in the moment – you need to move a lot, take long strides around the lanes through the forest at Cullen – and sometimes after you've been back home for just five minutes, you need to get up and go out again just because you can't sit still for a minute.

So sometimes you go walking as soon as you get back home and you try real hard to appreciate the beauty of the countryside all around you because you want to keep her and your anger and the sometime longing from driving you nuts. Mostly it doesn't work but you have to try and hold the past in its place even though you're powerless to stop the re-runs and the instant flashbacks that can take the legs from under you.

So you walk the lanes and your whole life plays regular or fast forward as it pleases, and you can arrive home in a jaded state even though started out to just take a walk, with no thought of turning it into any kind of stumble along Sad Memory Lane.

My feelings were mixed as I got back to the Old House and started heating up some water for coffee; I didn't know if I was staying or going for another stride around the block. I hadn't arranged for any visitors to come this evening and nobody just dropped in, not where I live. The place I live in is truly offside, as in buried in the countryside of East Wicklow, four miles from the town and two inland from Brittas Bay. It's a wonderful place for a writer who loves the countryside like I do. And even more especially since my monthly rent is just fifty pounds.

So Cullen Lower is a tough place to find and I had not made it easy for anyone to get to me since Nuala had gone. The phone number was different and I had directed my mail to a PO Box and generally done all I could to be left alone except for the few friends that really mattered.

But if you are to be found, if someone is meant to find you, they will reach you whether you want it to or not. It's like some power outside of you and your understanding, organises what's going to happen to you, so that when you think you're making decisions it's more like you're just making arrangements.

I'm leading up to this story that begins with a phone call, a ring-a-ding-ding out of the blue from a guy I do not know. This happening, even as I ditheringly watch water boil while I wonder about another walk or not. Decisions, decisions. In the instant I am saved by the bell.

You've heard it said 'a phone call can change your life'. Well, while many a call has helped create change in the roller-coaster of my existence, this latest one was going to take the biscuit. Of course I didn't know that as I picked up our old fashioned telephone receiver.

After I say a low key hello, it goes like this:
'Is this Lee Dunne?'
'It is.'
'Wow! I've finally got you, Mister Dunne.'
'Congratulations. Now who the hell are you?'
'I'm Richard Davidson calling you from New York City.'
My first thought is that something has happened to Nuala but Davidson presses on:

'I finally talked an Irish operator into giving me your telephone number – I told her it was a great career chance for you.'

'I'm still here,' I say, giving myself full marks for casual.

'It's about your play "Goodbye to the Hill". Right now there's a lot of interest in it for Broadway. And George Lane at the William Morris agency, he's keen to handle it for you.'

'How do people even know about it? Where did all the interest suddenly come from?' I know I sound calm but my heart is in overdrive.

'I directed a reading of the play at the Playwrights Forum here in Manhattan last week. Several well known Broadway producers turned up and they all want to get their hands on it.'

For a second I feel angry, like, I don't even know this guy and he's been directing my play. I cool it, remembering those curveballs the gods now and then let rip.

'At the risk of appearing ungracious, how come you were directing my play? I don't even know you.'

'Mike McAloney said it was okay.' I can hear that the guy is flustered and embarrassed and he's gushing on: 'He gave me the option and I directed two late night performances at The Guthrie. The audiences there loved it.'

McAloney! The dead arose and appeared to Mammy! Two years, not a word. And it has been on stage at The Guthrie. And I didn't even know about it.

'Hey, take it easy, Richard. You're going to have to back up a bit. Am I right that you've just jumped from a rehearsed reading in Manhattan to The Guthrie in Minneapolis and two performances of the actual play?'

While Davidson gets a cigarette going, I quit trying to be pejorative about beautiful, mad Mike McAloney. Suddenly I'm smiling as I remember the last sight I'd had of the crazy bastard, who for all his high-handedness and his ruthless streak and his paper thin talent, actually produced 'Borstal Boy' on Broadway.

'Let me tell you the story, Lee, and how Mike said it was okay for me to use the option.'

'McAloney's option ran out a year ago, Richard,' I said, just to keep the situation in perspective.

'Sorry,' Davidson says. 'I'd no idea.'

'Look,' I say in a conciliatory way: 'You've given the play the kiss of life, so I won't pretend to be mad. Just tell me how the hell did it all happen? How come you got it to The Guthrie? I mean the Guthrie's class.'

Implicit in this appreciation of that wonderful theatre out there in middle-America was the suggestion that Mike rarely paddled in what you could call classy waters. I sympathised with him here – I had seven or eight banned books to my credit. I was also the first Irish writer to have a Hollywood movie banned, a movie that I wrote and helped produce in Ireland, giving work to a heap of actors and technicians, but never mind that, the Censor said it was dirty.

Since I also had a sort of Technicolor reputation as a sexual athlete, I was not regarded as *respectable.* Thankfully, the latest batch of Irish females had eschewed the text their parents had suffered by and dropped the hand eight seconds after you kissed them, and all I could say was bless them all.

When had I last seen Mike McAloney? That was October '78 in Dublin. He sat through the Wednesday performance of *Goodbye to the Hill* at the Eblana theatre and like me he knew right away I had a hit show on my hands.

Mike looms large, as in nobody goes asleep while he's on, and as he greets me that Wednesday night with his Broderick Crawford handshake he is *on in Technicolor.*

He goes: 'Kid, you got the whole enchilada here. Family life, social deprivation, a love story, sex, and you got laughs coming out of the fucking woodwork. Kid,' he shakes my hand still, like he's trying to hurt me: 'On my dead mother's life, I am taking this wonderful fucking play to Broadway."

You can't help liking a guy who talks like that about a play you've written. In this instance I had also directed the show, built the set and decorated it, using every bit of wood and curtaining I'd salvaged from the cellar of the two hundred seat theatre situated between the between the buses and the fish in the Liffey.

That night Mike and I went for a late curry and I had a great time laughing. He is one of the funniest guys around, so colourful he could light up a dark room, so loaded with great stories about actors and producers and show business generally that he is wonderful company for a night out, but not more than twice a year.

A lot of people put Mike down but, in fairness, he gave me a two thousand dollar advance for a year's option on the play and had, by the time he left Dublin, convinced me he would take it to Broadway.

Richard Davidson's voice on the phone closes down my reverie. He is telling me: 'Mike flopped on my couch just as I was about to head for The Guthrie as an actor. He gave me a copy of your script, said there was a year left on the option. I read it on the plane and loved every bit of it. Truly, I think it's a wonderful play. A week after we opened at The Guthrie, I got the cast together and read your play to them. They loved it and agreed to rehearse it. We did two late night shows and our audiences loved it – they flocked to see it when we told them it was the American premiere of a new Irish play. And I can tell you the play stood up. It was wonderful and got a standing ovation both nights. We're talking Minneapolis here and it's my belief that Broadway audiences will just eat it up.'

'Let me get a cigarette, Richard. This is some kind of fairy tale and I want to remember every word of it.'

I was speaking truthfully really needing a few moments to let it all sink in. My head was already getting into a trip that could keep me awake for a week. You sit out there on the fringe for half a lifetime, or so it seems, and even the slimmest chance of being asked into what I call the magic circle is enough to give palpitations to the most pragmatic heart.

'Before you go on, Richard,' I heard myself asking like some vain old queen, 'Who played me, eh, Paddy?'

'A guy called Kelsey Grammar. He did a good job.'

I'd never heard of the guy but that meant nothing, so I had a smoke and went on looking out at the land rolling down to the sea, my eyes doing their own dance as Richard said, "When I came back to Manhattan from The Guthrie, Linda Sturner at the Playwrights Forum here in the city, she asked me to direct a reading there. I agreed but I insisted that I do a rehearsed reading of your play. Which I did with the cast from The Guthrie, and I can tell you it is the liveliest thing around just now. And this was just a rehearsed reading.'

'So what happens now?' I asked, not wanting to sound too anxious.

'Considering that established Broadway producers have shown interest in the play and that a top agent at William Morris has already declared his interest in handling it, the sky could be the limit. And I'd like the opportunity to take out an option myself, now that I know Mike's is long dead.'

'You gave the play the kiss of life. Mike gave me two thousand dollars for a year. How does that seem to you?'

This gave him some pause. 'I'd like to talk to a couple of people about it. Would you give me a little time?'

'How much time are we talking about?'

'If I could have two or three weeks – the party I would like to involve financially is out of town. Take a few days to get to him.'

He was surely entitled to that. After all, if he hadn't read it and liked it enough to direct it out at The Guthrie it could still be lying on his couch.

So I told him okay and he said: 'Great, thanks. And let me tell you again, Lee, I'm very excited by Goodbye to the Hill. It's a wonderful piece of writing, funny and touching, with a hard edge that ought to make it a winner on Broadway.'

chapter 12

When I put the phone down I went out into our glassed in porch with my coffee, leaving Neil Diamond to provide me with the gift of his genius. As *Longfellow's Serenade* wrapped itself around me I watched the sun dip as evening settled in.

There was a buzz inside me and that all too familiar wanting, wanting it to happen – needing the big dream to come through – began to have its way with me. Suddenly it was like I had ants biting my ass and I had to get up and do something. I had to get moving to distract me from the hunger in my heart, that old mad and angry hunger for a break that would alter my life.

I was grabbing my jacket, knowing it would be chilly down by the shore at Brittas Bay. I was actually walking out through the door when the phone rang again. I thought about letting it ring but the bug had got me and when I picked it up I was hoping it would be the William Morris guy on the other end of the phone line. And it was George Lane calling from New York City.

I stood listening while he recalled being at the rehearsed reading directed by Richard Davidson a week earlier. I can still hear George Lane telling me: 'It's my belief that your play can go all the way. It certainly ought to – it's a beautifully crafted work and I'd be honoured to act as your agent.'

The William Morris Agency is synonymous with show business worldwide. At some time or another many of the giants of writing and performing have been handled by this outfit. I'd even heard the name mentioned in movies so you'd believe I was pleased to be asked to be one of its clients and excited about how insistent Lane was that I come to New York to meet the people wanting to produce my play.

When the call ended, I took off my jacket and I built a turf fire for the evening ahead and sat down at my old piano to just get the world, its wonders and its woes out of my head for a little while.

Having built singing into my life though I'd had no vocal training or indeed any tuition on the keyboard, I started to sing my way to detachment from the ups and downs of the day.

I had put together chord accompaniments on piano for many songs that I had known all my life. I didn't read music, simply augmenting my singing just like we'd all been doing down the years with the three chord trick on guitar. That list includes Paddy Monaghan, Phil Lynnott, Peter Law, and a lot of other guys that one way or another, made the grade.

I really let it rip on the night of my New York phone calls. That's one of the bonuses to living in an isolated spot. You can bring the roof down with music without anybody coming to the door asking you to tone it down.

After ten or fifteen songs, I had let go of the wishful thinking and the pictures of what *could happen* if only *this and that* fell into place as soon as possible. Later that night as I was heading for the sack I decided I was like a trust fund waiting to be opened and I settled for that, even though I knew I was a long way from a deal.

How far away might a deal be? I had no idea, but well do I remember Milo O'Shea, words to me some months later in New York.: 'When a man tells you he is going to produce your play on Broadway, allow six years.' As it turned out, he was wrong but I'll tell you about that when we get to it.

As I drifted off to sleep in the countryside silence of Cullen Lower in County Wicklow, George Lane's voice kept dropping in, all the time urging me to come over to New York. 'You need to meet these people, see which of them you would be willing to trust with your play.' His last words 'which of them you would be willing *to trust with your play*' were so respectful of the work that I felt I was finally going bye-byes with a grin on my mouth.

But before I could leave Wicklow for Manhattan I had to do something that tore the heart out of me. This episode was all about cats, nine of them that my wife had left behind when she decided she needed a six-month trial separation. At my last After Care group I got the message loud and clear. Find homes for as many cat as you can and have the remainder put down humanely. In a nutshell, that was that, and I left the centre with the best wishes of my group, closer to tears than I would have imagined I'd be.

From day one in After Care the cats had been a bone of contention. I admit I had moaned a few times about Nuala just taking off and leaving them while she was taking her sabbatical from our marriage.

Nine is a lot of cats but since we lived in a house which seemed to have grown in a field, with the countryside right up to every angle of our home, we needed all the help we could get to keep the house rodent free. A Cuban Siamese, a present from my sister-in-law, Olivia, went one better. This tobacco coloured character with a head like a snake was actually fast enough to kill rabbits, which he left by the back door as though telling us he was earning his keep.

Through the caring and sharing of my group members I came to admit that I had been afraid of damaging my image in Nuala's eyes if I got rid of the cats, and I finally agreed to take responsibility for my part in the situation.

As I drove home that night I felt I'd be safe enough going to New York. I had lost all interest in booze and drugs and I was still going to meetings. And in the Big Apple you can go to AA around the clock if that's what you need to do.

I expected I'd just be away from Wicklow for a month or

so. Certainly that was the impression I'd given Noel Jones at the radio station when I told him about the excitement my play had caused at the Morris Agency. I didn't phone my wife until just before leaving because, for a day or two, I thought about not telling her I'd be in Manhattan, but of course I wasn't ready to be that brave, so I rang and asked her would I get to see her while I was in town.

I must have sounded pretty loose because in the instant she became very territorial about me. What I mean is, she sounded amazed that I, her husband, could possibly be asking such a question.

'What the fuck do you mean, do you get to see me?' For a moment there was a hint of concern in her very direct manner of speaking, and I enjoyed hearing it.

'You asked for a six month separation. Its only been four, so I'm just respecting what I agreed to when you left.'

'I have an apartment on West Twenty First so all you have to do is hang up your hat.'

'As long as you're sure,' I said, meaning it. 'You're inviting me back into your life, right?'

'Is this a new approach gleamed in After Care?' Nuala had never been a fan of the small changes that Reality Therapy had caused in me within weeks of my return home from the centre.

'I just want things straight between us. I've had to learn to live without you. I can go on doing that.' As the words came out of my mouth I knew that I meant what I was saying. And I felt good about that too.

'Before you leave Wicklow, what arrangements have you made about my babies?'

'We don't have cats anymore,' I said. Then as I began talking of Sam my missus banged the phone down.

She called me back within an hour, far from contrite but she wasn't riding any high horse.

'Just let me know when you're arriving. I'll be at Kennedy.'

I'd like to be able to say that my attendance at the *After*

Care Group in Rutland, and the whole new business of starting to grow up, had helped me be free of the need to live with my wife but it wouldn't be accurate. I was okay – I'd managed myself well enough during our separation, though at times I was tempted to just go and find a woman who needed me as much as I needed a warm body to hide in.

Those were the times when Reality Therapy supported you well. Nothing was barred. You could do what you liked. All that was recommended was that you be clear why you were doing whatever it was. You wanted to have sex with a woman, even though you were a married man, that was alright, as long as you didn't have to dress it up in 'I wouldn't be doing this if my wife wasn't a heartless cow who took off for her trial separation' or 'because I'm a writer, more sensitive than most guys, I need female companionship' or whatever bullshit you would have used before being exposed to the treatment in the Rutland and a year of *After Care*.

Obviously, I had not drunk alcohol nor used dope of any kind since leaving the centre, and though the odd time the mind played games with you – you wondered what it would feel like now that you knew what you knew – it was all bullshit. For me I knew I was through looking for the hit, finished hiding from the day in booze and drugs and sex.

I could slip yet into dreams of success that were a way of escaping from the day to day hassles that everyone has to deal with in their own way, but in all honesty, I still believed I would never drink booze or use dope again.

At Kennedy Airport I didn't see Nuala until she came up and stood in front of me. I soon realised why. She had a pageboy haircut – all her magnificent big hair shorn away like it didn't matter – and my first thought was 'she's having an affair'.

Something good happened to her when our eyes met and she came to tears even as she put her arms around me. I held her and found I was holding my breath in the moment, as though I could not believe this was happening and that it seemed to be so right and more than alright. It felt beautiful and it felt natural and when she kissed me I knew that whatever had gone down before her departure she had missed me deeply.

'You knew I was a flake when you got me,' Nuala's eyes were carrying tears, the flippant tone her way of saying I'm glad you're here.

We had a honeymoon night together after our four months apart and she never asked me if I had been with another woman in that time. All I felt sure about in the moment was that I was glad to be with her, though unsure of exactly where that was.

I guessed I was more attractive since I had attracted the attention of a number of Broadway producers. Like Nuala was nothing if not ambitious for me – ergo for her – and had never hidden the fact that she was interested in the main chance.

Anyway, I let the hare sit for the moment, deciding *least said soonest mended.* I had places to go, people to meet who, if things worked my way, could change my life by producing my play on Broadway.

Goodbye to the Hill the novel had been published in 1966 in Manhattan by Houghton Mifflin and then in paperback in 1967 by Ballantyne so I had some idea of how things worked in the Big Apple.

Fourteen years later I land in Manhattan again, sore that my second marriage is on the rocky road to god knows where. I take the balm offered in Nuala's embrace even though I couldn't in all honesty trust her to be there for me in any kind of crunch. But I moved into her apartment on West 21st Street and I let go of thinking about my life way back in the mid 60's.

It was now 1981 and I was involved in what could turn out to be a serious Broadway production situation. This guaranteed that I was going to need my head in good shape to deal with what was out there. This suggested that the question of whether I trusted Nuala or not really couldn't feature too heavily.

I suppose it was only natural that ego would step in the minute it got its chance. Had it not been for the benefit of my time in *After Care* where ego and self pity earned you nothing but derision, I might well have got into pointing the finger at Nuala.

I had dismissed her need to have a six-month trial separation as another example of what I called her insane streak, unable and subconsciously unwilling to allow that I was living alone because she wanted to be away from me. But however I dressed it up, her departure stated all too clearly: 'Lee, I can no longer live with you as things are.'

Being with her again, dealing with the adjustment of having to consider her presence and all of the day-to-day stuff, I found it hard going even though I still had strong feelings for her.

She had always been a stunning looking predator, a woman who went after what she wanted, and it was unlikely she had been celibate for four months. But so what? Compared to what could happen for me career-wise if things went my way, it was yesterday's bus tickets and couldn't be allowed to distract the mental and physical energy I was going to need

Within a few days, I am walking uptown from 21st Street to Sardi's, feeling in good form and looking forward to what lies ahead. Nuala had left the apartment at ten o'clock to head over to Doran's where she was the Maitre D and I had to grudgingly admit that we had been close within our embrace. I had this niggling need to push her away a bit, get my own back on her for leaving me. Childish shit, but seen in the moment which was what mattered. It meant I was aware of how destructive the addictive mind can be even when it's firmly resolved not to use again.

The man called Hobard had been very nice to me on the

telephone and I felt I could work with the guy. The story was that he was an experienced Broadway producer while his partner moved in the right circles to raise the production budget. They were both looking forward to meeting me he said.

My trouble with George began the moment I met him. In a way it was naïve of me to have expectations of how my agent should behave, even talk. George never got to charm school and today, older and perhaps a tad wiser, I would be the first to praise his openness along with the absolute lack of guile and his refusal to play the games people play.

When I told him I wanted to meet Hobard and his partner he almost came out of his chair.

'You do that, Lee, and your play will never go anywhere. He is not to be trusted and the lady is a dilettante with a rich and powerful ex-husband who will be catching a tan out at Montauk while she tells her friends how exciting it is to be a Broadway producer.'

It just might have been possible to hear something like this without a heavy reaction had it been delivered in a reasonable tone of voice. The bad news, as George saw it, delivered with a spoonful of honey. This was not the way of George Lane. He came at me bluntly, got my back up, so that I immediately wanted to meet the ogres Hobard and Bregman.

Had George, at that point, said, look let's go and have a cup of coffee and kick this around, I might have handled it better. But he didn't because this was not George's way of doing things. In fairness to him he told me right up front just after we shook hands for the first time: 'Here's the story. If we get lucky with the notices, I can do wonders for you. Should we get mauled by the critics, I can do nothing.'

Rick Hobard was the kind of guy that wore charm like aftershave and he looked like a sophisticated villain from one of those old black and white movies as he greeted me at Sardi's like I was the king of somewhere dropping in for a bite of lunch.

'My partner, Betty will join us very shortly, Lee,' he said as he shook my hand with a well practiced grip before he allowed the head waiter to lead us regally to 'your regular table, Mister Hobard'.

Betty Bregman turns out to be a Liz Taylor look-alike but wearing an open expression like she doesn't have anything to hide. Rick has a stealthy air about him. Later, I realised he saw himself as mysterious or something. In the minute, they seemed an unlikely pair but not so when I learned that while he was the professional producer – five plays On Broadway and five plays Off Broadway – she was the party that would raise the money for the production of my play which they were already referring to as 'Casey'.

While I was coming to terms with the name change, they eulogised about the play, washing away any reservations I might have had, while they assured me that they would never allow me to get away from Manhattan: 'We have to keep talent such as yours right here in the Big Apple.' This is a verbatim quote from Betty Bregman.

Some guys might have demurred modestly, even mounted a half-hearted protest, before succumbing to such flattery. I would love to say that I did just that but I can't. Not me. I wasn't seduced or inveigled or captured by such hyperbole. Oh no. Me? I dived into it from the ten metre board – dove head first into the embrace of all that flannel and agreed to let them produce my play even though I hadn't met the other people my agent had lined up.

In fairness, Hobard and Bregman produced a Writer's Guild contract – a standard form designed to give the writer as much protection as possible from producers that didn't play the hand *According to Hoyle*. And, right there at the lunch table, they gave me a cheque for two thousand dollars, which was very acceptable for a year's option.

Then they told me that Timothy Hutton was keen to play the lead – he was still hot after winning the Oscar for Best

Supporting Actor in Robert Redford's 'Ordinary People'. They even showed me a rough drawing of a theatre poster which read: 'Timothy Hutton is Casey on Broadway' and I had no trouble about agreeing that it was very eye catching.

When I told George Lane what I'd done he was shattered and we parted company immediately. So in an instant, I had managed to divest myself of this giant of an agent – a man with clients like Harvey Fierstein with his wonderful 'Torch Song Trilogy'.

It's almost too sad to relate but this is how it was and I would have plenty of time and no shortage of reasons why I might come to regret my shallow behaviour. It had been on the cards that George and I wouldn't last long as a team because I just couldn't stand exposure to my agents sandpaper personality. But a guy would want to catch himself on.

Whatever, I blew a major connection in the theatrical world of Broadway though I felt nothing but immense relief when I left his office for the last time. So I was confused enough to be going on with in my day to day but I couldn't have known the twists and turns that were about to come upon me.

The Broadway production of my play, was, ostensibly launched with a small cocktail party at Sardi's with no shortage of Great White Way people there to drink its health and may god save all who sail in her.

All play productions take quite a while to make it to a stage, any stage anywhere at any time, but to bring up the curtain on a Broadway show of any description is a story that automatically comes under the heading of *Long Distance*. And some take longer than others. Like, the musical 'Nine' actually took nine years to get from the signing of option contracts to opening night. And there are many more examples of just how difficult it is to bring up the curtain on any opening night.

Nuala was more than pleased that I had made a deal and I took her out to celebrate the signing of the option agreement.

She was particularly pleased to hear that Timothy Hutton was seriously keen to play the part. She thought he even looked like I did in the pictures of me at around twenty years old when most women thought I was really something.

Within a few weeks I was able to tell her that I had talked to Timothy on the phone and he had nothing but great things to say about my play. He was also enthusiastic that Colleen Dewhurst should play his mother and I was sold right there. I mean, this is an Academy Award winner saying to me, 'Colleen and I, we've just done a movie together and it was a wonderful experience, Lee. She was like a Mom to me and having her there on my Broadway debut would bolster my confidence mightily.'

He waxed enthusiastically while Rick Hobard and I just smiled at each other. The idea of having those two names above the play's title was enough to make any heart do a jig of delight. And you do well to cherish those uplifting moments because there is no guarantee how long the bright spots are destined to last.

During the next three weeks Hobard asks me to drop by his office three or four times to talk casting possibilities and ask me how I was getting on in Manhattan. It was like he was staying in touch and I appreciated this. Because he acted like he was my friend I was comfortable enough with him to comment that Betty Bregman never seemed to be there in the office with him when I called in.

I remember well how Rick looked up from the pictures we were studying of actors that might possibly be players in *Casey* which was now, officially, the title of *Goodbye to the Hill.*

'She is supposedly raising the money we need to produce the play. That's her main function though she expresses interest in learning the whole production trip.'

That was all he would say about Betty just then and I let it go. The truth is I never got to know Rick. Our relationship, though friendly, was strictly business, no talk about home life or whatever, and once or twice, when, quite unusually, I spotted him walking alone, he seemed to move like a Will O' The Wisp, like a man who had learned to make himself halfway invisible as he moved along.

Just four weeks after I signed the option agreement I had very good reason to remember a really nice guy at the American Embassy in Dublin who had handed me my visa to the States just weeks earlier. He was a reader and he had liked some of my novels and he took the time to warn me: 'Mind yourself in Manhattan – there's a lawyer for every few hundred people – if you can be there for more than a few weeks without somebody slapping a writ on you, you have a benign divinity sitting on your shoulder.'

I took this as colourful conversation and I asked him was the city as tough as people made out. 'Your typical New Yorker is a decent guy, they talk tough, straight out, but the heart is in the right place with most people there. It's a hell of a city – the Irish built it, the Italians run it and the Jews own it. Have a good time, Lee,' he gave me a firm handshake, 'and stay out of court.'

As always, Betty is the very soul of courtesy on the phone, a model of *extremely polite* and apparently very interested in how I am doing just now. But once the pleasantries are out of the way the lady comes right to the point.

'Lee, I'm sorry to have to tell you this, but Rick and I have terminated our partnership.'

I said nothing simply because I didn't know what the hell to say. The thought 'where does that leave me?' crossed my mind but she went on: 'So, you have to choose which of us you want to work with.' I was appalled. To be put on such a spot just didn't seem fair.

'Don't do this to me,' I said guilelessly: 'I made a deal with your partnership. Surely, if you two are parting company, the deal is off.'

Staying with her pleasant mode she said: 'That's not how it

works, Lee. You really do have to pick one of us.'

'Well, if that really is the case, then I have to pick Rick.'

Betty sounded more than surprised when she said: 'Do you mind telling me why?'

'It's not personal Betty. It's just that he has produced ten plays while you have not been involved in production. I'd have to go with the Pro even though I'm sure you can raise money.' I bit my tongue not to say that I knew Rick wasn't happy with her lack of success in this department.

'And you're certain this is your final choice?' Betty said as though she expected that, if I thought about it for a few seconds, I would change my mind.

'As I said, Betty, it's nothing personal.'

'Fine, I wish you luck. 'Bye.' With that Betty hung up, while I stand there shaking my head at the prescience of the guy at the American Embassy in Dublin who had casually warned me about Manhattan's litigation syndrome.

Next morning a large man delivered into my hand a writ suing me for colluding with Rick Hobard to deprive Betty Bregman of her rights to produce my play 'Casey' originally called '*Goodbye to the Hill*.'

chapter 13

As I looked at the legal document I was holding in my hand I felt as though an enemy had a grip on my heart and I felt angry enough that I yelled 'Can't anything ever just happen? Does there always have to be some fucker to take the good out of everything?'

When I told my wife the news she was as devastated as I was and I had nothing to give her in the way of a helping hand back to comfort. Like, we had a stage play that was considered a hot property – Rick Hobard claimed he was still devoted to it – but, raising money was not his forte and though nobody came out and said it, I got the feeling he was not a man who had engendered a lot of trust in those around him. That being said, I never once heard anybody connected with the Broadway scene say an actual good word about anybody else. In fairness to them, they rarely spoke ill of each other but praise equally was scarce around *The Great White Way*.

Rick didn't sound the least bit surprised when I told him about getting the writ from Bregman. A moment later he told me he had received something similar. 'Have you got yourself a lawyer?' he asked in the most matter of fact way. I was more than surprised: 'Me? What do I need a lawyer for? I haven't done anything.'

'Drop by the office this afternoon,' Rick said: 'It's in your interest to do so.'

Later that day he assured me that the smart thing to do was get a lawyer and he offered to introduce me to the guy that he had used the last twenty years. I nodded my head and told him I'd think about it. Then I got to the real reason for my visit. 'What the hell happened that split you up?

'It isn't all that sudden,' Rick corrected the impression I had of the situation: 'When I pushed her about Danger Money,'– he was referring to the *up front* money any producer needs to get things moving while the work to raise the entire financing of the play goes on – 'She looked at me as though I was crazy. She had led me to believe she would come up with it herself, say twenty thousand dollars or so. She said that wasn't going to happen and when I pointed out that she had not raised a dime in two months,

she just told me she didn't want to work with me any more, that we were through. And that was it.'

'And had she been working at it, trying to get the money? Did she even get money people to meet with you?'

He shrugged his shoulders softly. 'Any time I was at her place in The Hamptons she talked a lot about Casey. She waxed like a producer and her house guests were making all the right noises.' He snorted derisively: 'She couldn't get a dime out of anyone I met there and I began to see that she didn't have the gift, hadn't the right touch to help people part with, invest their money. Lee, I'm sorry. The mistake was mine, taking her on. I thought that with her ex's connections she could and would come up with the money.'

'So what happens now?' I asked.

'I believe in "Casey" with all my heart,' Rick could wax dramatically when the chance came his way: 'I will do all I can to raise the money.' As he spoke my heart hit the floor since there wasn't even a hint of self-belief in his sound. It was like he knew that nobody would give him money to mount a new play.

That night I took my wife out to dinner, and when I felt the moment was right I mentioned that I might just go back home and stay with the radio show. Clearly I was bitterly disappointed but Nuala dismissed the idea. 'We have a hot play. Hobard and Bregman gave you two grand for the option – that happened only because they know the play is a runner.'

This made sense to me and I said I might go and talk to George Lane, see if we could find a way to work together.

'You don't deserve to put up with that asshole,' Nuala said with some fire. 'You deserve an agent with some kind of heart.'

This cheered me up, like really having my wife on my side was a bonus. So often in the past she had shot me down, told me to forget ideas that I thought worthy of a run around the block. But I heard no cheeriness in my voice when I told her I would have to find some kind of part time job since the advance from my ex-producers had just about dried up.

We got a bit nostalgic after that, and over dinner it was all about Wicklow and our old house and I admitted again that I had half a mind to go home right away. Nuala said she felt that way too. 'But we have to find a way to help get *Goodbye* off the ground.' She was so adamant, her jaw like a rock that I felt the future of our marriage rested on the success or failure of the play.

Later that night, even though we made love, I couldn't have argued with her. The spark had gone from our joy in each other and I don't mean just in the sexual department. As I lay there while Nuala drifted to sleep it seemed to me that the plays fate was a metaphor for our marriage. If it clicked we would have good reason to be up and merry and cheerful together with the much needed money to make the path smoother, and if it went down the tubes, I just couldn't see what I could do to change things for the better.

It was clear in our new early days that she wanted me just as much as I wanted her. The sex thing was there as strong as ever between us from the minute we shared the sheets for the first time in four months. So I thought, 'Let's see how we get along. I know I can survive without her. I'm not the cripple

I was when she left me weeping in Wicklow.'

Overall, being with her again was alright but dealing with the adjustment of having to consider her presence and all of the day to day stuff, I found it hard going, even though I still had strong feelings for her.

At the same time I knew I'd stopped running on the inside and I felt better about myself. This was to be expected – serious people wanted to meet me about my play. That my work was good enough, or commercial enough to be in some kind of Broadway situation was enough to give anybody a lift.

I wouldn't see Betty again for a good while, but I stayed in contact with Rick who was very philosophical about the hold-up while we waited to go to court. I wasn't in such a comfort zone even though I had accepted that this kind of thing was par for the course on the Broadway scene.

I soon learned that being served with a writ was something that happened all the time in the Broadway situation. As Hobart's lawyer greeted with what seemed like genuine warmth I realised why all the lawyers you met in Manhattan were easy to deal with, all very pleasant and smiling a lot, unless you were the opposition. Like, no matter who won the latest contest, or whether it was settled out of court by mutual agreement, the lawyers were the guys who always came out bucks ahead

Then, right out of the blue, another twist in the tale happens, and I shake my head again in wonder at the way a door opens while you're still reeling from the one that just slammed in your face.

What happened was this.

Within about a week of my inception into *Writsville*, Nuala rings me during lunchtime. The moment I heard her voice I knew that something was cooking (well, she was Maitre D' in a restaurant) because she wasn't built for small-talk during the working day.

She's calling to tell me that a couple of lawyers, regulars

that lunched there several days a week want to read my play.

'They're okay guys,' she quickly assures me, knowing how I hate the way every other punter you meet is going to make you famous or rich if not both. 'My asshole-geiger-counter is on the ball and I know from Jimmy Hanly (the bartender at Doran's) that they are money guys.'

I manage to strangle the life out of the sigh that is right there in my throat, though of course I feel like telling her to forget it. I am raw from the left turn my dream of Broadway has taken and the very last thing I need is a couple of New Yorkers who are in need of an ego trip that will get me precisely nowhere.

Chances are the guys are married, living in Brooklyn and going into Doran's on a regular basis because they would like to be intimate with Nuala's body which really is something.

Nuala is still talking, like she is trying to make a sale and it occurs to me that it would be very good for her if she happened to find the angels who would actually produce the play. She is enthusiastic while I've been feeling down so I thank her for doing what she can to keep the dream alive.

Then she mentions this pearl she dropped on the two lawyers while serving them lunch. 'I indicated that Jose Quintero wants to direct the play, okay?'

As a matter of fact, this wasn't all that accurate, but since she had already done the deed, I said, 'Sure, why not.'

As it happened, the week before when Rick and I were pondering possible directors, I wondered would he ask Qunitero to direct the play.

Rick waxed blasé about speaking to the great director. 'Of course I know Jose very well and I consider Casey a play worthy to be offered to him.' He sat there like Socrates in one of his trances for perhaps a minute. Then he shook his head sagely and said he would sleep on it and get back to me. So far he had not done so and you didn't need to be Einstein to work out he wouldn't go near the great director when he hadn't two dollars to rub together.

I was smiling as Nuala kept the call going to reiterate that the lawyers were genuine guys and whatever. Had I not been the half mad romantic that I've always been, I might have told her to forget it right there and then. But what was wrong with keeping the door open? I mean, was it at all possible that thanks to a hint of deviousness on the part of my good looking wife – dropping the name Jose Quintero was a master stroke – might just have attracted an angel or two.

Jose Quintero, the man from Panama, was a giant of the theatre. In recent times he had resurrected the works of both Eugene O'Neill and Tennessee Williams, and was as hot, if not hotter, than he had ever been.

I'd mentioned this to Nuala – she didn't comment at the time but the name and the details I'd laid on her had obviously made an impression on her mind. Apparently, the information had made enough of an impression that she was willing to bend the truth with a view to gathering interest she deemed worthwhile. Like the two lawyers.

I had to admire the way she had developed the truth a tad, in that mythological fashion, that fey way, that great Irish women can do, without prejudice. I knew one terrific woman, a devoted practicing Roman Catholic, who never mentioned her extra marital affairs to her confessor because he was a gentle, womany kind of man, and she though it might upset him. This rates as the most devious alibi structure, even a new level in the art of minimising, as I've ever come across, but I didn't mention this to the lady in question. No more than I suggested to my wife that she was guilty of what Winston Churchill referred to as 'a terminological inexactitude' when she told the Quintero strand as something definite.

As I would later discover, it was the fact that Quintero – whom Nuala had never heard of before I mentioned his name – *wanted to direct the play* that really captured the interest of the two medical malpractice lawyers.

That lunchtime, I walked over to Eamon Doran's place on

Second Avenue and met the two guys. They were American, born of Irish parents, and you didn't need to be a mind reader to see they were decent people. I do realise that today the words lawyer and decent form the perfect oxymoron, but this was a good while ago, and my first impression of Harley and Kain would turn out to be right on the money.

After the chit-chat in the restaurant, I left the script with the two guys who had asked me to meet them back there at Doran's at four o'clock that afternoon. When they left, Nuala sat down with me and said, 'What do you think?'

I had to smile. 'I think you should be a writer's agent, that's what I think.'

This response pleased her and she touched my hand on the table, not the kind of gesture Nuala performed in public. 'No matter what's gone down between us, you deserve a real shot at success. Nobody could work harder or be so willing to go on learning. Somehow, we have to hang in till things work out.'

How fickle is the human heart. A few hours earlier I was wondering how much longer I was going to hang around New York and Nuala. Then, an accidental good happening takes place and the woman I married till death us do part gives me a few kind words and I melt like fucking chocolate left in the sunshine. The heart so hungry to be loved, appreciated, so slow to let go of all the conditioning that showed up on the screen during the Rutland course, afraid to really go in there and find Lee, just in case he wasn't worth offering to the world.

I sat down with Bob Harley and Tom Kain for the second time that day while Nuala was sitting in the back of the restaurant pretending to read while she was silently doing novenas for a break. Wild and wicked and wilful though she was when her urges fuelled her madness, she never quit praying and believing in God. This was the same God that the nuns had drummed into her without ever knowing a thing about the girl that hid all her real goodies from the world and from herself.

Within minutes, Bob Harley, speaking on behalf of Tom Kain who was a James Joyce freak, and two others I had yet to meet, told me they wanted to produce my play for Broadway with Jose Quintero directing.

I told them I was interested but pointed out that there was a caveat by the name of Betty Bregman.

Bob told me they knew this story from my wife. He and Tom Kain both said that Betty's claim was a joke and they would – through a couple of show biz lawyers they would hire – blow her case right out of the water.

I asked if they would give me that in writing and Bob Harley produced a typewritten agreement which acknowledged the status quo at the time of signing – which we would do within fifteen minutes.

The contract revealed that they were prepared to give me an advance for seven thousand, five hundred dollars for a two-year option on the play which they would call *Goodbye to the Hill.*

Clamping down on my need to yell *There is a God*, I accepted the offer, signed the agreement, and was then handed a cheque for the agreed amount of my advance by Bob Harley.

When I asked the guys if I might buy them a drink to celebrate the deal they didn't argue and within minutes they were drinking champagne while the wife and I sipped coffees and ate dangerous desserts that were adverts for a trip to cholesterol city.

Within days they guys introduced me to a woman called Elva Oglanby who next day channelled my script to Jose Quintero and the following weekend I got a telephone call from the great man himself.

Because of my interest in writing, I devoured all the news of those involved in books, theatre, film, and I had actually read Jose Quintero's autobiography 'If You Don't Dance They Beat You' which helped me love the man before I had the honour of meeting him.

I say *the honour of meeting him* from my heart. I mean, this was a theatrical giant whose handling of the work of Eugene O'Neill and Tennessee Williams had launched him into orbit in recent years and his first words to me were: 'Lee Dunne, I love, love, love your wonderful play.'

Need I tell you I worked hard not to blubber as he went on to invite me to lunch – he checked the day – we were speaking on a Thursday – would I come to lunch on Monday when he had a quiet day and we would have all the time in the world to talk about *Goodbye to the Hill*, and get to know each other.

On the following day, Friday, I was floating as I walked down town, sight seeing the Statue of Liberty – for the tenth time at least – and taking a ride on the ferry out to Staten Island.

I stopped at a coffee shop and had a rice pudding and a cup of java and I was smoking a cigarette when a question that had never occurred to me before arose in my mind. It concerned the last third of *Goodbye to the Hill* and I was more than surprised when I heard myself musing: 'Is it best for the play that Harry leaves before the end? Since Paddy has to go because of how he changes as a result of what happens to him, and since Harry does not and never will change, should he not remain like a metaphor for Ireland, which, to Paddy's mind at this time is like a country frozen in aspic?'

This question, arising three years after the play had first hit the boards set off something in my head, something that wasn't going to quit and before I knew it, I was back up town turning the key in the lock of the apartment on West Fifty Seventh Street.

I was still getting used to the latest pad – we had moved in just a week earlier – but this did nothing to impede whatever it was that had to be written. By Sunday afternoon, the work finished with me and I got another coffee before I read whatever had come through me.

I mean that just as it reads. The work just happened. There was no question that it was Lee finishing the work. It was like the play itself saw to its own needs and the rewrite of the last third wouldn't leave me be until it was ready to let me go. After which I had no doubt that it was for the benefit of the play, that it was absolutely right though I did wonder how Quintero might feel that I was still working on script.

But not for one second did I doubt that what had happened was for the best and I had no hesitation about taking the freshly typed pages with me when I went to have lunch the next day with the great man himself.

Quintero, who had a huge apartment above the *Café des Artistes*, welcomed me with a hug of such warmth that I loved the guy from those first moments. Then he stood back and allowed me to pass into his home.

When we got to the discussion of the play, Jose began by saying again how wonderful it was, how touching and how it seemed so faithful to the condition of poverty that permeated the action. Then he said: 'And the boy is so wonderful. How he loves the girls and the older woman, and how he loves to fuck them all. It is quite wonderful in its glowing innocence.'

Now he looked at me for several moments. Then he said: 'But, since we are going to be partners, writer and director of a great play, I have to tell you that something goes wrong for me in the last third.'

He paused and I could see that he was registering the effect this statement might have had on me. Without pause or even a moment of doubt I made my own presentation. "Would you be willing to read these pages?'

Hardly taking his eyes from my face he took the rewrite and sat back. He put on his glasses and began to read and I just sat there in silence until he put the pages down and greeted me with a smile to light up a dark room.

'Goodness.' Jose was incredulous. 'Nick, come and join us.'

His partner came in from the kitchen. Jose spoke in awe as

he said: 'Lee has done the work I would have asked of him to make his play perfect.'

He shook his head and Nick stood there laughing heartily. 'Congratulations Lee,' he said, while Jose said to him: 'Lee has done it as though he worked from the notes I made last night.'

We celebrated with freshly brewed coffee, Jose and Nick being off the booze, too. Later, Jose and I read the play out loud and I felt like running to the window to tell Manhattan of my astonishing good fortune.

Within days, Jose and I, along with Bob Harley and his lawyer pals, Tom Kain, Arthur Perry and Jim Brown, met with a top Broadway manager who would be responsible for the day to day running of the play. I saw Bob give him his advance cheque, which meant we really were in business.

Bob handed Jose an envelope containing a cheque to cover his Up Front money while I stood marvelling that things had turned so quickly positive.

I actually felt a bit breathless because it seemed that the clouds *lowered upon our house* by beautiful Betty Bregman had gone with the wind. Like Rick Hobard she was not mentioned by name. So, for the moment the lady was forgotten but, unfortunately, not gone.

Within days Harley and company had a writ slapped on them from the same woman, which meant that they too were now going to the Supreme Court of New York *for interfering with her right to produce my play.*

I felt like I'd been kicked where the sun never shines and again had an attack of angry self pity. Jose was philosophical and more than willing to believe Bob Harley and his partners, who were convinced to a man that Bregman's would be blown out of the water within minutes of the case going before a judge.

Nuala was furious and angrily said something I hadn't even thought of. 'She's looking for an offer. She wants to be given a hundred thousand dollars to take a walk. It has to be that.

She knows she is going to be told to fuck off by some judge, since the partnership she was half of no longer exists. I know nothing about the theatre but even I can work that one out.'

While she was letting off steam, I had to acknowledge that her observation was based in good old fashioned common sense. A moment later, I was remembering George Lane at the William Morris Agency saying: 'You sign with that pair, your play will never happen,' while I'd been hoping he wasn't as prescient as he deemed himself to be.

In fairness to George, I had to admit to myself yet again that I had dived into the seductive embrace offered by Hobard and Bregman in Sardi's. In retrospect it was totally irresponsible but I knew I had to forgive myself for diving in without even going back to my agent to run the details of the proposed deal past him. Like, it was no good beating my self up for being such a fool. I needed all my juice for whatever else was going to turn up on the day-to-day screen.

With hindsight, I felt I could see Rick as he might have said to Betty: 'We take this young man for lunch at Sardi's he will sign up with us.' This didn't take any kind of genius – the guy survived in a pool with sharks and barracudas at every depth – somebody like me riding over from Ireland on a dream – Rick knew he could wave the wand of experience and make my reservations disappear before we got to the coffee.

To visualize the memory of *getting the treatment* in the world famous restaurant, I tried to console myself that most guys would have done the same thing. Like, two apparently serious Broadway people that could be bothered to roll out the red carpet? A very enticing image when few people know your name or your work, ergo hard to resist and I felt I knew a lot of writers that would have welcomed their offer with open arms. But in all honesty, I failed to find the consolation I sought – just for once my old alibi structure wasn't working the oracle. I had made a major booboo and there was no getting away from it.

Thanks to the pragmatic response of Nuala's pithy diatribe

against Bregman, it occurred to me that had I chosen her, and not Rick Hobard, he would have been suing me and my new team of producers for the same reasons she had laid down in her writ.

Instantly, I was again remembering the guy at the American Embassy in Dublin, his voice reminding me that whoever won or lost, the lawyers came out with a hearty appetite for more of the same.

In more ways than one I was getting baked in Manhattan. The weather was truly glorious but just too hot for me, and as day followed day I seemed to have another layer of innocence, or perhaps ignorance, falling off me like sunburned skin.

I was still seeing Rick the odd time without Betty's name arising between us. When I asked him what his present position was he gave me one of his mysterious little smiles – nothing if not enigmatic – suggesting we put all that aside until after the Supreme Court hearing.

When you consider how quickly things had changed from wonderful to awful before quickly turning good again thanks to Bob Harley and the other guys, I said nothing. But I wondered how he could sound somehow hopeful. When my team won the hearing in the Supreme Court, he, Rick would no longer have any say in what happened to the play.

At the same time he was calm enough about things and I figured that having produced ten plays he had been down this road before. I like to think that I learned right there from Rick the wisdom of not saying anything you didn't have to say. Things could change in the blink of an eye, turning all the opinion and ostensible wisdom to dust, so if it didn't have to be said, keep your breath to cool your porridge!

I did tell him the play would not be called *Casey*. He had no feeling about that, admitting it was purely a commercial decision on his part – the kind of title that could entice a star like Timothy Hutton to come aboard. I could see the smarts in that but I asked him about respect for the work and the relevance of the title to the action of the play. He didn't argue, saying that sometimes in the production of a show you had to live with things you would rather not have to, but he slipped me another lipful of enigma as he said: 'But you have no concept of how utterly impossible it is that any Broadway production ever gets to opening night.'

He was right and since he was not being smart-ass or angry with me, I accepted what he said. And I didn't bother to tell him that in my view *Goodbye to the Hill* remained a perfect title for my play. I believed that it was particularly good for a New York stage play particularly since I had read William Goldman's 'The Seasons' I knew that the Jews kept Broadway alive – you only have to look at the names of producers, check out the long list of benefactors to the arts, theatre and opera and you will see this for yourself. And William Goldman said: 'Just about every Jew has a relative, an ancestor that said goodbye to some hill somewhere, whether it was Ukraine or Bessarabia or wherever.'

Meanwhile, I get a book agent at William Morris, a really bright go-getter kind of a guy called Robert Gottlieb who read three or four of my novels and said he'd be very happy to handle me.

The second time we met in his office we talked about a book I had outlined called *The Ethics of the Fathers*. Robert had fallen for the story when he read my twenty page outline and said he would like to show it to some publishers with a view to getting me a commission to write the book. This sounded very heartening to me and I told him, 'Go ahead, I'm in your hands.'

Robert was a very agreeable guy and he would make time to talk, go to lunch, which was something I needed in an agent.

Not that I expected friendship as a guaranteed part of the client/agent relationship but the fact that he would bother didhelp me feel better than I had done with the acerbic but ultimately honest George Lane.

When I brought up my experience with George, trying to find out what made the guy tick, Robert said nothing, and by his silence made it very clear that he had nothing to say. Another lesson example of 'don't say anything you don't have to say'.

chapter 14

That first time in the Manhattan, I was like Gloucester, *sent into this world scarce half made up.* Innocence and ignorance make for an uncomfortable blend, imbalance being the rocky road you have chosen to travel even though you claim it just happened to you.

Being nothing if not resilient, I went on my wanton way there in New York, drinking too much booze, in and out of affairs and no shortage of one-night-stands, and certainly once *in love* which is the same as saying in lust, insane, because that's what it was to me, a young married man with kids who thought he was *Jack the Lad* when he had a skinful.

When, finally, I had to pick up the tab for my wilfulness I did it with good will, many a year spent paying the instalments on the pain I had purchased on the drip for myself and my children. The hardest part to bear was the knowing what my children went through – having done nothing to deserve what happened to our family – because daddy hadn't shown any inclination to grow up.

There was no cure for the condition, but the passing years would help all of us get things into perspective, and in time I came to believe there was no blame, no blame at all, though *responsibility*, and the lack of it, was there in lorry loads.

And I had to allow the light of acceptance on my part to shine on the pictures until they were burned indelibly into my mind so that I might not forget where I could be taken again if I didn't take care of myself.

Thank god for time, considerate time which was there too, to help a guy realise that if you get very lucky you live long enough to pay your dues.

The second time around, the time of living in Manhattan in a marriage that had run out of road, enduring the ride on the switchback railway that the play's production had turned into – I returned to the feeling that I was still discharging my debts.

This being said, I found it difficult to feel grateful while the fresh demands were being made on me – the bloody court case for one thing, and for another a wife whose appreciation of me went up and down in keeping with my fortunes and some inner clock of hers that every so often seemed to go tock–tick.

The perennial optimist in me had to believe that all this would change in time. So that I can say now, if you don't like the way things are going down, stick around. Like death, change is inevitable. And more often than not, change is for the better even if you can't see this, or don't want to accept it, in the immediate moment.

I wasn't in the Supreme Court when my producers and their lawyers, and my lawyer acting on my behalf, and Hobart and his lawyer answered the writs served on them by the lawyers of Betty Bregman.

This didn't bother me one little bit since I was sick to death of the whole circus. Besides, I was having a chat with an editor at Harper and Rowe about my outline for the book I wanted to call *Ethics of the Fathers*.

The editor, Buzz Wyatt, and I, kicked the outline up and down the length of itself for an hour. Then to my surprise and delight I was offered a very decent advance to enable me to go away and write the book.

The deal was that I would get half the money up front and

the other half on acceptance of the final manuscript. This means that when the publishers say the book is fine and they place it in the 'to be published basket' the scribbler gets the other half of the advance.

After that you were really in the lap of the gods. By this I mean that the book has to sell a serious number of copies if you are ever going to get another penny. Like, you have to pay back your advance, which is really a loan against sales and any book has got to sell very well before you earn anything else from your story.

Should you be fortunate enough to get well reviewed and should your publisher spend money on publicity – which very few publishers do – you may cover your advance and go on to earn some real money. For a new writer to have this happen to him in America is very unlikely.

In recent times Frank McCourt really cracked it with his story 'Angela's Ashes' but he is the case that proves the point that it rarely happens.

I was anything but bothered as I got my advance cheque from Harper and Row. As a matter of fact I was smiling inside and glad that something had come along to help me live with the anger I felt at Betty Bregman as she continued to step all over my trip.

Not that Harper and Rowe had given me a small fortune but they were buying me the time I needed to write the story. And I felt good that I wouldn't have to lean on my wife financially. A lot of the time I didn't like her enough to let her buy me a meal.

We were getting along, just, but she worked hard for her pay and I needed to hold up my end of the tentative arrangement that our once happily married life had turned into.

I'd been prepared to take a job while I was waiting for my play to be up there in lights but I wasn't legally entitled to work so I was, in the interest of not being deported, keen to stay within the law.

If you got lucky with a play you could go from being broke

to *well-off* in a very short time. Like the author of a play was entitled to a royalty of ten per cent of the gross box office takings, less three hundred dollars. This was the arrangement worked out by the Writers Guild of America and can turn a pauper like me into a millionaire within a couple of years. As you can imagine I was hooked onto the dream of getting that lucky – and when you think of people suing each other over the rights and this whole bunch of lawyers wanting to actually produce the play and spending good money to take the possibility forward – you'll forgive me for dreaming in Technicolor.

When I got to Eamon Doran's to tell Nuala about the book advance from Harper and Rowe, Bob Harley and Tom Kain were having lunch. In my innocence I was jumping up and down as I expressed my surprise that the court hearing was over so fast. So they had been right – it had been thrown out and we were free to get on without any more bullshit?

'Well, not exactly, Lee, not exactly,' Bob Harley said to burst my bubble, going on to tell me that the judge had decided to pass the case on to the American Arbitration Association.

'But you said it was all bullshit, that Betty had no case,' I protested, not unaware that I sounded angry. 'You said your lawyers would blow her out of the water in a matter of minutes.'

They began to explain that in the Supreme Court of New York a judge never made a decision unless he absolutely had to – in a kind of a nudge-nudge way they suggested that cases were passed on as much as possible since it kept lawyers working. They weren't that surprised, so they assured me, and expected to win the hearing at the American Arbitration Association.

In fairness to them, they didn't sound bothered or worried. As a matter of fact they didn't even sound surprised, and they were as good humoured as ever considering they had already lashed out quite a bit of money.

So I let go of my ire and my angst and my need to yell out one more time. But in my mind I was asking the question, 'Can anything ever happen, and happen right, for a fucking guy who just wants a fair fucking shake. Does he have to go on getting fucked by this fucking woman, who is living high off the hog and, according to my wife, and my producers who are also fucking lawyers, is really looking for them to make her an offer of say a hundred thousand dollars to take a fucking walk?'

Bob called this 'nuisance money' going on to assure me that what Betty was doing was not in any way personal, reminding me at the same time that had I chosen her as my travelling companion along the *yellow-sick road*, I would have been facing a writ from Rick Hobard.

I asked Nuala to get me soup and a sandwich in a hurry, making out I was starving, which wasn't true. I needed the fast food as a mask because I felt sick to my stomach. So much so that my good news from Harper and Row was stuck in my craw like the worst form of indigestion and worse than that, I didn't even want to tell them about it. What I really needed to do was go away somewhere and cry my fucking eyes out. But I sat there trying to look like I wasn't stunned.

As I went through the motions of eating the soup, I began to seriously realise that I still had a lot to learn about Manhattan and how to live in her.

For a start, they had a double-speak going on that was too subtle for me, leaving out George Lane and Jose Quintero. George was unique with his up-front-no-bullshit way of laying things on you. And Jose had been forthcoming right away about the rewrite needed for the end of the play. But my producers, for all their decency and their skills, had a lingo going that gave me problems. But then, they were lawyers too!

I broke bread and kept my head down at the table in Doran's trying to ignore the reminder dancing on my mind that I had made a grievous mistake in telling George Lane bye-bye.

Up to this time in my life, I had usually said what I thought, and I had assumed that most people in the world did the same thing. There on Second Avenue, eating soup and a sandwich I didn't want, I let Tom and Bob carry on speaking as though I wasn't there while I did a very good impression of a starving scribbler.

Being gentlemen, they left me alone and I got my thoughts lined up to help me cope with this new-speak that was all around me.

Like, the guys *had known they were going to win in the Supreme Court*. They practically chortled at Betty Bregman's accusation that we were trying to deprive her of her rights to produce my play.

They said her claim was total bullshit, that they would blow her out of the water in a matter of minutes.

The scenario doesn't play out quite like this.

As a matter of fact the script that went down is basically the exact opposite of what *they had known would happen*.

And here we are in Doran's with me eating to stop me yelling obscenities, all the while listening to these two decent men verbalising how it is going to be when we go before the Arbitrator at the American Arbitration Association, whenever that is supposed to happen.

At no time did my friends – and in fairness, they were my friends and my supporters – consider that we could lose the Arbitration case, any more than they could tell me when we would get a fucking hearing.

I had believed them, taken their word when they had pronounced with such certainty on the *blow her out of the water* scenario, and now I was supposed to be cool even though the verdict, which was not a verdict at all, had left me feeling like I'd been slapped across the face with a wet fish.

Sitting there looking into my soup, I knew I was taking on another negative reaction, another self defeating mode. But I couldn't help it and maybe *I wouldn't help it*. I was so fed up with all the noise we can make with our mouths that I was fit to be tied.

In a way this is a good example of how we screw ourselves. Like, even though things were temporarily on hold, I still had my deal with Harley and company. And I was being assured by the guys, who were risking their money and egos and whatever, that all would be well. Not forgetting the cheque in my pocket from Harper and Rowe.

Yet I was raging inside to the point where I felt I could vomit at the drop of a hat. Ridiculous, of course but *I Want–I Want* stuff always made me mindless. So I knew instantly that I needed more than ever to fall back on all that I had learned in Rutland and in the *After Care Group* to help me keep my head together.

I was still going to AA meetings, glad to have the rooms to go to morning noon and night. And it was while I was coming from a meeting which took place in the back of a book store that I found a booklet that was going to have an influence on my life.

I'm not talking about miracles or anything like that – in fact it would take quite a while before this new direction became inculcated into the texture of the life I led – but from the moment I picked up the *Science of Mind* magazine in that bookshop, I felt real hope that I could make a good life for me and mine.

The word *visualise* on a small magazine cover catches your eye as you are leaving a bookstore and you buy it without even checking out the contents because you have long needed to look at the idea of visualization. Nothing more than that but in the moment it felt so important that I could taste it.

I got back to the apartment and I read the booklet from cover to cover. It was filled with articles of a spiritual nature, each one of them giving me a lift. I was very taken by *The Daily Page* which provided the right kind of fuel to help anybody get through the day-to-day hassles life throws up, without taking on the usual ration of stress which, like most people, I felt came with the territory.

Of course, this is not a fact, but it takes more than the reading of a magazine – it takes time and study and a hunger for change before you can put this sort of stuff to work in your life.

Obviously, there is very much more to *Science of Mind* than I have indicated here, but since this story is about my play and my writing career in general, I'll just say that the new blueprint I had discovered for a day's living was precisely what I needed at the time. And for the next nine years, by daily studying the monthly magazine for an hour, I came to a sense of my own worth that up to then was beyond my imagining.

In a sense Science of Mind was like the Fellowship of Alcoholics Anonymous where you could not buy a pinpoint of sobriety for a hundred million dollars, but you could get it for nothing if you were willing to go to any lengths to find it.

Through a combination of AA meetings and the study of *Science*, I was soon feeling better. Without effort I was finding a peaceful space to stand in while I looked at all that wasn't working out the way I wanted it. This alone was a priceless gift which arrived in no time at all, and I revelled that I was no longer totally imprisoned by my *I Want It Now* agenda.

I should admit that when I find something that I feel is good for me, I go for it with all that I am. And if there are rules or techniques that need attention and practice, I apply myself a hundred per cent. And what's more, I actually expect to feel better than I did before I got started. This approach has always worked for me, so within weeks, and despite the fact that our date with the American Arbitration Association was two months ahead, I stayed cool. And shortly after this, I had my head well into the book I was contracted to write for Harper and Rowe.

Of course, I was constantly in touch with Bob Harley and Tom Kain and I saw Jose a couple of times a month. When we met all we all did was talk about the play and its environs –

all of those connected with it focussed on mainly one thing – the departure of Betty Bregman from our lives and the Broadway production of *Goodbye to the Hill*.

I was also getting to know Elva Oglancy, the lady who had arranged for Jose Quintero to read the play. Elva lived with her mother and two teenage sons in Manhattan and pretty soon my wife and I were seeing the family about once a week.

Elva was an entrepreneur of real vision, but she was never too busy to quit encouraging me and, indeed, does so to this day forty years later. She was a genuine talent for finding talent and she had virtually invented John Curry the great ice-skater. She also brought Robin Cousins to the peak of his career and was responsible for putting us together so that I would write a film treatment for the world's best skater who was good looking enough to be a leading man. I was well paid for my work and though the film never got off the ground, it was just another example of Elva creating positive things for other people.

Her mother and I became great friends, and I was like some kind of uncle to her sons Andrew and Struan. Meanwhile, I had no idea Elva was *talking me up* to all kinds of people in publishing and theatre and that she would soon be responsible for helping a minor miracle happen in my life.

The American Arbitration Association meeting was put back because Betty pleaded ill health and I have to admit I did lose my cool for a few minutes. But, thanks to the insight gained through my daily study I knew that I didn't have to do this to myself. There was simply nothing to be gained by getting angry while the energy burned-up was a total write-off. Pretty soon I realised that the automatic anger arising over something I didn't like was no longer an option. In a way it became very simple, since however strong my reaction was to anything, I couldn't get away with it for more than a few seconds. After which I was calm enough to release the self-defeating thought and prevent that old habit making a come-back.

However, one day I was as low as a snake's belly with what you might call Father's Blues, feeling overcome with a very real need to see my children.

It had been eighteen months or more since they'd been to stay with me in Ireland and as it looked like I was going to be buried in Manhattan for some time. I was feeling kid-sick and needed desperately to be with Sarah and Peter and Jonathan if only for a few days.

I'm not what you could call a religious person, but I found myself sitting on this afternoon in a quiet, cool church, willing to let any possible Higher Power know that I was desperate to see my kids who lived in London.

I suppose you could call this a prayer, a muted plea to help me see my guys, but I thought of it as putting a wish out there in the hope of getting a result. As I went on sitting there I began *visualizing* my three children and I having a meal together in London. I just let the picture sit there for a little while and then I felt okay about going back out into Manhattan to face whatever was waiting for me.

Just before I left the church, I heard myself saying: 'If you can hear me, please help me to see my children.'

This may well have been the most sincere plea I had ever deposited into the universe, and I felt good when I realised that I didn't even check to see whether anybody sitting close by had heard my prayer. It just didn't matter.

This seemed like another bonus, another tiny freedom from one more self-defeating-habit, one where you waste minutes and hours of your precious time on earth caring about what other people think.

In that church I had spoken from the heart without even a blush, no thought that it was simply ridiculous to ask point blank for something you wanted in the worst way. Smiling, I went on to say, 'Please help me find a way to visit with my children in England. I hurt for a sight of them – I lost them because I drank too much. I'm well now, though sore for the loss of their company.'

I left it at that, not getting into the nitty-gritty of how my kids saw me, acted around me, whatever. I knew that we hadn't talked out things that needed to be aired regardless of how painful the process might be.

Jonathan had come to confront me at Rutland with his mother, Jean. She really had put up with the worst of my shit, and said so in spades. But he, bless him, wanted only to talk about the good things I had done and refused to put me down. Strictly speaking, he wasn't helping me but I wept in bed that night with the feeling of love I had for him all over me.

The pair of us had faced each other, hearts broken, while my ex, bless her, really tried to put the knife into me because she honestly believed it would help me.

When I left the church in Manhattan I felt some kind of relief from the pressure of my need to see my kids in London. This alone sort of validated the exercise for me. I had given no thought to the humility that had to be in place for someone like me – a militant agnostic by the time I was fourteen – to have expressed my need for help, but, I didn't get into any heavy expectation just because I had verbalised a begging letter to some power greater than myself.

Come on, even if it was remotely possible that there was a Higher Power that could give people a dig out when they really needed it, there had to be a very long queue ahead of me – a line of souls far more entitled to assistance than I was.

Like, when I was drinking, I could go out *for one* and not come back for a week. Where, then, was the love of my children and this desperate need to see them?

Five minutes after I got back to the apartment at 57th Street and 9th Avenue the phone rang and I picked it up expecting it to be my wife. I hadn't called her yet today at work – as you know, my head had been elsewhere. When I was offhand about giving her a bell, Nuala tended to seek me out more than she normally did. We never talked about this but I liked it when she sought me out.

Our marriage was by no means out of trouble but deep down I was still hoping that we could work things out and stay together. I knew that this would take a lot of work – since I'd been through the course in Reality Therapy, Nuala and I were in different places and I didn't know if we would ever truly meet again.

The phone call was from Bob Harley and his first words to me were: 'Hi Lee. You and I are booked on a flight to London tomorrow about this time."

Even as I write this, I have to make a real pitch to you the reader, asking you to please believe that the words attributed to Bob Harley, the Medical Malpractice lawyer turned Broadway producer, are the gospel truth. And that I was hearing them within an hour of my pitch to the heavens in that cool afternoon church.

'Run that by me again,' I said, 'and go slow. I want to be sure I'm not day dreaming.'

Bob laughed. 'Elva just called me from London. She's over there doing business with a hot producer, called Bill Kenwright. You know of him?'

I most certainly did. Bill Kenwright was a major theatrical producer, controller of something like forty to fifty theatres all over England and he was just as addicted to Everton Football Club as I was to Manchester United.

Bill had once been a regular in Britain's most famous television soap *Coronation Street* and had been a compulsive gambler. He was also a well known nice man, a decent skin, who was more than willing to take a punt on a new play if he thought it was a live one.

'He wants to meet you to talk about a UK production of *Goodbye to the Hill.* Elva says you should bring the television series idea. The one called 'The Days of Dizey Davis' – have I got that right?'

I told him he had it right and he said: 'And you're to bring the treatment for your other television series, this one's called 'Ace High'! – Elva says bring all three – Bill Kenwright wants you to meet Hannah Gordon – she's a big star over there and Elva thinks she is the ideal actress for this eh, Dizey Davis.'

Bob was as excited about our trip as I was, but for a different reason. Elva had lined him up for a personal meeting with Bill Kenwright, so he wasn't just going to London as my US producer cum lawyer.

Nuala and I had dinner at the Siam Inn on 8th Avenue – my favourite place to eat, to celebrate another wonderful phone call. Like me, my wife was full of admiration for Elva Oglanby. She it was who had brought Jose Quintero into my play situation – now, while she was in London setting up an ice skating show for Robin Cousins at the Victoria Palace under the Kenwright production banner, she could make the time to sell me to such a powerful man.

She had also arranged a total bonus in the shape of the impresario's willingness to pay all expenses for Bob Harley and me. We were booked into the Marriot Hotel on Grosvenor Square and though I didn't know it until I checked in, there was an envelope waiting for me containing a thousand pounds to spend while I was waiting to meet the man.

Chapter 15

On the flight to London, we had barely left Kennedy when Bob fell asleep. This suited me and I took out my little book of musical chords to pass the time.

A month before I had bought a small keyboard of two and a half octaves, having finally decided to risk finding out that I just couldn't make music.

I'd wanted to play piano all my life but had never dared to give it a shot because, very simply, I was afraid to fail. I've already mentioned a mate in Dublin, a brilliant photographer called Paddy Monaghan, who was naturally musical. He gave me some tips on guitar so that pretty soon I became adept at the Three Chord Trick.

Three chords may not sound like much but you can have a lot of enjoyment with them provided you can sing the melody line. I had been doing just that – singing acapella – since I was five years old, so I could carry a tune without any problem and I'd been blessed with a good memory for both lyric and melody.

I was still scared about jumping from guitar to piano but what finally caused me to buy a small keyboard in Manhattan was the fact that I was living on my own again. Nuala had gone back to Ireland for a break from the pressures of earning a living in Doran's and being around my play situation which seemed to have been going on forever.

I didn't mind her going. In fact it relieved me in some way, though of course I missed the regular sex and soon started to allow my Single Man's eye to walk around the block.

I caught this inclination early and made the decision that I didn't want to go back to my promiscuous ways and so I got the keyboard and started in on trying to make music. If nothing else, the application to the study would keep me out of bars and clubs and at a safe distance from booze and drugs and the guilt I knew I would feel if I just got laid because I was feeling entitled.

When I sat down at the keyboard the first thing I did was write in pencil from Middle C up – C D E F G A B C – then did the same thing backwards from Middle C going down on the left hand side.

My intention was to take the three chords I had learned on the guitar and transfer them onto the keyboard. As I marked the keys I thought this was a childish way to go about things but I didn't let it stop me. And so I made a start.

When you think about it, learning to play what you might call rudimentary piano is not brain surgery. Like, a guy who can be a channel for books and plays and soap scripts and movies and short stories and newspaper articles by the hundred and have his poems published in *Hayden Murphy's Broadsheet from Trinity College,* surely he can put some chords together and work out a way to marry them with the singing voice.

This being said, I wasn't talking about it to anybody. Come on, I was over forty years of age and I couldn't have played *Twinkle Twinkle Little Star* for God's sake!

Shut up! I yelled to the little prick in my head who was trying to put me down again. 'I can sing, I can carry the melody line and I'm going to do it.'

Because I sound better singing in the key of D, the first chords I practice on the keyboard are D, A7 and G. The idea is that I play the same chord on both hands, literally just hitting down on the notes either side of Middle C while I carry the tune.

The singing of the melody line is all important in relation to coming at the music from such an ignorant perspective. This means you have to know the song, you have to be able to sing the tune, and of course you have to love the whole idea of making music in the first place.

I'll admit right away that it wasn't easy. But it was and remains simple. I kept it that way – simple – and pretty soon I was making headway, so that even with my shaky confidence I was hitting the right note sooner than you might expect.

And I'm here to tell you that within a week I was actually making some kind of fist with songs such as 'Galway Bay', 'Help Me Make It through the Night' and one of my favourite jazz standards 'All Of Me' all of which you can handle with just three or four chords, once you are singing the melody line.

You'll understand that Buddy Greco had nothing to worry about, that none of my friends were going to have to purchase tickets for my concert at Carnegie Hall. But let me assure you that right away I was having a lot of fun. It was wonderful and I was very excited when I added a new chord to my repertoire. So much so that I vowed I would make some kind of music and sing some every day for the rest of my life.

After I'd been enjoying my new hobby for about six weeks, I shared the elevator with my next door neighbour. We hadn't spoken before but I said good morning – not a widespread habit in New York – the city was a tricky place in which to be sociable, full of people scared to make eye-to-eye contact.

Untypically, my neighbour responded in a very friendly manner, 'Pardon me, sir, but am I addressing the gentleman who has been entertaining me with those wonderful easy-to-listen-to-songs that are such a joy to hear when they are performed well?'

I swear to God this is what the guy said. And he spoke in the most matter of fact way. As a reflex, I actually started to apologise for disturbing his leisure time – I thought I had kept the sound down to the minimum, but there you go.

This very gentlemanly, Ivy League type American nice guy assured me he had been very happy to hear the songs I had been singing. I smiled as he mused about a line from 'These Foolish Things' that goes 'a tinkling piano in the next apartment' and I went out into the Manhattan morning sort of floating along on the first compliment my musical effort had earned.

It was unbelievable and entirely wonderful that this stranger had been pleased with the overall sound I was producing of an evening – who could ask for more than that? As I thought about it over and over, my spirits soared and I felt glad I'd taken the risk of doing something I had been scared of forever.

Okay, so now I am on the plane going to London with Bob Harley to meet Bill Kenwright and Hannah Gordon and spend a few days at the Marriot, with my children coming in to have dinner with me the night after Bob and I unpack our bags.

Elva Oglancy is there to greet us at the Marriot and when we are settled in she tells me that Bill and Hannah are keen to talk about all three projects and that a meeting will be fixed up within a couple of days. Then she gives me the magic envelope containing the thousand quid for my walking around expenses and I only just stop myself from looking up to the heavens to yell thanks.

Silently, I do offer up my gratitude which, just then, seemed the right thing for me to do. To see my children and to be in a position to offer them a meal was something that seemed totally impossible just two days earlier. And that in itself was surely something for which to be grateful to a god unknown.

I felt little in the way of joy as I greeted Sarah, Peter and Jonathan, simply because my heart was like a great bruise underneath my shirt and as I was hugging each of them I realised more than ever how much I missed living with them. I probably hugged them harder than they would have wished and no way did they reciprocate to the same degree. Also there was no hiding the vibes, anger and pain and resentment that I felt coming my way.

They were good looking people, Sarah, my first born being a real beauty, a good mix of her parents dark looks. She had almond shaped eyes and a brain larger than mine. She had the kind of nubile figure that turned a guy's head, but more important to me than all her goodies was the feeling that she was a real nice girl. As the evening wore on I found myself liking her more and more, and after a wine or two my trio were talking and laughing their way through our first meal together in a sinfully long time.

Peter at twenty, was two years younger than Sarah and he had the blonde good looks of my mother's people, the Rogers of Ranelagh in Dublin. This had been a seriously dysfunctional family with hard drinking sons including my Grandfather Rogers. He and his brothers between them drank and gambled away the considerable family fortune so that by the time he was marrying my grandmother they were experiencing what it was like to live in the real world where poverty knew no favourites. *The poor bewildered man* was how my mother described her father – of whom I was and am the living spit – who died from alcoholic poisoning at the age of forty-one. So again life gives me a reminder that nothing comes out of the stones in the road.

Peter was already a member of MENSA with an IQ over 160, his first novel already written. He was a shade taller than me with an athlete's body, cynical blue eyes over a smile that was going to captivate a lot of ladies. He was more English than I had remembered maybe, partly, as a result of whatever problems he had with his Irish father.

My youngest, Jonathan at eighteen, was a small giant already. He was built like an All American running back called John Riggins but he was carrying thirty pounds he didn't need. He was the real comic of the trio, so sharp and smart and quick that he was deadly in any battle of words or wits. He was good looking too, and already vowing to be a millionaire by the time he was twenty-five. I didn't doubt it. I had said of him from the time he was five-years-old, 'If we can keep him out of jail he'll surely be a millionaire.'

I felt blessed to be in the company of three healthy ongoing young people that I was flattered to know. Having played a part in their arrival on the planet had always given me a good feeling – our dinner party seemed to me like the beginning of a fresh start – I certainly hoped so.

While the food in the Marriot restaurant was excellent and not just by hotel standards, my children and I had a few rough moments – Jonathan, who to my mind was drinking too much too fast, got very smart assed with me and I lost my cool for a few seconds. In fact, I was giving him an earful by the time I realised what was happening. Peter seemed quite distant even before this and had moved further away by the time I tried to back off my heavy father routine. Sarah seemed to be on the fringe looking in, and all in all I was, by the time I watched them drive away, feeling that the evening had been a complete disaster. I realise now that this was not the case but I had been so emotional that I was angry with myself, feeling I had let myself down in the eyes of this trio that meant so much to me.

I was also mad at myself for trying to impress them, hoping they would like me a bit more than they had done when they had arrived earlier in the evening.

For ten minutes after they had driven away I walked around Grosvenor Square hoping that the peace of it – I was immune to the traffic noise, having driven a London Taxi for six years – would help me lose the fear that I had driven an even bigger wedge between my children and myself. It's hard to know, when you feel like the villain in the script. That night I did, still, feel this, since my alcoholism had been the driving factor in Jean's ultimate rejection of me as a husband,

and her love for another man.

My head was spinning under the power of speculation so that all I was sure of was that I hurt a lot and than an aspirin wasn't going to fix what was wrong with me.

The walk helped some – by paying attention to my feet touching the pavement, I got back into the present moment and by the time I went back into the hotel I didn't feel so bad.

Before going up to my room I took a look around the hotel. I don't know what I was looking for, maybe hoping for a little late night music.

I stepped into a lounge the size of a football field with enough furniture to give the Ideal Homes Exhibition a run for its money and a carpet to caress the ankles. There were enough standard lamps to light Central Park but to my surprise only a couple of the lamps were lit and there was nobody in the vast space.

My eye fell on the grand piano under a single standard lamp and I almost gasped at the boldness of my next thought. I was actually shocked by an uncontrollable urge to go over and sit down and tinkle those high class ivories. I could hardly believe it.

Up to this moment, I had never touched, never laid my hands on a real piano keyboard. I had never even sat down at a piano, never mind a Grand Piano, and I was truly nervous even as the thought developed muscles and I knew I was going to have a go.

First I had to nip up to my room to get my little book of chords, so excited by the prospect ahead that I was sweating just a bit as I came back down to the lounge.

I probably knew my mini-repertoire of songs by now but I knew too that my nerves were doing their own dance and I would need the symbols over the words so that I didn't make a mess of my first touch on a Grand Piano.

Then, just to be on the safe side I use my biro to write the symbols on the keys to the right and left of middle C, just as I had been doing during the couple of months I'd been making a little night music to help keep the gremlins away.

With this important aid to a faultless performance in place, I am set up, ready to go, probably just as nervous as I would have been had I been sitting in front of an audience in Carnegie Hall. Alright, a bit of an exaggeration but I was actually sweating a bit more than I'd been doing a few minutes earlier.

In moments I was singing the words of *Galway Bay* to my own Grand Piano Chord Accompaniment and I make no bones about admitting I was deeply moved by what was happening.

After this I go to work on *Me and Bobby Magee* before I tackle *All of Me* and in no time at all I am singing one song after another, the worry about my kids, the possibilities for my career, whether my wife really loves me or not, all given away to the world.

This is one of the most exciting benefits of giving yourself to the music and the words of the songs you sing. You forget all the stuff that's standing in line *to make your day,* so that if you ever had a seriously great-aggro-free-day when you were a kid, well, it's like being transported back there.

So I'm having the time of my life until there is a frisson of change in the air, as though the space had been invaded. Its got nothing to do with seeing or hearing but somehow without even looking up you suddenly realise that somebody is standing where seconds before there was nobody.

I get such a shock that my heart probably misses a beat – for a few moments I feel like the little kid caught with his hand in the cookie jar – ridiculous, of course – like what was the big deal? If I'm breaking a hotel rule or whatever, prison hardly seems like an option.

I glance up from the keyboard and there is this guy standing there, well, swaying slightly is more accurate, a nice looking, big, amiable sort of American tourist who is feeling no pain, no pain at all. And in the moment he makes everything alright when he says in a slap happy, three parts pissed sort of Texan drawl: 'Gee! I didn't realise there was entertainment.'

Had I not been sweating so much – there were globes of damp the size of soccer balls expanding from under my arms – I might have started laughing. The dryness in my throat made that impossible but in seconds I heard myself saying: 'Oh I'm just a guest here, having a little tinkle on this lovely piano.'

The guy nods and asks me straight out: 'Can you do *All the Things You Are?*'

As it happened, this had long been my favourite love song in the whole wide world – I had loved the music of Jerome Kern, generally called 'the Father of the American musical' for fifteen years and I had the chords right there in my little pocket book.

So within a minute, there I was singing on my very first appearance out of my apartment on a real piano to a seriously appreciative audience of *one* – a guy who left me smiling in response to his praise for *the entertainment.*

A short time later, still staggered by the experience, I am back in my room and just about to take a shower before going to sleep when I remember something I absolutely have to do right away.

Within a minute I am back downstairs in the lounge and again I am at the keyboard. This time I'm not there to make more music – this time I'm using my wet face flannel to clean the keys an octave either side of Middle C.

I mean, can you imagine the face of the professional pianist the next evening when he sat down to play cocktail music for the high and the mighty at that Grand Piano in that Grand Hotel!

A few days later I had a brief meeting with impresario, Bill Kenwright and the delightful actress Hannah Gordon. We had a nice time – kicked around the three properties I had brought with me – the play, the two series for television– and we went away to think about how we might work together on one or more of the trio.

Both Bill and Hannah were complimentary and even kind, nice people and we got along really well. We were supposed to get together again in a few days but it never happened. They were both so busy, so into so many projects that they couldn't find the time to meet me again on that trip. That's how it can be sometimes in show business, publishing, films – you can go from having nothing positive happening to suddenly finding yourself up to your neck in a number of different productions or whatever. At this time it was all go for them but essentially no go for me.

When I got back to New York, I was talking to my son, Peter on the phone, expressing my gratitude for the trip and the couple of occasions when 'I was able to buy dinner for you guys'.

'I'm still gaping at the way the trip happened, like some kind of miracle really,' I said, going on to tell him about my kind of praying plea to a god unknown in the church in Manhattan.

I described to him then how, within hours, Bob Harley had phoned to say he and I were going to England next day to meet Bill Kenwright, all expenses paid. When I finished describing this *little miracle* Peter allowed that it made a wonderful story. 'But if I may,' he says adroitly: 'I suggest that next time you pray for a trip, pray for a fucking deal as well.' I started to laugh and in moments he had joined me, both of us knowing we would dine out on the story in the weeks and months and maybe even years ahead.

Within days of my return to Manhattan, I find myself enduring the news of another postponement of the Arbitration hearing. This time Betty Bregman has changed her legal team, and, fair enough, her new lawyers need time to read up on the case.

I didn't moan or beat my breast on this occasion because I felt it was unfair to Bob Harley and everybody else involved.

They had to be disappointed too, but they never laboured it the way I'd been doing, and I was grateful that the penny had dropped for me before they justifiably told me to shut the fuck up.

I might have seen it at the time but I didn't ever grab the obvious fact that I wasn't ready for the degree of exposure that came my way that time in Manhattan. Yes, I'd been there before and I had spent three months there, but I'd been insulated from much of the reality due to being stewed a lot of the time.

Waiting for the new court date to arrive I aimed at shelving any negative thoughts that arose about Betty. I knew she was entitled to do her thing even if it inconvenienced me a hell of a lot. I did find myself wishing I had graduated with a couple of years of *After Care* under my belt – the phone call from Richard Davidson had put paid to this possibility – I would surely have been in better shape to deal with the sleight of hand that passed for normal in New York New York.

For one thing I would not have left George Lane simply because he did nothing to win your vote as Manhattan's Nicest Agent. And I might well have resisted the charm and the flattery that Rick and Betty laid on me at that first meeting over lunch at Sardi's.

The fact that I am not missing my wife is not bothering me. In fact, I feel relieved that I don't have to listen to her angst over the latest hold up.

Meanwhile, I am having trouble with the novel *Ethics of the Fathers*. This is hard to take because it has never happened to me before in all the years of trying to make it as a writer.

Usually I sat down and the stuff came as naturally as letter writing. I wondered was it the pressure of my wanting that was holding up the usual free flow of words that came my way. Was it my angry, hungry need to have my play free of this court case bullshit so that we could get on with the production? Was this what was eating away at my ability to work?

I tell you again that I knew next to nothing about the whole writing process, I just accepted that it happened to me as naturally as sweating. I had to write, had to be there watching the words come up on the page, which is how it had always been for me up to this block on *Ethics*.

In the years since that time, I've come across a school of thought that believes you are not a real writer unless *you have to do it*. I don't know about this but I had become all too aware that my ability to do my thing which was write and write and write had suddenly gone down a cul-de-sac without me realising it.

This thought grew until I became convinced it was all the hassle over the play that was screwing up my ability to tell the story and *not try to be a writer*. So now, as we prepared to go into the Arbitration hearing I felt that a change of scene might well get me back to my normal routine. The idea that I might go home to Wicklow to write the book found its feet in the moment and the taste of it in my mouth was very welcome.

The day before the hearing opened, Nuala arrived back in Manhattan and walked straight back into her Maitre D' role in Dorans. True to his word that her job would always be waiting for her, Eamon Doran welcomed her with open arms: 'She has class,' he said to me every time her name came up, 'I never had anybody as classy as Nuala work for me before.'

I didn't say anything to Nuala about maybe going home to write Ethics because I was afraid she might think I didn't want to be around her. We got laid a lot after she came back but we were still dancing around each other without what I'd call any natural, easygoing happiness there between us. The sex drive between us was like a drug and the fact that we could acknowledge this probably helped us stay together as long as we did.

It saddened me though that I didn't share everything with

her. Even on our good days now we were not as we had been before she took off for her six month sabbatical. That I kept something as matter of fact as a possible trip home to write Ethics to myself, shutting her out, the deep down hurt of her going, of her needing to get away from me corroding my day to day to the extent, that I didn't even want her opinion about whether I should head for Wicklow or not. In a way, it was as though I was saying I am not your business.

Meanwhile I was building my repertoire of songs on the keyboard, wishing I had a real piano at my disposal in New York. Then I bought a second hand guitar in a flea market, smiling inside as I gave free rein to a crazy idea that had long tickled my fancy.

A couple of days practice and I was flying high on my old three chord trick though I only played my music when Nuala was out of the apartment. There was something I needed to do with the guitar, something that had always appealed to me, and I decided I was going to realise a long cherished utterly insane ambition. But only after the American Arbitration hearing was out of the way.

Chapter 16

During the first day of the hearing, I sat and listened to Betty who had sworn an oath to 'tell the truth and nothing but the truth, so help me God'.

I'm not saying she told lies but she did relate a story, create a picture of what she claimed had taken place, that wasn't in the script I'd been reading.

When the good lady finished her statement, her ex-lawyer who had become her chief witness now laid down his version, which supported fully the creative scenario painted by his client.

Following Betty's ex-lawyer the appearance of her ex-husband seemed to me to be a master power stroke.

Martin Bregman, never likely to be mistaken for a nice man, was a big wheel in the movie business. He had produced 'Dog Day Afternoon' and 'Serpico'. He was also credited with discovering the actor, Al Pacino. So he was a real heavyweight and he was soon in there pitching for Betty while displaying the demeanour of an alter boy. And he made a good witness.

Fortunately the man had his wires crossed and was thinking about some other deal that Betty had been hovering around. So he was talking out of his ass, which Rick Hobard proved to one and all when he submitted his statement later.

Rick told the truth as I have written it about his partnership with Betty who was to raise the money while he would teach her how to become a producer in her own right.

Not a single dollar had been produced – she had agreed to put in some of her own money but this had never materialised. When he asked her for a cheque she demurred. He pointed out that scripts had to be printed and bound along with the printing of a proposition for investors.

The production company (Rick and Betty) also needed petty cash to take potential investors to lunch and so on, these being the first steps to mounting a production. When he reminded her that she had agreed to produce the early finance herself she told him she would never put a dime of her own money into the play.

Since she had already invested a thousand dollars – her share of the advance to me – he was surprised and shocked, and bitterly disappointed. Rick was a good witness, really like a brilliant actor playing a part, managing to wax sadly as he told this to the Arbitrator, without going over the top.

He continued to explain that at this point Betty made her decision to sever their partnership which had led to the present situation. Rick then denied truthfully that we had ever colluded to deprive Betty of her rights in the matter, which he deemed to be none since the partnership with which I had made my deal was no longer in existence.

Rick had agreed to be a witness on my behalf – his evidence was intended to show that I was the innocent party here. This move on my behalf didn't mean he had turned into any kind of angel. It was clear as a bell that he was hoping he would be part of the production situation once we got Betty out of the picture. I said nothing to disabuse him of this notion even though I felt that Bob Harley and Tom Kain wouldn't touch him with a bargepole, if only because they didn't need him.

He went on to say that to his mind Betty had in effect dissolved the company that held the option on the play. When Rick finished giving his testimony the Arbitrator brought the first day of the hearing to a close.

On the second day, I finally got my chance to speak and I told my story without any frills. I was sitting on a lot of anger and I made no attempt to hide the fact. In all honesty, I couldn't have behaved any differently, all the frustration and anger that had been shelved, let go, bottled up, whatever, all of it was there brimming over the lip of the cup so that I was powerless to stop it spilling into the room.

Somehow I got through the story of my seduction at Sardi's without sounding like a victim – admitted I was flattered to be talking to Timothy Hutton on the phone – spoke of feeling fortunate to have attracted the attention of Hobard who had a very respectable track record as a theatrical producer. I allowed that Betty had been courteous, encouraging, she being the one to say, 'We have to keep your talent right here in New York, we can't afford to lose you.'

An arbitration hearing is not the same thing as a case in a court of law. Yes, you have your lawyers and the opposition have their legal team, and essentially all the participants are facing the man, the arbitrator who is himself a lawyer and the judge and jury but you get a chance to tell your story without all that yes and no stuff that can make a mockery of justice.

As it happened, I was at the opposite end of the oval table set directly facing this conservative looking gent who gave nothing away thanks to a natural born poker face.

My showbiz lawyer – hired by the Harley quorum – Gerry Cotura – moved in his chair that was half facing the speaker. So now Gerry is looking almost directly at me as though he is willing me to be brilliant.

So like all the other witnesses I get to make a statement – really getting time to say my piece,

'When Betty called me and said she and Rick had parted company, she insisted I had to choose one of the other of them in order for the production of my play to go ahead. I told her I had no desire to make any choice at all. This phone call telling me they would not be working together any longer had come out of the blue – the very last thing I needed, believe me – she insisted I had to choose between her self and Rick. I refused several times but she was so insistent – I tried digging my heels in, repeating that I didn't want to choose anybody. But, she would not let go – she insisted again and again, until finally I told her that if I had to choose I would choose to work with Rick.

'She seemed surprised and said something like: "Why on earth would you do that? He hasn't got a dime."

'I told her Rick had never pretended to have money, that he was the experienced Broadway producer, and that I felt his track record – five plays On and five plays Off Broadway, was my best bet in terms of what was best for the play. I didn't say to her, though it was on my mind, that while her agreed part in the process was that she would raise the money, Rick had assured me that so far she had not managed to find even one investor, in other words she hadn't come up with a dime. She asked me if I was sure I wanted to work with Rick rather than her self. Again, I said I had no wish to choose either of them but as she had put me in this impossible position, I chose to work with Rick. She seemed to accept this, wished me all the best and put the phone down.

'Next day I am handed the piece of paper accusing me of colluding with Rick to deprive her of her right to produce my play. I felt I'd been pole-axed, the dream of a production turning into a nightmare because of this rich bitch fucking dilletante...'

Betty's lawyer stood up and objected to my filthy language. The Arbitrator, who clearly felt my rage, told him to sit down. He then said that since the other witnesses had been allowed to tell their story in their own way I was entitled to present my story in the manner most natural to me. He then gave me the nod to carry on.

I took a sip of water and caught the eye of Gerry Cotura silently mouthing the word 'sorry' in his direction. At that moment he was facing me so that the Arbitrator could not see his face and he mouthed, clear as a silent bell –'Keep going' which would have made me laugh had I not been so angry.

By the time I finished telling my side of the story my shirt was wet from my perspiration and I felt that the Arbitrator believed me. In the circumstances, I couldn't have expected any more than that and when the man concluded the proceedings we were informed that his verdict would be rendered to us at the earliest possible moment.

Afterwards Bob and the others told me I had blown the Bregman case out of the water. This didn't impress me since it was what they had expected to do when they got to the Supreme Court about a hundred years ago.

Besides which, I didn't need to be boosted by bullshit – I needed somebody to tell me the date when the Arbitrator's decision would reach us. My legal team couldn't do that so I let it go. But I knew in my heart that it wouldn't be tomorrow or the day after.

As I headed back to the apartment I felt that the situation had reached a kind of natural Time Out. Like, there had been a lot of positive talk that was waffle to me – the projections were all of success – the Arbitrator finding in our favour – followed by a hugely successful production of the play. I said nothing but knew I was setting myself up to go home and write the novel for Harper and Rowe.

I checked my money which was running low and I had to think hard about how I was going to raise the funds to finance a trip home. The fare was just part of it – I would have to keep myself in groceries and the like while I was trying to get Ethics into book form.

With the intention of putting all thinking and all scheming on hold, I decided to live out the fantasy I mentioned earlier, it being on my list of things I had to do before I kicked the bucket.

Now my crazy dream to take a guitar and go busking for just one day is finally going to happen. This had been right up front in my mind for so long that I couldn't remember when the idea first landed on me. That didn't matter – it was something I needed to do and I was going to go for it.

Maybe it was about to happen because I felt hemmed in on both sides by situations I wouldn't have chosen to be dealing with at this time in my life. Like, despite the fact that I'd been honest with my evidence, I had no say in how the Arbitration hearing was going to work out.

Meanwhile, I was stuck in a marriage to a woman I was crazy about despite resenting bitterly the fact that I didn't know how she was going to be, what sort of mood she would be in, from one minute to the next. I went on trying to remember not to react and not to expect anything but recently I'd been so fed up with her that I had faked good sex when she was in the mood and I was anything but.

When I'd bought the second hand guitar, I'd picked up a big hat at the same time. Not a cowboy hat exactly but one of those big wide brimmed jobs you see Aussies wearing to keep the sun from frying their brains. When I tried it on I added a pair of shades and felt happy enough that I wouldn't be recognised by anybody I knew. But just to be sure, I picked up a red scarf on the way over to Fifth Avenue for my busking debut.

I keep checking myself out in the store windows as I walk along with the guitar on my shoulder and I reckon that the hat and the shades and the scarf together do hide my identity.

I do consider how daft this all is. I mean, here I am in the bright lighted star studded centre of the world's greatest metropolis – the city where something like a hundred and forty different languages are spoken at any one time – and I am disguising myself in case somebody sees ME busking on Fifth.

So, daft, stupid, ridiculous, yes, but in a way it sort of defines the scribbler in me, like it shows that while you don't have to be crazy to scribble a bit, it certainly seems to help. I instantly forgive myself for the put down – with my luck somebody from Dublin could just come up from the subway and there I'd be singing fucking Galway Bay.

I pick out my spot across the street from St. Patrick's Cathedral and I fold the soft guitar case into a sort of bowl – this to be the place where the punters will throw their donations for my singing and strumming.

Now I am about ready to rock but apart from the buzz of actually tackling this wild idea, I have a need to earn something, this being the test as to whether I am any good or not.

Like, if punters drop a coin or two it ought to mean you sound okay. So I needed to find out since praise for my singing had been in short supply since I made my debut when I was fifteen years old on the stage of the Marymount Hall in Harold's Cross, Dublin a long way from Fifth Avenue in Manhattan.

I make sure that my hat and the shades and scarf are all in place and moments later I am singing the tale of Molly Malone.

This is one of those Irish songs that have been popularised in the English speaking world for many years and I am soon getting a nod of the head from a passer by and the odd coin or two.

In five minutes I'm wishing I had a throat mike. Like the noise on Fifth could drown a US army brass band. But I press on regardless and in next to no time coins are dropping into my collection unit (the soft guitar case shaped like a bowl) and one or two people actually stop and listen for a minute or two before going on their way with a wave of encouragement to me.

I do 'The Isle of Innisfree' before I unashamedly drag out 'The Old Bog Road'. This song, which I love even though it hits an all time low in sentimentality – it ranks alongside 'There's a Bridle Hanging on the Wall' which I also love, god help me.

The bog road song is about *the mother* and, though it is as corny as Oklahoma, I find myself moved by it, and again I notice how some people actually stop for a few moments, one or two clapping their hands before moving on.

I now hit a D chord and get off on 'Me and Bobby Magee,' giving the great Kristoffson song all I have, without trying to compete with the traffic noise in the interest of staying free of a hernia.

I do a few more country songs and then start to repeat the Irish ones. Since my audience is moving, as opposed to *the audience was moved,* I don't think there'll be any complaints about the repetition of my tiny repertoire.

After half an hour, my fingers ache but I press on thanks to the encouragement of those decent New Yorkers who drop coin after coin and even a couple of five dollar bills.

I'm just thinking about taking a break when, coincidentally, I am joined by a very large cop. This silent blue suited giant looks like he'd be more at home milking cows in Donegal than throwing shapes just across the street from St. Patrick's but I don't comment on the fact. In fact, I try to ignore him in the hope he will just disappear. This does not happen and since I am unsure of the etiquette in relation to buskers getting arrested, I just keep on singing.

Fair play to the cop – he waits until I have milked the last drop of sentimentality out of 'The Old Bog Road'. Then he tells me in an accent that reminds me of Pat O'Brien, the actor who starred in a lot of black and whites when I was a kid: 'I like your singin' pal. Do you have a per-mit?'

'No,' I say with a grin: 'but I've got Mother Machree and The Isle of Innisfree.'

This goes over like a lead balloon – I can practically feel his arteries hardening – which makes it abundantly clear that my effort to be bright and cheerful and interesting hasn't got to first base.

'You did right to pass on the *Stand Up*, pal.' The nod of his head suggests that the day had been going real good until he met me. But there is no malice in his glance which would have set paper on fire. 'I'm just making a guess here,' he tells me in an offhand way: 'You don't have a per-mit right?'

'Right,' I tell him trying to sound like I really appreciate his prescience. 'So what does that mean, officer? I mean, it's not a criminal offence, is it?'

The guy may have descended from mountain men but he knows a rhetorical question when he hears one. He sizes me up like I'm a nut but harmless and I feel good because I don't mind what he thinks of me. Like, I came out here to shake the blues and whatever has been getting in the way of the writing and this has already happened in a major way.

The other bonus is the degree of sheer enjoyment. Its been so great that I have already considered dabbling in busking as a serious part-time thing. I mean, I love singing and strumming and there is money to be earned on the streets. And since being here in a neat little scenario with a big Irish cop, who could quite easily be earning a living as a human cement mixer, is about as bizarre as it can get, and I like the overall flavour of the day regardless of what's going to happen any minute. Like, it's real good, it's life happening, and I'm willing, if necessary, to take a whole book of tickets from the cop even if they're not for a raffle.

'Here's the story, pal. You and your busking, you just got through for the day. I catch you again and I'll be arranging for you to meet my friend The Judge, got it?'

'Obviously I need the money or I wouldn't be out here,' I lie just to see what he'll say.

'Spare me the story, Mick.' He makes the name of the Irish stereotype sound pejorative: 'I got enough stories of my own to fill a book.' I bite my tongue not to say: 'Maybe we should collaborate', but he crosses the thought by saying: 'Get your act off the street.' He gives me a look that could burn paint off a door. 'I'm serious, I see you again busking and it's no more Mister Nice Guy."

I watch him move off and turn to put the guitar into its case and that's when I notice that this is no longer where it was when last I checked.

That's right. My bowl shaped soft guitar case with my

busking earnings in it is no longer with me. It's gone. And I don't have to think hard to figure that the plastic case didn't come with legs or wheels. So somebody has helped it disappear into the noon of the day.

I burst out laughing. Like for someone to rob my busking money while I am being warned off the street by a cop as big as a taxi cab is really a bit stupendous, and I knew I'd have given anything to have the nerve of the guy who performed this remarkable deed.

The cop has stopped a few yards down the block and I yell at him, just to see what he'll say: 'Hey! Officer! Somebody's ripped off my collection.'

He shakes his head, giving me a grin that's pure nylon. 'I guess that's Show Business, pal!' He opines, looking like he's eaten up with sympathy before he walks away swinging his stick like fucking Pat O'Brien.

I find myself grinning now because I'm remembering a cop story Jose Quintero told me a while before this, a story about a traffic cop and John Cranko, the great British choreographer, who was in New York working with the Royal Ballet.

The story goes that Cranko steps onto the street at a junction just as the traffic cop is about to give right away to the seething mass of cars and buses and trucks that are pulsating to get away.

Seeing this little English poof actually begin to cross the street, the cop slams his hand up to indicate 'nobody move'. At the same time he blows his whistle, making sure everybody sees his hand signal.

The shrill blast of the whistle shocks John Cranko severely enough that he drops his cane. He stands there looking helpless in the moment, like someone not knowing quite what to do.

The cop steps over and bends down. Then he picks up the cane, and quite theatrically he slaps it into John Cranko's hand. He now asks, as only a sarcastic New York traffic cop could: 'What d'ye say, Little Fairy?'

To which the miraculously camp Mister Cranko, while tapping the cop of the shoulder with the cane replies, 'Vanish!'

I'm chuckling away to myself while I'm removing the shades and the Aussie hat when I see Darby Charles mincing across Fifth Avenue in my direction, doing, incidentally, a good impression of John Cranko.

Darby is dressed to kill, dark grey suit, white shirt, red tie, and if it wasn't for the mince in the walk and the clear varnish on his fingernails you'd never have known he was as queer as a three dollar bill.

'Isn't that a funny thing,' Darby casts a glance at a black guy in jeans that establish he is well endowed in the lunchbox. 'Well, look at the meat on him.' He turns back to me. 'There was I just coming from Mass and Holy Communion and I thought I saw you talking a cop.' His accent is like a breath of County Tyrone in Northern Ireland which makes sense since he is from Omagh. 'I looked again,' he continues, 'and thought you were in shades under a hat as big as an umbrella. What's going on?'

'I was busking and while the cop was basically suggesting I go home and sing to the wallpaper, somebody ripped me off.'

'Busking?' Darby makes a kind of a moue with his mouth as though he is allowing that some people do strange and funny things. 'No wonder you weren't answering your phone. I left three messages with your service.'

'I was going very well till the cop came along.' I tucked my busking shades into Darby's top pocket. The fact that he knew who I was on the other side of Fifth meant they weren't of any use to a guy trying to hide his identity: 'A present,' I said, 'just in case you want to look lewd and mysterious.'

Derby pulled the shades out with his fingertips, looking at them as though they were toxic. 'I wouldn't wear those to my own funeral. You really have to go for the best, Lee, tacky just doesn't suit you. You're too good looking for tacky. He smiled: 'Now now, don't look at me like that. It wasn't a pass, well, not a real pass. No point. You're so heterosexual it's hard to believe you're a writer.' He made another moue with his mouth. 'Come on, sweetie, I'll take your downtown to lunch, if you'll pardon the expression.'

We went to a Burger King where for my money you got the best hamburgers in Manhattan. I listened to Darby chattering away about his friend Julie, an ageing queen he had adopted a few years before. At the same time I'm thinking about how much I ate out in Manhattan. Back home Nuala and I probably ate out ten times a year. Here it was about twice a day and just about everybody seemed to do the same thing. Which reminded me that I'd read somewhere that on any given day there were eighty thousand restaurants in the city.

'Poor Julie, she could not go gently into that soft Six O!'

I caught Darby's drift and meant it when I said: 'You should have reminded me. I wanted to give him a birthday present. I like old Julie.'

'In which case you will never refer, while in *her* company, to *her* as *He*, and you will eschew for all time while she is within earshot, from your lexicon, the word *Old*.' His look stated how seriously he hoped I understood. I gave him a smile and in all innocence I asked: 'You gave him a little party, did you?'

Darby pulled a face that suggested there had been a minor earthquake or something equally trivial. 'I bought her a video of the most magnificent studs jerking off. We didn't say a word, just sat her down with a glass of Dom – special occasion, the big Six O, and hit the button. The next thing Julie sees is a massive phallic in the huge hand of a black boy you'd want to eat.' A bell seemed to go off in his head: 'Well, not you, I mean, but would I? Oh my God!' He sounded appalled: 'And me *coming* from Holy Communion.'

He put a French fry into his mouth in such a precious way that I burst out laughing. He silenced me with a look. 'Well, this dark demigod goes to work and a minute later Julie cries out. We all thought she was having a heart attack, the poor thing. When the black stud hits his orgasm, Julie actually faints, Dom all over her zip which pinched her erection while she was reaching for herself. They kept the poor thing in St.Vincent's overnight, so distraught she wasn't fit to be moved. Just goes to show how careful you have to be when you pick a birthday treat for a dear friend, especially when she is hitting the Big Six O.'

I was giving attention to my cheese burger, wanting to laugh like a drain but all too aware of how touchy County Tyrone gay men could be.

'Why were you ringing me three times anyway?' I asked.

'I think I can put some bread your way if you want.'

'Tell me the story.'

'Could you read a book, then write a what? Break it down like, to say, fifteen hundred words?

'I've written loads of book reviews for newspapers. What's this book about?'

'Y'know these arabs I work for right now. Well, while I'm working my boobies off setting up a trust for their eldest son, he is spread all over Manhattan eating pussy and banging chicks like he is in training for a pussathon or something. He should be, should have been, studying hard for the last few weeks – reading this book and writing a fifteen hundred word essay, I suppose you'd call it – this to impress the shit out of the people who have to try and educate these rich little Bedouins who should have been left in the desert with flies up their nose.'

'How much will they pay?'

'Thinking of you, mentioning my intimate friend, this great Irish writer, and making you sound like the guy that wrote the Koran, I suggested you would do it for me as a favour for twenty five an hour. How does that sound?'

'Sounds great but tell them thirty an hour and I'll give you ten per cent agents fee, okay?'

'The problem is.....' He looked tremulous and I stepped in

to save him any further discomfort:

'Ali Hard-On should have delivered the paper yesterday.'

'You're a mind reader, too.' Darby was relieved. 'I'll drop the book at your apartment on my way home this evening.'

After lunch I headed for Fifty Seventh Street and Ninth, Avenue thinking I'd take a hot bath and maybe a nap. To tell you the truth, I was feeling a bit worn after my busking gig. It wasn't demanding once you got going but getting started, hitting that first chord on the street, that had pulled a lot of juice out of me.

When Darby came by later he brought two books with him. On closer inspection the horny student's father had discovered that his son was even further behind in his studies than they had first believed. This created no problem for me especially since Darby had made the deal for thirty an hour, the only caveat to my feeling that I'd had an actual windfall being, that I had a lot of work to do in a very short time.

To make a long story lengthier, I finished up by earning twelve hundred and sixty dollars for the work I did to keep the priapic student in the running for his degree. My pal Darby was delighted with his commission and I had the bread I needed to fund my Irish trip and the writing of Ethics.

When I told this to Bob Harley and Tom Kain that I was going home to write my novel it seemed to me that they were relieved. I would be gone for some months and even the slow grinding mills of arbitration should have sorted out the wheat from the chaff in that time. Fair enough.

I called Jose who greeted me with the news that Bob had called him, assuring him that, after the manner of my diatribe against the injustice designed by La Bregman, victory to our side was guaranteed.

I made no comment, told him I was going to Ireland to write the novel. Jose wished me well – he would be ready to go to work on the play the moment he got the good word. Before we said goodbye he said to me: 'Do not be down hearted, Lee. This is par for the course in the production of any play in New York. The theatre attracts all kinds of people who are looking to make a fast buck, unlike us that write and direct slow plays and novels because we have to. Please stay in touch. Let me know how the pages are coming for you.'

Nuala said much the same thing before I left for Kennedy. Tell me how the work is going sort of thing, no word about it being a sacrifice that we, as a couple, were making, nothing romantic or emotional. We were more like two people who were tired enough of playing the games people play to just, for once, not saying anything that didn't need to be said.

chapter 17

As it turned out I got a good deal from the airline that meant I wouldn't leave New York for almost a week and I decided to try and make a start on the book even before I left. On my first day at the desk I get a phone call and this time it's the Scarlet Pimpernel himself, Mike McAloney.

Right away he is bellowing down the blower, chewing my balls off for not letting him know where I was and what my new numbers were and whatever. This was Mike's approach when he had failed to call you for a year or two.

I said quietly: 'They seek him here, they seek him there, that mother fucker's everywhere...'

'Alright, alright already, I haven't been in touch because I've been busy in Canada working with Donald O'Connor on my musical version of *Harvey*.

I hear him inhale on his cigarette and I can picture his smug Broderick Crawford expression as the name of the Hollywood legend with the dancing feet and the wicked smile has landed on my heart. Not to mention the great story of Harvey.

My God! That Mike had actually got his hands on the rights to stage *Harvey* as a musical.

Trying hard and failing not to sound incredulous, I say, 'Are you telling me you've been working with Donald O'Connor?'

'Don't sound so fuckin' surprised you Mick prick. I knew

O'Connor when he couldn't get arrested – I gave him the job in *Harvey* because I like him as a hoofer. No big fuckin' deal. Me and Leslie Briccusse put the show together after I sweet talked Old Lady Chase into giving me the rights to produce it as a musical. Nobody could get within a mile of the old broad, but yours truly, the guy who is going to make you rich and famous, you undeserving shit – your friend and mentor, me, charmed the panties off the old doll and the show is made for Broadway.'

'I didn't know you could write words and music,' I say just to take some of the steam out of the belligerent bastard's piss.

'Fuck you, scribbler,' he yells, taking another drag from his cigarette, his chest sounding like its got holes in it. 'Briccusse wrote it, me giving him a lot of ideas.'

I bit my tongue not to say, 'I'll bet Leslie Briccusse really appreciated your input,' substituting the line 'You got Leslie Briccusse to work with you. Wow!' I exclaim just to remind him I've been around the block. 'Did you have to pay him a lot up front?' I ask out of pure badness. Like, genius though he might be, Briccusse would have to get up very early in the day to get any kind of serious money from my buddy Mike.

'Pay him my ass!' he yells. 'He ended up investing in the show it's such a fuckin' winner. You are one of the very few asshole writers I have ever given a fuckin' dime to, and where the fuck did it get me, answer me that.'

I heard the way his tone got stretched as it usually did when he was elasticating a tale beyond what was allowed. This meant he was laying the bullshit on with a trowel. I said nothing. I'd get the whole story whether I wanted to hear it or not, next time he got pissed in my company.

That was Mike, the good hearted charlatan that you couldn't help loving, not even when he fell short on another promise he had intended to keep 'because I love you, you prick, and not just because you are the greatest fuckin' writer walkin' around at the minute'.

That same evening, after I'd had a fruitless day at the page, he and I are having dinner when he begins talking about my play as though we signed our option agreement last month, and he is the sole keeper of the rights. He knows better – Davidson and he would have been in touch.

Before I can comment, he hits me with: 'So be nice to me, especially as I'm buyin' the fuckin' dinner.'

'I've got something to tell you,' I try to make it sound like a warning but Mike never picks up on stuff like that. He has some built in filter in his brain that blocks out whatever interferes with the scenario he's running with inside his head.

I tell him the story that had finally taken me and my play into the American Arbitration Association hearing a few days before and I warn him that the option is tied at the minute, that Bob Harley and Tom Kain and others have invested money into the production while we wait for the result of the hearing. I tell him how Jose Quintero wants to direct it, and that I have every good reason to believe it will happen.

He kills his brandy and takes a deep drag on his cigarette and indicates to the waiter, with the aplomb of a Roman Emperor, that a refill would be a very good idea. Now he gives me his attention, failing miserably to hide the derision that is dripping from his eyelids.

'Leaving the Spic out of it...'

My reaction is so severe that I feel my eyebrows have hit the ceiling and he sets out to placate me with a hand gesture and a contrite expression. 'It's okay, take it easy. Quintero and I go back a long way. I call him Spic to his face. And he calls me Meehall, the Gaelic for Michael.'

'Is that what that means?' I say, feeling I could put a knife into him while I think he is so slippery the blade would probably slide off the bastard as I tried to stab him.

'Spare me the Stand-Up kid. Forget it. Quintero apart you are in the middle of something that could be called Amateur Night in Fuckin' Dixie!'

He sips brandy while I try to hide my grudging admission

that, in a way he is being proved right by the events that have unfolded since I signed up with Rick and Betty.

'You are right now having dinner with the guy who took fuckin' "Borstal Boy" to the Broadway stage.' He pointed a finger at me like a stop sign. 'That wasn't a great play and I've yet to meet anybody finished the fuckin' book.' He quaffed a real belt of his fresh drink.

'But fuckin' Behan was a great draw, people buying tickets hoping the crazy fucker was going to stumble on stage and tell the actors they were a bunch of assholes like he did with that Joan Littlewood production of The Hostage at the Garrick in London, fillin' the fuckin' theatre for weeks afterwards.'

He exhaled dramatically, pulling my strings, always needing to be producing his fucking monologues like he was Orson Welles.

'Regardless, it was your fuckin' buddy here, Michael Quinn McAloney, who got 'Borstal Boy' on the Great White Way and though a lotta fucks hate me for making it happen, they can suck mine before they can deny I did it. It was me who opened that show on Broadway.'

His slant on the story was pretty true though he left out the input from Burton Kaiser out of Chicago. I said nothing. When Mike was flowing he didn't need any feedback. Besides, there was something about him that suggested he could make things happen again, like an air of confidence that seemed real rather than the one he usually wore like cheap aftershave.

He went quiet, donning the nosebag for a few minutes, munching away as though it was his last supper. As I watched him eat, my heart went out to him. He was like a great big kid who wanted you to join him in a game that he knew would be a lot of fun. He seemed so innocent despite all the West Coast shit he donned like a suntan that I felt like hugging the crazy fuck.

When he surfaced, pushing away his half eaten meal like it

offended him, he lit another cigarette, took another belt from his drink and started on about Eli Wallach playing 'Harry' in *Goodbye to the Hill.*

'Let Michael tell you something, kid,' McAloney could wax confidential, as though he was slipping you a secret you could sell to the Russians. 'Anne Jackson's in love with the *Ma* role. Five minutes after she quit reading the script she turns to me and she's talkin' with a fuckin' Dublin accent. I couldn't believe my fuckin' ears. And if she takes the play, Wallach'll run to get aboard as Harry because he is still crazy about his missus and loves workin' with her. Are you gettin' my drift.'

I said nothing – he was on a roll, needing nothing from me but my attention.

'What I need from you is this, kid. I need you to turn Eli on to the role of Harry. He's scared, that's all that's wrong with him. You go and meet him, hit him with Harry, the Harry you wrote better than any Irish character since fuckin' O'Casey came up with Fluther and Jockser. You convince Wallach he can play Harry and we are in fuckin' business. Forget these fuckin' ambulance chasers you've been dickin' around with.'

'They're medical malpractice lawyers,' I cut across him, 'and they are good guys, so watch your mouth.'

'I'm offering you Anne Jackson, a legend, her husband, Eli Wallach, one of the best actors around. He'd've won the Oscar for Maggio in "From Here to Eternity" if *The Chairman's* pals hadn't scared Harry Cohn out of his balls. And get ready for this, kid –I have Sean Cassidy creaming himself to play *Paddy.*'

I know that my jaw drops because of the gleam of sheer delight that dances through his booze shredded eyes. Sean Cassidy. Jesus! This is a stroke of genius. Typical Mike. To come in from Left Field and hit you for a home run that knocks all your reservations right out of the ballpark.

Truth is, I believe him since Jack Cassidy is one of his closest drinking buddies and he has known Sean since he was a kid. This really is a time to be impressed and without blowing any smoke up his ass, I tell him I am deeply impressed.

He abuses his cigarette, sucks the life out of it, the cunning gleam that is his trademark riding high in his eyes as he sits there savouring every second of my concession.

'Fuckin' right, kid, be impressed.' He gives me absolution for all my failings. 'Sean Cassidy playin' *Paddy* you're gonna get panties thrown at the stage every night. I've been around the block once or twice and I know I can get the financing with those three names – all the bread we need to give your great fuckin' play the production it deserves. And you, you start thinkin' about ten per cent of the box less three hundred dollars per week while the play is on Broadway. So go meet Anne and Eli. They're sweethearts, lovely unpretentious, real people behind the actor shit. So you get him for me kid. Annie's already in the bag. Go get him. Fuck it kid! We deserve the cream, don't we?'

When I left Mike, I walked back to the apartment thinking that there could be no harm in talking to Eli Wallach and Ann Jackson. Like, you could have ten pokers in the fire in that Broadway situation, ten possible groups of people who were going to put your play on, and still the show might never see the light of day.

The problem, so I was beginning to realise, was that people rarely said no. If you were *out*, as in *you weren't going to be doing business* they simply didn't return your phone calls. This was nothing personal. They didn't call because they had nothing to say to you at the minute. But they hadn't said no, just in case things changed, as they could in any given minute, and then they called you without either of you referring to the hiatus. So you never heard anybody say 'I've been dropped' or stuff like that. You did hear people say 'he's not returning my calls' which the Shah of Persia might have said when Jimmy Carter saw the writing on the wall for him a while before the Ayatollah Khomemi returned home from France.

It was like *the games Broadway people play* except it's all too real because of the money involved. It's all about money and the chance of making it, or stealing a whole lot of it that attracts people who will fight to get involved – if only to become such a pain in the ass that you will give them a hundred or a hundred and fifty thousand dollars to just go away.

So, why not go see the two stars Mike wanted in the play. On a personal level it would be a treat for me, a joy. I'd never seen Ann Jackson work but my admiration for her husband went all the way back to 'Baby Doll' up to the 'Magnificent Seven' – a master actor.

Knowing that Mike had given them a script that did not include the rewrite I had presented to Jose Quintero, I took a copy of the new script with me when I went to Riverside Drive where the great acting duo lived.

Nuala came with me because she wanted to meet the two stars and partly because we had found some of our old magic in the feathers the night before and she was still all over me like honey.

She had put in a special effort to go meet the Wallachs and I have to say she was a showstopper as we stepped off the private elevator that had taken us up to their penthouse.

Anne Jackson was there to greet us with a Dublin accent that sounded perfect while an aproned Eli Wallach – he was cooking hamburgers – rushed out to say a quick greeting of welcome before he went back into the kitchen.

It has to be said that the Wallachs were just delightful, so kind to us that I was hoping – box office apart – that things would work out for them to be in the play. Just to be around them, working with them, apart from the honour of having them in something I'd written, would be a great time for me.

After we had eaten we sat in comfortable chairs and in answer to Eli's request that I read the play to them, I stood up and set about giving them a real taste of Harry Redmond.

They wanted every nuance and inflection that I had felt in both the writing and the directing of the play for the stage. It was clear that they loved the play and I was very much at ease as I started to perform.

Since I knew every line in the play I could move and act, strut and fret, go through all the feelings and actions of the quintessential Dubliner, *Harry*, whose main claim to fame was, as he boasts to the young hero *Paddy* who is worried about not having regular employment: 'I've never had a job, not even part-time.'

Something wonderful happened to me right there in that penthouse living room overlooking the Hudson River. *Harry* seemed to take me over so that I had no sensation of acting the part. Nor did I feel I was throwing Harry-type-shapes for the Wallach's – I was just being, or had temporarily become, the layabout Dub who was strutting his stuff, showing off his goodies in his own inimitable, unenlightened way.

When I ended my offering, Eli and Anne applauded and applauded while I suddenly felt shy, embarrassed to receive such approbation from two great Broadway stars.

They couldn't say enough about the work and the way I had brought Harry to life and they asked me, if I could recapture a scene between Harry and the eighteen-year-old Paddy which I was only too happy to do.

The scene is between the pupil, Paddy and the mentor, Harry, who *talks* but, *does* very little, while Paddy *listens* and *does it all*.

The story is set in *the Fifties* when the poor of Dublin were really poor. And where a survivor like Harry could be cynic, philosopher, doggerel poet, incipient alcoholic and last but by now means least, whoremaster, all in the course of an evening cadging drinks in one of the pubs he was not yet barred from.

Harry has his very own slant on life, like if somebody was to ask Harry what does the word *poverty* meant, the reply would likely be something like, 'Poverty means if you don't wake up with a Hard-On on Christmas morning, you'll have nothin' to fuckin' play with all day!'

So, once more with feeling, I gave myself to the scene they wanted to enjoy again, and was so taken by the experience that it was the standing ovation that Eli and Ann and Nuala gave me that brought me back to myself, back down to earth.

Getting the opportunity to perform that segment of the play for Eli and Anne was an honour and the generosity of their response left me steeping in gratitude. As we left them they assured me they would be talking to Mike the next day and they looked forward to meeting me again.

I was floating as Nuala and I stood on Riverside Drive waiting for a cab. I was buzzing like a bee, due entirely to the inner glow I felt at having *delivered* Harry. I hadn't been reading any script back there. I hadn't been acting back there. It was like Harry had taken me over for whatever time the scene took, an experience I wasn't likely to forget in a hurry.

Then Nuala said quietly: 'What happened back there?'

'How d'you mean?'

She was shaking her head under the street light. 'It was amazing. You stood up and it was as if you became Harry. Like you're my husband and you were no longer there.' She was looking at me in something approximating to awe when she said: 'I'd no idea you could act like that.'

She was impressed enough that I didn't doubt her or question her motive, not for a second.

'I had no sensation of acting.' I felt humbled as I said it, moved, and even a bit shocked by what had happened to me, and I gave her a hug which she turned into a passionate kiss.

As a cab came to a halt beside us she said, 'I want you in the worst way.'

My wife was rampant during the cab ride to the apartment and we were like hungry teenagers for each other until we lay satiated on the bed, Nuala very gentle and loving in the glow of several orgasms. We were both smoking cigarettes and I knew I should have been bursting with gratitude for what had just gone down between us.

Sadly there was a jagged edge to my mind that shut out even a hint of comfort because I was wondering would my partner have been feeling so cosy about me if I had made a mess of the offering to the Wallachs.

The morning after that memorable happening, I meet Mike McAloney in an apartment on 8th Avenue where he was flopping on a friend's couch, once more with feeling.

He had called me around ten which would be like daybreak for him. He is looking at me as though I have another head, then he tells me straight out: 'You were too fuckin' good kid. You scared the shit out of Wallach. He said that if he rehearsed for a year he could never take Harry where you took him last night. He said you were incredible. More than that, he put Anne on the phone to back him up. She raved about your performance, and I mean she fuckin' raved.' He smoked fiercely. 'Remember who we are talking about here – a couple of fuckin' giants – and they said you have to play it, that nobody is going to do it better.'

While I sat there dumbstruck, Mike killed his cigarette.'The exact words were 'nobody's going to do it that good.' He shook his head. 'You are full of fuckin' surprises, y'know that!'

I said nothing because I didn't know what to say. When he had a fresh cigarette burning he went on looking at me as though I had two heads. Then he said: 'The fuckin' play can be a knockout on Broadway. Eli and Anne think it's wonderful. They feel about it like I do and they're right.' He stood up, his mind made up about something and I said, 'What?'

We get into the elevator to go and eat breakfast. He is reiterating the same script to me like he's trying to beat it into my mind when a bunch of fags bustle in on the floor below. He goes still as a rock while the fairies go waxing all glitz and gabby talk in musically high voices with all that breathless giggly stuff that I lived with when I worked with bunches of them in the Merchant Navy.

I thought they were wonderful that morning, all bright

eyed and bushy tailed, chattering away like parakeets about tinsel and literally flowing out of the lift like a gush of late spring.

As they floated ahead of us across the foyer McAloney is waxing angrily and he grunts at me, 'I hate fuckin' fags.'

'So stop doing it then,' I say, knowing I am risking life and limb since he could homophobe for America.

He goes through the revolving door at such a pace that I know he is trying to injure me and I'm burying a severe need to laugh as we hit the street.

'Only the testimony of the Wallach's is standing between you and a trip to St.Vincents.' As he warns me like this he actually bursts out laughing. 'Fuck it! They're just a buncha busy little assholes.'

Now I laugh. You have to give credit where it's due and he slapped me on the back with enough force to let me know I was forgiven, but only just.

We walk up 8th and he turns to me right there in the street: 'I'm asking you right now, will you agree to play Harry?'

'If you're serious,' I said.

'Any doubt you could do it for a Broadway audience? Don't shit me now. Just tell me the truth.'

'I can do it.' I bite my tongue not to say 'because I wouldn't be doing it – I'd let it happen like it did last night.' I didn't want to get him ranting and raving about 'all that fuckin' method shit' or whatever.

'You do what you did for the Wallachs,' he paused and I knew he wanted me to believe that he was very serious about what he was telling me. 'You repeat the performance you put on for Eli and Anne and we're in business.' He raises his arm and a cab glides to a halt beside him. 'Gimme a twenty, will ya?'

I pass him the note and he throws his holdall onto the back seat of the cab. He turns and nods to me, steps into the Yellow Cab but sticks his head out again: 'I'm going to Chicago to see Joyce Sloane. She's my partner at Second City.

We have to find the bread for your play. And you, you prick! You're going to be the first Irishman in history who wins two Tonys – one for the play and one for playing *Harry* the way you did for Eli Wallach.' He nods, business done.

Then as though as he's been struck by a really significant thought he yells: 'And fuck you!' With those immortal words he slams the door and the cab takes off and I stand there shaking my head at my crazy life.

Getting back to the apartment, I'm still remembering how excited Mike was by the response from the Wallachs. Hard not to be excited but I'm not holding my breath that he's going to make a miracle happen by the weekend. Besides, where the play is concerned, everything is on hold until we get the decision of the American Arbitration Association.

Just days later I am on the plane to Dublin, taking with me Bob Harley's promise to let me know the moment he gets word of the Arbitrator's findings.

Then I start to scribble down all that has happened – just dates and salient facts relating to my time in Manhattan. When I get through making the notes – the basis of this book as it turns out – I am startled to remember an episode that I hadn't thought about for so long until it hit me out of the blue on the flight out of Kennedy.

I have to take you back now, back to the Americans, Ed and Michael Gifford, decent people and well heeled, that came to the Oscar, saw the play and claimed they wanted to produce it on Broadway.

I finally sent Ed Gifford a copy of the script and he rang me to acknowledge receipt of it, promising to call me in a week or so which, unlike McAloney, he did.

Ed continued to say very good things about the play and assured me that within a month he would have positive word for me. So it's back to waiting even though Gifford is the most positive guy you ever talked to.

The thing is that, as someone trying to make a living from

writing, you can't just sit around waiting for some guy to make you rich and famous. You have to keep putting the work out there. I've said it before – you stick ten pokers in the fire and if one of them gets warm you have the grocery money. And if one of them gets hot, well, you might even have jam on the bread and butter.

In this context, I had particularly high hopes for a thriller called 'Ringmaster' that I'd sent to a London publisher fully expecting it would be snapped up. This was a hell of a story, much of the plot given to me by Freddie Forsythe while we were fishing together down in Spain for eight or nine weeks.

Shortly after I got back from that trip I typed up a solid outline of the story and some time later I wrote it out in three short bursts called Ploy – Gambit – Check.

If you don't know about Frederick Forsythe you must have been living under a rock.

Freddie was the brilliant journalist who left the BBC over their stance on Biafran blockade back in 1967.

After that he took a Time Out to write his thriller 'The Day of the Jackal' which became a world wide best seller. Freddie wrote many more very readable thrillers, all of them hugely successful, becoming a multi-millionaire, which could not have happened to a nicer guy.

While he and I were sitting in a little fishing boat nattering away, nobody would ever have suspected he was a household name worldwide. Even in the province of Valencia – out in the sticks of Spain– waiters knew who Freddie was.

During our time catching lots of little fish, Freddie and I talked writing – he admired *Goodbye to the Hill* almost as much as I did Jackal, which to me is the definitive thriller post World War 2.

Anyway, he suggested I write a thriller, since novels don't sell as well and I agreed. By the time I came back from Spain I had the plot of *Ringmaster* there on paper, much of it down to Freddy and I was looking forward to writing it.

To create *a time window* during which I would write

'Ringmaster' I doubled-up on my output of scripts for the radio serial 'Harbour Hotel,' and I soon had the show four months ahead. I had written the first 750 episodes of the soap and would ultimately contribute 1,200, quitting just before the bubbles started coming out of my ears.

This meant I could write thriller pages for a week before doing a bit more radio work, then more of the thriller, and so on. I'd already asked Noel Jones – my script editor on the show – to read the pages as they came off the typewriter and he was only too happy to help me out.

I gave Noel the manuscript in the three lumps described earlier: Ploy-Gambit-Check and a few weeks later I got his phone call to give me the news about the book.

Noel was not just a brilliant guy, he was also an honest man and when he called me after he'd read the final part of the book he said simply: 'Sleep the sleep of the just, you fucker, you have written a cracker.'

The truth is that I felt it was a terrific read, a story that never quit and I was more than surprised when it was rejected for the first time and then when it was rejected again and again.

In all *Ringmaster* was rejected ten times, so you might understand I was beginning to wonder was I nuts. And was Noel Jones, truly, one brilliant guy, equally nuts, or what?

Finally, I asked a mate, John Boorman, the film director, if he would do me a favour and read the manuscript. I vowed that if he said it was crap I would throw it in the bin. 'I could be on an ego trip, I don't know,' I said to John. 'It just seems like such a good read, I thought it was a shoo-in.'

John rang me a few days later and said: 'It's wonderful, mate, I couldn't put it down.'

He said it would make a cracking movie but of course I didn't ask him to do it since he would be working two and three pictures ahead and wasn't waiting for me to come along and give him something to do.

The very next day after John had called me – it was a

Sunday – I was out picking blackberries in the lane by our old house – when I got a call from my book agent in New York.

The agent, a lady called Lois de la Haba, who had taken me on via a recommendation from Gordon Thomas, the Welsh born, Irish domiciled social historian who was always willing to help a fellow scribbler. Lois was elated to tell me that Michael Korda, a powerhouse author, and the top editor at Simon and Schuster, had made an offer for *Ringmaster.*

chapter 18

I was very excited and more than happy to get this much needed confirmation that my self and Noel Jones and John Boorman were not gobshites. We three had believed, without reservation, the thriller was a hell of a read, but after ten rejections you could be forgiven for beginning to wonder.

Lois goes on to say that Korda loved the book but was even more interested in the writer, and that he wanted many of my books on his list. Naturally, I was delighted that a publisher of Korda's stature even knew my name, let alone considered me a writer worth having around.

I was disappointed though to hear that Korda offered a minimal advance of only eight thousand dollars. That being said, of course I would accept the offer – not every day of the week somebody like Michael Korda comes-a-calling. Lois asks me how Ethics is coming and I tell her I'm getting good days but it's too early to say if the writing is any good or not.

An hour later, Nuala makes her Sunday call from New York moaning about everything. She wants to be home in Wicklow. I bite my tongue not to say: 'Sure and after three weeks here you'll want to be back in Manhattan.'

She might have said: 'Back in Wicklow with you.' But she didn't and I wondered was she involved with somebody and maybe having a tough time with it.

Whatever, she pissed me off and I told her she had *alcoholic arse.* This means you are always sitting in the wrong seat, going in the wrong direction, and never where you really want to be. She said she was going to take a break, go with her brother to the Bahamas or somewhere. I made no comment because in the moment I didn't care what she did.

When we quit talking I couldn't help wondering if my feelings about her – all peaks and valleys – would ever become less extreme.

Coming on the phone like that, dumping her tale of woe was just typical. Being totally consumed with herself came so naturally. Years later I would come to see that this part of her character only bothered me so much because I was her twin here, in that I was totally consumed with me.

But that day as I deliberately didn't say anything about the offer from Simon & Schuster I was just protecting myself from her predictable response – absolute delight at the acceptance, then bitter disappointment that the advance was only eight thousand dollars. The fact that I was about to be handled by one of the giants of the literary world would have been no balm at all to her need that we make some real bread at last. Whereas, all I could do was harvest the pages, drawing great satisfaction from the work, and try to quit hoping for a best seller. Some hopes!

Living alone, I did a lot of hill walking and felt no need for company and, to my surprise I didn't even cast a glance at any particular woman, not even when I went into Dublin for a day.

This didn't stop me looking, admiring lots of women – as the fella said: 'Just because you're on a diet, it doesn't mean you can't look at the menu.' In the minute I was content with a stint of celibacy, hoping my monastic pose would help me add some sliver of quality to the words coming through from my muse in the sky. But I couldn't have guaranteed that the no sex routine would last for very long. Old favoured habits die hardest of all.

Then Bob Harley gets news to me that the Arbitration Association lawyer has found in our favour and that Bregman was no longer in the picture.

Bob mentioned that while we did win hands down he had to return to Bregman the thousand dollars she had paid out as her half of the original advance to me.

There wasn't a bloody word about any compensation to me for the time my career and the play were on ice because she was playing games.

All in all, I responded warmly but I was still feeling the effect of the weeks spent buried in my room with 'Ethics'. I might not have been like this had I been able to tell if the book was any good or not.

Finally, after four months at the Old House in Wicklow, I deliver the manuscript to Bud Wyatt at Harper and Rowe in Manhattan.

Nuala and I are again sharing the apartment at Fifty Seventh Street and Ninth Avenue and we are getting along alright. She certainly welcomed me back and without her gushing in any way she let me see she was impressed by the size of the manuscript.

Meanwhile I make a list of all that I am involved in on the career front.

There's *Goodbye to the Hill* with Jose Quintero to direct, the producers to be Harley and company.

There is Ed Gifford who says he wants to produce the same play and will get back to me in a month or so.

There is Mike McAloney – I have not heard a word since he took my twenty and bid me adieu with a touch of Anglo-Saxon repartee, the words *Fuck You* being his idea of a completely unrehearsed witty answer. Indeed, he who was drooling to produce the same play since he heard such good things about it, and about my performance as Harry, that when last seen he was fantasising about me winning two Tony's – if you don't mind!

I am also now waiting to hear from Buzz Wyatt at Harper and Rowe to hear his verdict on Ethics.

Meanwhile, I am saying nothing to anybody about the

other players in my career scenario because I have finally got the message about *don't say anything you don't have to say*. Like they are juggling their balls in the air hoping that one will bounce high and make a lot of money, and now I am doing the same thing in a much smaller way. It's part of the games people play in the exciting playground called Manhattan.

I am soon seeing the Giffords who live in a startlingly beautiful house on Park Avenue. They seem to like my company since they invite me every couple of weeks and since they serve wonderful food, I am happy to join them. I say nothing of this to Nuala, remembering how she had gone many times without any word as to where she was going or who she was going with.

Ed remains very positive while he waits for his personal investors to make up their minds about how much they want to put into the play. I like the way he talks. With him it's never a case of *if* they are going to invest, but rather *how much*. He was one of the most confident, coolest guys I have ever met.

Now I get word from my agent to go and meet the great Michael Korda at Simon&Schuster on Sixth Avenue, or to give it its proper name Avenue of the Americas.

I had read one of Michael Korda's books, 'Power', on the plane over from Ireland. In this hugely successful book he tells one and all how they should act, behave if they want to have power and its accompanying wealth. He advocates that you put your power into action at every given opportunity. For example, when a guy like me is coming to meet you – you leave him sitting for some minutes before joining him. You are never to be found waiting for him to come and join you.

Ideally, you leave the guy facing the wall behind your desk which is covered with pictures of you and famous and wealthy and extremely powerful people – or words to this effect. Then you make your entrance like the powerhouse that you are.

There was a truck load of this kind of stuff and I gave up on the book early on, harbouring the distinct feeling I wasn't going to like Mister Korda.

I may be some kind of slap happy innocent but I've always believed that all people are equal. Sure you meet those that can test you in the severest way at times but I have tried to live up to this ideal. Ergo, though I hated *the Korda approach*, I tried to keep an open mind on the possibility that he might have been a decent and caring kind of man.

As it happens, when I emerge from *his* elevator on the 14th floor of the Simon and Schuster building, I am shown into Korda's office and offered a chair facing the wall behind his desk which is covered with pictures of *the great little man* and a host of the famous and the rich and the powerful, the galaxy including people like the Kennedys and some film stars and other children of some lesser god.

Being some kind of dumb Mick, I ignore the chair and make sure I am standing looking out the window when Michael Korda comes in.

He shakes my hand, tells me he likes *Ringmaster* greatly and that he hopes we will do many books together. He ventures the view that the book can sell in big numbers – 'A political thriller, an SAS killer wiping out the top men in the IRA, with a great love story in there, my idea of a huge seller, Lee.'

I admit to being happy to hear him say so but I think it's fair to say that Michael Korda and I didn't like each other. Later when I thought about my churlishness in not being in my seat gazing at the images of this literary giant, I could understand how someone who could write what he did might find me unappealing. Yet, at the time he gushed about wanting me on his list and I lapped it up without wondering if he really meant it.

Our meeting was brief and essentially all about the book. I can't remember much about what passed between us but I am positive I asked him to check out whether or not we could use 'Ringmaster' as the title for the story.

He seemed puzzled by this request but I felt it was such a good title that it might have been off limits for us because someone else had used it recently.

To make my point I showed him a possible design for the cover that I had sketched out myself. 'Something for your designer to kick against, if nothing else,' I said, not meaning it.

The idea I had was this: A cartoon ringmaster, a black figure cracking a whip which forms a circle. Coming at you through this hole are some of the real figures in the book – Harold Wilson the British Prime Minister, IRA gunmen, with Nemesis the goddess, turned into a One Man retribution unit called Steve Gunn, conned into being a Hitman for MI6.

I felt that the title 'Ringmaster' was perfect for the book. The whole spy situation is called 'The Circus' – the Ringmaster cracks his whip and all kinds of people start to jump through hoops.

This may have been a tad fanciful but Korda allowed that it was pretty good and at my request promised he would have the title checked out, just in case we might have to come up with something else.

Knowing that I was dealing with a publishing giant, I left the matter there and assured him that I would be happy to offer him my next novel. With that we shook hands with his assuring me that he would publish the book in the following April.

A few days after this, Lois de la Haba rings me to say that Korda was happy to be working with me. I was surprised but didn't say so. She was excited that he wanted to read my next book – she had climbed some kind of mountain in getting this guy interested in one of her authors and she was entitled to be excited. Like a lot of other people she thought Korda was a god and now she was doing business with him and I was happy for both of us.

Lois was a nice woman, well meaning and caring, and I

hoped we would work well together. We had got off to a good start by her signing me up with Korda, no doubt about that, even if he had been tight as a duck's arse with the advance.

Moaning aside, I felt bucked to be in Korda's stable and I was already aware of the next plot forming for a second book about Steve Gunn.

Some weeks go by but neither Gifford nor any of the other possible producers of my play is setting the world on fire in the fundraising department. Jose Quintero is away in Europe or Hollywood – he would direct a movie or two – so we were all holding our breath that he would return hale and hearty and ready to go with the play, which, according to Bob Harley, would be fully financed by his group in the not too distant future.

Bob's assurance arrived just in time to help me deal with the disappointing response of Budd Wyatt at Harper and Rowe.

Buzz just didn't like *Ethics of the Fathers*. He felt I had spent too much time giving out information about the period – the book was set between 1902 and 1922, instead of just taking the reader right into the action, letting the period emerge as it needed to, which is what tended to happen when you were doing the job right.

I could accept I had failed to do this and that the book had suffered as a result. I had no heart to go back to it at the time so I put the manuscript on a shelf where it sat for twenty years before I ever gave it another thought. But that's also another story.

It was sickness – as in the disease of alcoholism – that, and nothing else, had been the glue used to bind Nuala and I into a couple. We had been ill enough – while thinking we were fine because we were *in lurve* – that we had found alibis for anything and everything we wanted to do on our wayward way to the present and in doing so we had betrayed the rules of AA and indeed the rules of common sense.

We had been steeped in delusion from day one. As time went by it was clear that we had very little hope of the constant balance any long term relationship needs if it is to survive in anything like harmony, which surely has to be the bottom line in a marriage that is in any way worthwhile.

Although I was not free to leave her or encourage her to leave me, I vowed in my heart to let her go. I became willing to put my feelings on ice – just live with her for whatever time it took for one of us to get the courage to leave. Meanwhile, I set out to feel good about the overall interest in me and my work.

That same night, I felt good as I went to dinner at the Gifford's house on Park Avenue. To me this was a mansion and it was dressed well in the trappings that only serious money can buy.

Ed Gifford actually hugged me when he let me in and I felt a wave of affection for the big guy. Michael gave me both of her cheeks while her perfumed fragrance and the press of her breasts against me actually got me aroused. If she had any notion of this she was too much of a lady to let it show. My guess was that she was a loyal and devoted wife.

Ed had invited some Manhattanites – sophisticated types including a gay television personality, a fat guy who had a lisp you could photograph. He had this tiny wife-guy who gasped over the food presented and begged Michael for the recipe of several dishes as though his/her dainty existence depended on receiving them.

The dinner party was in my honour and Ed said wonderful things about my play and about my talent while I sat there wishing that, just once, I could just accept what was on offer.

When Ed announced that his lawyers were drawing up a contract between us in relation to the play *Goodbye to the Hill* there was a round of applause from the guests and the fat, poofy guy embraced me and tried to give me a kiss which I managed to avoid without giving offence.

It was a lovely evening spent with Ed and Michael Gifford, the other guests just dressing in the Gifford style, and when I left them I was touched by how decent Ed had been to me even though I hadn't yet seen a dime of his money.

Within days Ed Gifford had sent a contract to Lois de la Haba who within hours had me up to her office on what she called a matter of the utmost urgency.

Her problem was that there was a clause in the contract which stated that Ed Gifford was free to sell the option on to another party if he chose to do so.

He also wanted a two year option by the way, whereas Lois would only give him one year with an option to extend if both parties agreed.

I didn't have a problem with any of this. Like I had seen how Ed Gifford responded to the play at the Oscar the night he had taken Michael to the fringe theatre 'to catch a little Shaw' and I believed deep down that he wanted to do it.

Lois was adamant: 'You could be tied to all kinds of people, even unscrupulous people, if he were to sell his option on to them. We know nothing about Mister Gifford – the Mafia are always on the lookout for ways to put their money into legitimate situations, the theatre being one of them.'

I tried to protest but she insisted she knew more about the scene in New York than I did, and that there was no way this guy was getting our agreement to what she called that *carte blanche* clause in his contract. 'You're a hot writer, someone who is being published by Michael Korda.' Lois said his name the way some Catholics sound when they talk about Our Lord, and I had to suppress my need to smile. He might have been a powerhouse but my over all feeling about the guy was that he was a little ballocks.

Lois goes so far as to beg me not to talk to Ed Gifford about the contract unless she is present. I reluctantly agree with the lady since I have signed up as her client and because I felt I had to back her judgment here.

Right away this creates a problem with Ed Gifford and

within weeks he has told me I am a damned idiot to listen to this crazy woman and that he is washing his hands of me.

Not only that, he tells me that he really liked me, that he felt like a father to me and that he would have ensured success for the play because he knew how to do that and he had the clout to make it happen.

As he put the phone down on me I felt like something had been ripped away inside me. It was like part of me knew that he really was on the level. But then the big question arose in my mind — if that was absolutely true, why would he not agree to lose the clause giving him carte blanche to sell his option on?

Within hours, Buzz Wyatt called me from Harper and Row to confirm they were not interested in talking a rewrite on Ethics. He said he wasn't prepared to get into it. He was very close to retirement and didn't need the hassle.

Remembering the saga of rejections that 'Ringmaster' had been through before Korda had arrived like the Seventh Cavalry, I tried to keep my sunny side up. But I was sick in my heart at being struck out twice in a matter of days and before I knew it, I had jumped on a plane and was heading for Ireland.

chapter 19

Within a few days of arriving back in Wicklow, I was working away in the room I called my office, writing what I could remember about the last few years. Meanwhile I went on studying Science of Mind and remembering all I had learned at the Rutland Centre. In this area, my main aim was to detach from old ideas, to find a place without peaks and troughs where I could learn to live on the level, in the now, feeling grateful for all I had, even if sometimes it wasn't enough.

The Old House had been sadly neglected so I began doing the maintenance work that was needed. The garden was a total shambles and I did some tidying up on a daily basis, working three and four hours every other day as my birthday and Christmas approached.

I had no memory of enjoying birthdays. In the early years the family was on the floor so enough said. My one abiding memory of a Christmas present was the one roller skate I got wrapped up in fancy paper from a nurse during a party for poor kids in the Adelaide Hospital in Peter Street.

Those days were tough and very few poor people had any chance of presents at Christmas. In my case – being born on December twenty first – I was competing with The Big Chippy – Jesus himself – which meant no contest.

But I liked Jesus, respected him even though I dismissed his story overall by the time I was twelve years old.

Later on I decided he was the first man who believed that he was a Universal Being. Somehow *he came in* knowing that in back of our humanity there is *Being*.

This connects everyone with everyone, since we are all illuminated by the one light. This light never dims even when it is buried under the cover and the weight of our desires and wants and our inability to believe in anything other than that which we can touch and feel and see and possess.

Early in March, I get an urgent phone call from Michael Korda at Simon & Schuster. He tells me right away: 'We have a problem, Lee. We have just found out we can't use the title Ringmaster, and we need a new one right away. And, one where we can substitute eight letters for the word *master*.'

I'm shocked and angry and somehow stunned. I mean, here I am dealing with one of the powerhouses of publishing in the United States and this guy has checked out the title – which I had asked him to do many months earlier – just weeks before the book is due to be published.

Korda presses on because, as yet, I haven't managed to find my voice. 'The problem is that the review copies have gone out to the West Coast as *Ringmaster* and we need your genius to rescue the situation.'

'Ringleader,' I say, knowing it is the only one that will fill the bill.

'Brilliant,' Korda gushes. 'I expected no less. You have saved the day.'

'Of course Ringleader has nothing to do with the story. I mean it'll do, but...' my voice trailed off because I could feel that he had already left me even though the line was still open.

'Thanks Lee. We'll be in touch. And good luck to the book.'

He was gone and I was left there feeling like I had been raped. I tried all my positive exercises but nothing could stop me from feeling low about the book's chances of getting any serious attention. It was a very good story and worthy of good reviews but going into stores under two different titles it was already dead in the water. Certainly, Simon & Schuster were not going to do any advertising. I mean which title would be used in an ad for the book? The situation was the stuff journalists and comics make gags about, especially when it involves a high profile guy like Korda. So I knew, and I would prove to be right, it was a shutdown and the blackout on another dream.

In May I'm back in Manhattan to a warm welcome from my wife and a night of energetic sex that did me a power of good. By the sound of Nuala the next morning it had no been any hardship for her either and I hoped the good vibes between us would last.

I was quickly into a meeting with Jose Quintero who said he had found me a top class play agent at the Morris Agency. 'I waited for the right moment to talk to this lady agent – we are old friends but she will not handle just anybody.' He smiled. 'She trusted me when I said I had found a great playwright.'

I gave the man a hug, smothering my emotions, so grateful to have made such a friend of such a man.

You may wonder whatever happened to Lois de la Haba, the lady that didn't trust Gifford. Well, we parted company because I really felt we had lost a live one in Ed, when she might have found some way around the impasse between them. Then I had to deal with the Korda/Ringmaster debacle, so that all in all, I just didn't feel I wanted to work with her anymore. She was philosophical and we parted in a friendly way. I feel sure that Lois, like me, never heard from Michael Korda again.

I wrote to his boss at the publishers and I complained about the treatment, or lack of it, that my book had received.

Guess what?

Surprise-surprise!

I didn't even get a reply.

Bob Harley had been behind my move back to the Big Apple. 'It would be a good idea for you to be here. That's if you still want the play to go on.'

'Does a fish swim?' I asked him, telling him I was ready to return to Manhattan but that I had very little money. He offered to give me a part time job typing up legal briefs of an evening and I said you're on.

During lunch at Doran's I asked Bob and the ever good and generous Tom Kain if they were pulling out of the play production scene. Bob said no, but there was some kind of caveat in his voice that I couldn't figure out and I just let the hare sit for the present. Before we parted, I agreed to go into Bob's office on the following Monday to talk about the work situation, and as I shook Tom Kain's hand, he gave me a wink and said, 'I'm speaking for all of us when I tell you, all we want is to see your name in lights on the opening night of *Goodbye to the Hill*. Jose will tell you more when you meet him.'

I gave Tom a hug and Bob Harley shook my hand ferociously, a few tears sitting on my eyelids as we parted company.

As I left them I couldn't get over their decency. The catch, the caveat in Bob's voice earlier when I had asked were they pulling out – that was to do with the guys not wanting to be in the way of the play going forward. When Tom said that Jose would tell me more, I knew from the great man himself that he was already working on the situation. This gave me hope again because Jose had a lot of clout at this time and remained head over heels in love with the play.

I was only back in the apartment at Fifty Seventh and Ninth Avenue when the phone rang and I was speaking to Jose. Two days after this, he introduced me to Janet Roberts at the Morris Agency and I could only feel privileged to be in this lady's company.

Janet was a legendary agent and an old friend of Jose. She

was in her fifties, gentle in manner, but, according to Jose, very tough when it came to the protection of her clients.

She had read my play and said she loved it. 'I believe it could do well on Broadway,' she said in her low key way.

One thing I felt right away was that this lady wasn't in the bullshit business. She was far too successful to have fooled around and it was she, rather than Jose, who dropped the pleasant bombshell that we were all actually waiting for a major Broadway producer to appear at any minute. This theatrical giant was coming, so Janet Roberts assured me, to meet with me. He had read the play, adored it, and with Jose directing was very keen to produce it.

'Provided he doesn't have too many balls in the air at the same time.' Janet was shuffling papers as she spoke but you could hear that good down to earth stuff in her voice, something you didn't get a lot of in the theatre business.

Jose inclined his head to concede the point but we had no more time for discussion since the door opened and the man himself entered like a halfway decent Roman emperor.

He was lanky and beautifully suited and coiffed under a mane of white hair over a Roman nose, his gleaming teeth a tribute to the artistry of his dentist. This was legendary Broadway producer Harry Rigby.

He stood there beaming at us, one languid hand raised in the air in greeting as he said with a grand smile: 'How do I look for a guy just lost a million dollars!'

You have to admit it was a great entrance line. Clearly the guy was a top drawer shaper as well as some kind of theatrical magician.

At that moment he had Mickey Rooney and Ann Miller starring on Broadway in a show called 'Sugar Babies' which was a major hit with several touring companies travelling the length of America with the same show. And I have to say that to be in the same room as a man who was employing a couple of screen legends such as Rooney and Miller gave me a rush, and all the more so since he didn't seem to be taking himself all that seriously.

The million dollars he had just lost had gone down the tubes on a show called *Collette*, a musical about the French writer that was mauled by the West Coast critics and was stillborn.

After he had shaken my hand and blown a kiss to Janet Roberts and shared a hug with Jose he sat down and told me right away that he loved my play. I waxed appreciatively, looking to Jose to see if he thought this was a genuine compliment.

Jose nodded his head sagely, assuring me that it would work out and I relaxed. A few minutes later as Harry and Janet got down to talking the business end of the proposed production, Jose stood up and announced: 'Lee and I are going to lunch so we leave you to discuss your business. Talk to you both later.'

With that we left the office and headed for the elevator. Jose took my elbow and gave it a squeeze. 'You cannot be blamed for being sceptical after what you have been through already but Harry is a live one, and it's my belief he will produce your play.'

A little later, as we ate a diner lunch, Jose said to me: ' I was reading the play again last night and yet again I was very touched by your answer to Mister Hayes the office manager when he asked why you had not included the truth about your young brother Larry who died of the TB.' I was deeply moved by Jose's sincerity, remembering the passage from the scene where my hero is being sacked by his boss.

Paddy had got the job, believing that he and his mentor, Harry had fooled the office manager with a story so outrageous that nobody would make it up. As it happens Hayes was a man of compassion who on hearing how desperately the lad was lying to get the job, let his heart overrule his reason.

But we are at the come-uppance stage in the story and the plethora of lies has come home to roost:

Hayes
Did your brother Charlie really drown in Manchester?

Paddy
No sir. But we did lose my little brother, Larry, TB killed him.

Knowing he is listening to the truth, Hayes asks:
Hayes
But why didn't you tell me about Larry?

Paddy
Ah, he was a great kid, sir, I couldn't put Larry in the middle of a pack of lies.

I find I have recited the lines for Jose who sits there with his Caesar salad, tears hovering on his eyelids.

'It is one of the most beautiful moments I have ever found in any play. And you know, Paddy is right, which means you were right to put it down on paper just as you did. You must go with your truth. If you sell out your truth, one day when you go to that place inside yourself where your truth rests in waiting, it will be not there for you because you cheated on it before.'

Over coffee Jose told me he was about to leave Manhattan for a time. It seems he had been offered a theatre in Chicago free gratis. I would learn from Elva that evening that the offer was genuine because influential people there wanted Quintero working in their city and were prepared to pay well for the privilege. It was no surprise that Jose would never have talked about himself in that way – at the lunch table he responded modestly to my delight at his wonderful news.

'Of course I will direct your beautiful play on any stage anywhere at any time.'

We went on to discuss the arrival of Harry Rigby on the scene and Jose assured me that unless it was simply not meant to happen his old friend was the man to do it.

'He has the clout to get you the stars your play deserves and he has the backers – he will not be scraping around like Hobard and Bregman.'

That same evening I visited with Elva Oglanby to tell her about Jose bringing Harry Rigby into my life and she was very happy about this. 'You have two hot names right there, and with Janet Roberts minding your back, everything should work out just fine.'

She then handed me a cheque from Robin Cousins' people, a serious payment on the film treatment I had written for the world's best skater but she wouldn't hear of taking a dime commission. That was how Elva was and I didn't argue because I didn't want to offend her. As I saw it, she and I would do many things together, but I vowed to myself that she would never regret having helped me as much as she had

Her mother lived with her at the high-rise apartment on Ninth Avenue and we had a jolly time afterwards that evening. Before I left, I was singing songs and strumming on a guitar belong to Struan, one of Elva's sons, for one of the sweetest old ladies I had ever met.

She was a survivor of the London blitz in World War 2 and eighty-five years of age, bright and bubbly as a glass of champagne, in love with me since we had first met. She loved all the memories that the Old Tyme Music Hall songs that I kept in my rep for older people, had brought back to her.

So within weeks Harry Rigby throws a dinner party for Siobhan McKenna and me at a very fashionable restaurant – this, with a view to seducing the great actress – theatrically speaking since Harry was as queer as a three dollar bill – into signing on the dotted line as Ma Maguire in *Goodbye to the Hill*.

Siobhan had already been asked, privately, by the great producer to take on the role, and now he was bringing the offer out into the public domain.

In her *after-dinner* speech Siobhan, always a very nice woman to me, complimented me on the force and power of the play, but she had to decline the role because she felt she was too old to play a woman with a twenty-one-year-old son, which was the age of her eldest boy, Billy.

In fairness to her, I thought she was right but Harry didn't care about her age, and she wasn't that far outside the range where she could have handled Ma.

It was her drawing power that Harry was after because this lady could still pull them in at the box office on Broadway. Irish people that rarely went to the theatre turned up when Siobhan McKenna's name was over the title.

And let's face it, she was so talented she could have passed as Ma, but she was an honest woman and didn't feel right about doing that. I thought, fair play to her, even though it meant we had to go looking for another name, which meant more time in the trenches of uncertainty with no guarantee of anything at the end of it.

Now Maxwell Caulfield comes back into my life. Max was the young English actor who caused a sensation as 'Entertaining Mister Sloane' who walked naked around the stage causing palpitations for the Blue Rinse Brigade which returned again and again to sit gaping, goggle eyed, at nature's very generous endowment to the new leading man.

Max in his twenties was married to Juliette Mills who had been a TV star. I had first talked to him at the Cherry Lane Theatre just before I got involved with Hobard and Bregman

He was a very talented guy and he read my play in a night and came back saying he'd love to play Paddy. I didn't mention this to Hobart and Bregman because they had dropped Timothy Hutton's name for the role and even Max Caulfied naked couldn't compete with that.

A couple of weeks later, Max got what he hoped would be his big Hollywood break when Alan Carr came in for him to play the non-singing lead (a mistake in a musical, surely) in

Grease 2. So Max was whisked out of my life – ended up in a bummer of a movie – following Travolta who had lit up the screen – was always going to be a tough act to follow.

Anyway, here was Max back on the scene when I got to Harry Rigby's apartment after a coy phone call, 'You simply have to come by the apartment, Lee. Jose has dropped in from Chicago, we have the lady owner of the theatre in Philadelphia where we're going to open *Goodbye to the Hill* and,' Harry paused for effect, 'there is another guest, a surprise guest, that I'm sure you'll be delighted to see.'

The surprise guest turned out to be Max Caulfield and before I can even say hi to anybody he grabs me in a bear hug and asks me quietly: 'Am I really going to play Paddy in Goodbye?'

'You were my first choice,' I tell him truthfully.

He smiles and gives me a dangerous handshake. 'Do you remember what else you asked me that night at the Cherry Lane?'

'I asked you if there was any chance Juliette would play Clare.'

Clare Kearney is a forty year old woman who seduces Paddy and thereafter buys him clothes and gives him money provided he goes on laying her out of her mind, which being a well reared street-arab he does with alacrity.

'She'll do it,' Maxwell assures me.

'Have you told Harry?'

He shook his head. 'I was waiting to run it past you.'

'Ten out of ten,' I said, seeing the publicity angles attached to that possibility.

Now Harry is all over me like a rug. Introducing me to the lady theatre owner from Philly who would later tell me frankly that she regarded it as an honour to have a Rigby production in her place, remembering then to mention that she loved my play, 'read it right through in one sitting'.

Jose gives me a hug and mentions that Colleen Dewhurst has expressed a real interest in playing Ma. 'And she would be delighted if we had Timothy Hutton playing opposite her.' He spoke quietly as he usually did. 'They made a movie together and they are just crazy about each other.'

Jose is still calling the play *Casey*, so Harry had not yet told him that we are going with the original title. This wouldn't bother Quintero but Harry liked to keep his little secrets until he was ready to drop them.

I decided not to say anything to Harry about Maxwell being my ideal, though I wanted to say it, and let him know at the same time what a coup it would be to have Juliette Mills, known coast to coast because of her television series *The Nanny*.

Even as I was deciding to let the hare sit, I was smiling at the irony of what was happening to me. I was the guy who hated all the bullshit that had come his way, and here I was storing up my own little secrets until the appropriate time came along to reveal them. The outsider had thrown his hat into the ring, already sucked in to playing the games people play around Broadway.

At about seven o'clock that evening Harry had a brainstorm and announced that despite Siobhan McKenna's reservations about her age, he still wanted her to play Ma in *Goodbye*.

He was so hooked on the idea nobody gave him an argument and he announced he intended ringing her right away – 'Strike while the iron is hot ,' he said as though he had just dreamed it up.

He looks at his watch: 'Mmmm, seven o'clock' and he glances at me, 'What time is that in Dublin, Lee?'

'It's about midnight, Harry.'

'Is midnight considered *late* in Ireland?'

'Well, let me put it this way,' I offered as delicately as I could, 'On a Saturday night we have the Big TV show of the week – it's called *The Late Late Show* and it starts at nine fifteen.'

Harry throws his hands at me. 'Forget it! I'll call her tomorra.'

chapter 20

Within a month, Harry has quit returning my calls, Jose is in Chicago, and Mike McAloney might have been on the moon for all I know about his whereabouts.

I am seeing Bob Harley and Tom Kain with whom I have become mates for lunch every week and I am working for Bob, illegally, as a legal typist. I toil of an evening at ten bucks an hour with no shortage of need for my typing skills, so I am actually earning a modest living by working five nights from six to eleven.

My old pal, Mary Tierney, an actress and producer gives me a call and asks me if I could make the time to write something she could get her teeth into. Mary and I had always loved each other as pals and we were often there to encourage each other when the blues were coming down. So I took a *Time Out* from even thinking about *Goodbye* and over two days and nights – Saturday and Sunday – I came up with a four hander called *Off Beat* which Mary would produce – I still have the poster which reads *Off Beat Off Broadway*.

Mary played one of the leads and did very well, while a young Canadian actor, Paul Taylor Robertson was exceptional in the role of a cop who goes up on a roof to jump and finds an actor there about to do the same thing. I thought the play worked pretty well and we got one or two Off Broadway notices that were encouraging. But I hadn't been thinking *commercial* when I wrote the play – it came through my heart for Mary Tierney and we were maybe too far Off Broadway to attract the kind of people you need if the show is to go any further

Weeks turn into months as Harry Rigby and his very professional team get on with working the play into their agenda and since I am now getting a fairly regular phone call from the great producer, I sit back and let them get on with it. It's very clear that this big chance has slipped some way onto the back burner. This is par for the course when people are trying to mount a Broadway production, and though I'd like it to just get up and run, I am not beating myself up any more.

Meanwhile, Bob Harley and company – all of them really decent people – have backed off and left the field to the very successful Broadway producer.

I had mentioned their investment to Harry and their ongoing interest in things working out best for me. Harry wasn't at all interested, saying in a jocose way, 'I never produce by committee.'

My play situation now was very different to how it had been when I was having daily chats with Bob Harley and Tom Kain.

I mean, when you're dealing with somebody like Rigby you learn fast you don't ring up with 'Hi Harry, it's Lee. Just checking how things are going.'

People at Harry's level are throwing maybe six or seven productions up in the air at any given time. He is no different to all the other guys trying to get a play Up. They all go through the same motions with each possible runner, waiting for something to happen – the nudge that your play is *the most likely* – which gets it the spotlight and all the muscle that Rigby and his team can pull together.

Every other week I would get an update from the Rigby office about the possibility of this or that star about to be hired to play *Paddy*, who to my relief, was no longer to be called *Casey*.

It surprised me that Harry was looking at other actors – I thought he had settled on Maxwell Caulfield at that party on the evening Max told me Juliette would take the Clare role.

In fairness, while Harry nodded agreeably and assured me that Max was certainly capable of playing *Paddy* – 'if we have him nude in that bedroom scene with Clare – that should do wonders at the box office ' – he had never said, actually told me, he would hire him.

I had assumed Harry would use him after all that chat about box office and whatever. Not so. I would later discover that Harry didn't go for the idea that I had already met and given Max the play script way back in the Cherry Lane theatre before Alan Carr came in and whisked him off to the West Coast. As I said earlier, Harry had to be the top banana in every fold of his every production.

Ironically, I kept meeting Maxwell Caulfield in the street around Second and Third Avenue. He and his wife had an apartment there, then they were doing a play in a warehouse setting – clearly nobody was making any money on this one – and basically going for auditions with a view to getting a job to pay the rent. I liked Max a lot – we both had a lot of London under our belts and we were matey enough for a while there in Manhattan.

Meanwhile Jose was setting up his new scene in Chicago, giving me a call every week to let me know he was keeping an eye on Harry and my play and I appreciated this more than money. That this giant of the theatre could be bothered to stay in touch – but then we had been close from the first meeting – two guys that loved their mother and had never been afraid to say so.

I'm still working for the law firm of Harley&Browne, still with the five nights a week, typing up affidavits and letters and all kinds of legal stuff, even though, strictly speaking, it was illegal for me to be working in America. I was there on a visitor passport – my role as a writer allowing me to get a deal, take an advance – but to have an actual job was a total no-no. In this *illegal* respect, Manhattan was a revelation – I mean, it's no lie to say that if you pulled all the *illegals* out of the city's catering world, that huge industry would come to a complete, and I do mean complete, standstill.

As I've told you, my wife was working illegally for Eamon Doran. This very decent Irishman was also technically an illegal, since his paperwork had never been quite sorted up to this time.

Anyway, I'm typing and meeting a lot of terrific people in the law firm and I try on an almost daily basis to just leave the play on the back burner and get on with my life. Speaking of the day-to-day, I am hitting a lot of AA meetings and doing my morning study on my Science of Mind program and generally doing anything and everything I can to keep my head and my hopes together.

About now my wife returns yet again from another trip home to Ireland and we live and sleep together like a couple that's waiting for something to happen to show them what to do about their mediocre marriage.

At times I am tempted to throw the hat at it. Just pack up and go home and leave the dreams to fend for themselves. I really mean this – it was a real feeling at certain times but I would hear this inner voice saying 'you've put so much in, give it a bit more time' and I would relent and hang in there. The long wait as I called it took its toll on the marriage.

I'm not blaming Nuala but she had been at the end of the line when they were dolling out patience and tolerance. So, as you might imagine, since our latest hope seemed to have ground to a crawl, she was no fun to be around.

Harry Rigby makes time to meet me and buy me lunch and he tells me his principle money cow, a lady called Terry Allen Kramer, is off him at the moment but it won't last long. He assures me this happens every so often but he will die before he lets go of the opportunity to produce my wonderful play.

'Besides,' he assures me confidentially: 'Jose will put out a contract on me if I don't get "Goodbye" on the boards.'

When I finally get the call I've been waiting for from Harry Rigby personal assistant, Ray, I get a happy jolt of surprise. I knew then that despite all the polish and the promises, I did not think it would happen under Harry's production banner. I may be an optimist by nature but it's hard to stay up forever and ever when one thing after another goes almost all the way only to fall down at the last hurdle.

The message is we are going to start casting – the theatre has been booked in Philadelphia and that Jose Quintero passed on the message 'I can't wait to get started'.

At this point Jose gets a note from the great Colleen Dewhurst who is one of his closest friends. She of course married and divorced and married George C Scott but the word was that the lady and Jose would have been lovers had he not been gay.

So, great, they loved each other and she would do anything for him, so he was optimistic that she would want to play the role of Ma in 'Goodbye to the Hill'.

Colleen comes back gushing about the play and tells Jose that she would love to do it if I would just make it about the mother and the boy as opposed to it being about the Boy and the Mother.

This would mean that the truth of the play, the stuff that Jose had eulogised about from the moment he read it, would have to be turned on its head.

In fairness to him, he never said a bad word about Colleen but he couldn't hide being sick to his stomach that she would ask this of any playwright.

Nobody was blaming her for wanting the lead role but the idea that you can just chop a play up and fix it so that an actress will agree to do it left Jose speechless. Me too!

It goes without saying that things didn't work out with the precious Miss Colleen Dewhurst. As a result of this we lost Timothy Hutton which we expected. Anyway, I wanted Max

Caulfield to play Paddy – he had been my first choice like a hundred years ago, and I said this again to Harry Rigby when he had Nuala and me to his apartment for dinner.

This was a first, and of course, being Harry Rigby, the meal was catered for my wife and I, the great man himself, and his assistant, Ray, who spoke with a southern drawl that brought out the best in Nuala. Every time he addressed her she smiled in pleasure and wasn't shy about showing him her eyes.

During dinner Harry announced grandly, 'I am definitely doing the play, Lee.' He turned to Ray and said quietly, 'I have no choice. Both Ray and Jose think it is the best thing ever. I am almost of the same opinion. The freshness – it smells stronger each time I read it.' He nods at Ray, 'Just for tonight we'll mix business with pleasure.'

Ray opens a file by his hand and produces a contract. He passes it to me with a smile and an encouraging nod. 'It's the regular Writers Guild contract, no alterations or deletions of any kind. Would you like to take it away and read it?'

I look at Nuala and we shake our heads at the same time.

'No, I don't need to read it, thanks Ray.' I turned to Harry and raised my Perrier, 'I'm glad it's worked out, Harry. And I'm more than flattered that you want to produce my play. Thanks.'

Harry shakes my hand, rises and kisses Nuala on the face, indicates get on with it to Ray who now produces a cheque.

'Harry's customary one thousand dollar advance,' He passes it to me and I thank him.

'That's worth ten thousand...'

'A hundred,' Harry chirped in as he sat down again.

'...of anybody else's money,' Ray concluded. He raised his glass, 'To Lee and the play.'

We drank our various potions and Ray then said, 'This is the first time I have been certain it will happen under Harry's banner. And it will be beautifully produced, that I promise you.'

Hearing the truth of Ray's belief, I sighed in relief, 'I needed for this to work out,' I said, 'it's been a switchback ride.'

Next morning I get a call from Jose who is elated that Harry is definitely going with the play. As we speak, he assures me that his agent is finalising his contract with Harry to direct and he expects we can be in rehearsal in about four weeks time.

'Once Harry commits, things happen very quickly.' I can feel Jose's grin on the other end of the line and we share a few moments chat before getting on with the day.

A few days later, I'm heading for the Russian Tea Rooms to meet Harry and walk back to his office when I see Mary Tierney coming towards me. The moment I laid eyes on her I knew that something was wrong, 'Are you alright, Mary?'

'Harry Rigby died this morning.' She tells me quietly, her eyes finding more life in her concern for me.

I stand there feeling like I've been kicked in the heart, for a few moments I can't say anything.

'I'm sorry to bring you such bad news but I couldn't give it to you on the phone. It hasn't hit the papers yet.'

Mary takes my arm and we find a coffee shop. 'I ran into Joe Martin,' Molly holds a light to my cigarette and I inhale all the way down to my toes.

'When I told Joe, he said, "I guessed he must have passed away when he didn't turn up at the Russian Tea Rooms for lunch,' Mary sounded disgusted. 'Can you believe that?'

'After this, I can believe anything,' I grunted, trying to get a handle on my self-pity.

Joe Martin's sick joke was typical of Manhattan and how things resonated in the very showbiz fraternity. And I had in my time in the city laughed at some of it but I wasn't chortling in the immediate moment.

There was this thing among showbiz people – if they were in Manhattan they go to the Russian Tea Rooms for lunch. You can see them waving at each other in 'Tootsie' when Dustin Hoffman goes in there dressed up as the lady in question to fool his agent. I thought the food there was awful but nobody seemed to mind – it was the place to be seen if you were alive and kicking which, unfortunately for me, Harry Rigby no longer was.

He had died from a heart attack in his apartment, his death killing my dream of finally getting *Goodbye to the Hill* on the Broadway stage.

I felt bad about that – it just sounded like the death knell of my hopes and my dreams for the play, and the success we all thought I could enjoy when it finally got to opening night. And I felt awful about Harry dying, and apparently, dying alone, and I was sorry he was gone because he had been a terrific light and so encouraging to me.

In this mood I called Jose who was too grief stricken to do more than acknowledge my call and tell me though his tears that he would be in touch.

My next task was to get to Nuala before she heard it from somebody else.

This time she didn't hit the roof, didn't throw the head, didn't behave at all predictably. She put her arms around me right there in Doran's restaurant and she let her tears flow and didn't give me any argument when I told her quietly I was going home, that I had nothing more to invest in possibilities.

That evening we were agreed that we were going to go back home. In a few lines of dialogue we agreed we had given it all we could in Manhattan and I could admit that I had obsessed a bit in an effort to get the play on the boards. She admitted to pushing me, trying to force things, and she apologised. This was a first, and I mean a first – saying sorry wasn't something that came easily to my missus. 'It's time for us to go home together,' she said, and I nodded without speaking. It seemed right in the moment but I knew I was through hoping we would live happily ever after. I was gradually getting to the stage where I knew that the only real happiness, that feeling that you're okay was an inside job. Like, in the crunch you could only rely on yourself to get to the special place where you would no longer be a victim of the angst that life throws up just to keep you on your toes.

Out goodbyes were very casual. I'd say some of our contacts, especially Bob Harley and Tom Kain, were sorry for us on a personal level – disappointed too, that they were not going to be involved with Jose but, like me, accepting that the play was just not meant to happen at this time.

'It will though,' Bob said as though he knew it to be true, 'it will come again because it won't date. You set it in the Fifties and there it remains, so be patient, your time will come.'

On a lovely summer's day we returned to the Old House. Thanks to our neighbour-landlady, Joan Darcy it was clean and she had the old wood burning stove going well to warm the place up. I felt like crying and I could see that Nuala was close to tears. When Joan left we held onto each other and I had the feeling she was thinking something like, 'I hope we've done the right thing,' just like me.

On the kitchen table was a huge Welcome Home poster from Joan and the D'Arcy girls which made our home coming all the more emotional.

I made some coffee while Nuala went upstairs to start unpacking. I took a tray into the garden and she came and joined me at our outdoor table and we sat there smoking cigarettes and just taking in the land on its way down to the coast where the ocean was still as a muted blue painting.

It was too late for me to go planting anything in my vegetable garden, but all around us Billy Darcy's wheat and barley fields were golden in the sunshine and I got a buzz from knowing I would be there when it was harvest time.

The first couple of days we walked the half tamed paths through the forest above and up to the rim of Castletimon with the sea way down below and the patchwork texture of the East Wicklow hills at every turn of the eye.

In the evenings we eat and later talk by the open fire in our sitting room, both of us so aware of the peace, and laughing in wonder at the way we had dealt with Manhattan. Surprised almost that we had handled the massive energy and the huge noise and the fast forward movement of people all on the way to somewhere, many of them running to stand in line at Grand Central, or wherever, for their ride out of town.

'Do you think you'll really miss anything about it?' I wondered as I held a light to Nuala's cigarette.

She came back instantly with, 'Haggen Dass'.

'And the Siam Inn on Eight Avenue,' I suggested.

'How could I have left that out?' She was surprised. 'The best food I ever had, anywhere.'

She cooks dinner most days and I light a fire with wood I've cut myself and it burns good with the help of a few sods of turf. Without having to work at it, I know that these familiars are the salients of my life. I need to cut my own wood, set and light my own fire, just as I enjoy taking out the ashes in the morning because I've just been given another day. And though I've no idea what's going to happen – I have no work on hand that will earn me any immediate money – the given day seems all the richer because I am living it in Wicklow.

The first money to come through the letter box was a cheque from Irish radio for the repeat of a play of mine. A good omen, I thought, even though the fee was small.

A few weeks later I have agreed to take on the role of tutor to third level students for a Creative Writing course at a teaching academy in Dublin's Leeson Street.

As the man said *needs must when the Devil drives* so I signed up for the sixteen week course which was sponsored by a government agency called Fas. Nuala shot me an anxious look when I told her I had taken the job. 'Don't you need a degree to teach people?'

I wasn't worried, in fact I was excited by the challenge involved in facing a room of students wanting to write, and as usual, I chose to believe it would work out okay because I was me. This doesn't mean you automatically get the result you want but it does mean you don't end up in bits about any of it.

The routine worked out like this. I drove our car into Wicklow Town station and got a train that dropped me in Westland Row station for about half past eight. I walked from there up to Leeson Street, striding out, using the journey as an exercise bout. In the evening I caught a train that got me back to Wicklow around seven o'clock.

Nuala could get a lift into town to pick up our car – Joan made three and four trips a day – she would pick me up at the station in the evening. This happened Monday thru Thursday – I got a half-day on Friday – and I used both the train rides and my lunch hour at the Academy to get some writing done.

I had sixteen students, six or seven of them girls, and all of them, apparently, earning B.A degrees in one thing or another. I was soon surprised at how dim some of them were and within a few weeks I reckoned that two of them might have some sort of writing talent. Two of the girls were gorgeous and another, a young woman I hoped would make some kind of novelist, was a lady I could have been interested in during another lifetime.

It was hard work to hold the attention of most of the class. Some of them were into drugs and it showed, others were in some sort of emotional angst and all in all, their work was pretty dismal. One quirky little guy from Galway had genuine ability but he wasn't gifted in the listening department, reminding me of myself when I was his age. I helped him get a half hour radio play produced by RTE – Irish Radio – it had taken a lot of work, some of which I provided, but he deserved his shot, the play was good, and I was glad to have served as his tutor. I thought he could make a sound of some kind if he worked hard and learned to listen to others.

About halfway through the course Nuala said to me one evening as we sat down to dinner, 'Be great if you could get that job permanently.'

She'd had a few months of being back in Wicklow and had returned to her wont of walking around the garden, tending and picking flowers, baking bread and conjuring up fine meals. She was also into driving into the town to have mid morning coffee with a wealthy friend of ours, like a well-off middle class woman who never had to think about where the next few pound notes were coming from.

Since she was in good health and had many abilities with which to earn a good living, I'd been expecting her to take a job once she had got settled in again at the Old House.

Her eyes opened and she looked startled when she saw what her last remark had done to my demeanour. 'What?' she said disingenuously, 'what have I said?'

I told her without frills that if I thought I would have to do the tutoring job for the rest of my life I would slit my wrists. 'That you could even think of it amazes me. You knew what I was when we got it together. I never kidded you. I was and remain some kind of scribbler, and if you seriously wish I'm ever going to have a steady job, tell me out straight and we will part company with no hard feelings.'

She was stunned enough that I had the freedom to go on, 'Like, if you imagine for one second, that you are going to wear your floppy hat and spend summers cutting fucking flowers and winters reading novels by the fire while I take a fucking train out of Wicklow in the dark for six months of the year and come home in the dark of an evening, you are out of your fucking mind. So think about it, think about what you really want, and you are entitled to say what you want, you'll get no hardship from me for that, but you must allow the same freedom to me. This job ends on my birthday four days before Christmas and it is over and out for me. So you take a few days, make up your mind. Times in Manhattan I thought we would split. This may be the time, I don't know and right now I'm not pushing for that, but hear me – if we're going to be together, you'd want to start thinking about taking a job. I've no guarantee what the earnings are going to be like, and you know that.'

I got a commission a few weeks later from the Dublin Youth Theatre, when a director there, Eilish Dillon, came and asked me would I write a play concerning the house in which the young people worked to learn their trade as actors and designers, producers and directors.

The very idea of writing anything about this lovely Georgian terraced house in Upper Gardiner Street in Dublin was a turn-on to me and I came up with a play called Charades. It was a very simple story about a brother and sister living together in the family home. They turn into various other characters including their parents, so that through their brief encounters we get a taste of the life as lived by this family within the hearing walls of the home.

The house had been totally refurbished right down to the last detail so that it was as it had been when it was first built all those years before.

Since our audience had to sit in the living room along with the characters we could only seat twenty-five people for each show and it was incredible how closely the customers related to the goings on of the family.

This includes a game of charades which becomes far too revealing and the cost of the schism - Catholic mother, Protestant father, the children following suit – visits on this New Years Eve.

During the banter and the fun and the angst, there is a build-up to the party that will start to happen just before midnight, this being the last day of the nineteenth century.

At the interval, the audience are taken downstairs to the long double drawing room and are fed hot pies and handed toddies and glasses of wine, while all are waiting for their invited guests, artistes from the Music Hall to come and bring in the New Year with the family.

The artistes arrive and the party pieces begin to be played

out. The audience, sitting on the floor are also at the party and then at the right moment, the bells of the nearby church toll out the welcome to the year 1900, this Sound effect supplied by a tape recorder sitting on the rear windowsill of the drawing room.

The audience join with the actors and David Nowlan from the *Irish Times* and all sing together Auld Lang Syne. So that, if only for a little while, the schism in the family is seen for what it is, an idea that has no place in those precious moments of New Year.

For me it was momentous and I felt flattered that the DYT had chosen me to write the script which was brilliantly directed by Eilish Dillon. It had to be a good show because David Nowlan, who never cared for my work, gave it what, by his standards, was a good review. Amen.

Not that long afterwards I ended my stint as tutor of the Creative Writing class and my boss gave me a cash bonus because I had turned up for work every day. 'I couldn't believe it,' he said frankly, 'thought I might see you twice a week or what. You were great and I thank you for your example to the students.'

As I walked down to get the train home to Wicklow, I was smiling at the generosity of my students who had clubbed together to buy me a woollen sweater to die for. I felt doubly grateful for the gift because it meant I had reached them in some way, which meant everything.

They had also given me a card which declared 'Happy Birthday Lee' and as I read it in their presence before we parted for all time, I did well to hold onto my tears.

On the train going down home, I knew that by the time Christmas was over, I would be into writing a book. This might have to be a part time thing since I needed to go on earning some kind of money to keep the home fires burning.

When Nuala was driving me home from the train she said casually, 'By the way, I start work on the first of January. I'll be back in the sales game but I won't be staying away overnight. Is that OK with you?'

'Sure,' I said, striving not to qualify any word I had laid on her during my outburst about her playing Lady Muck.

As the New Year began, I was pondering all the ideas that were floating around about what might have been if this had happened and that other thing hadn't happened, all of it the kind of guff nobody needs.

I used the sense of touch to come into the present moment and I knew for sure that I was okay about being fifty-years-old. I knew too that while I didn't expect any miracles just because I was me, I did expect to be alive and well come next Christmas. This seemed to signify that I believed I'd have all I needed in the year ahead. And I asked myself *when did you ever need any more than that?*

The only answer I got was silence.

To Be Continued

Also published by Killynon House Books

PRAISE FOR LEE DUNNE'S PADDY MAGUIRE IS DEAD

The most detailed and horrifying expose of alcoholism written in this country. Amazingly, Dunne now holds the honour of being the most banned author in Europe.
Sunday Independent

In any other country, it would be regarded as didactic. Here it is branded as "indecent and/or obscene" because it reveals exactly and honestly what it is really like to be an alcoholic
John Broderick, Hibernia

ISBN: 1905706022

Also published by Killynon House Books

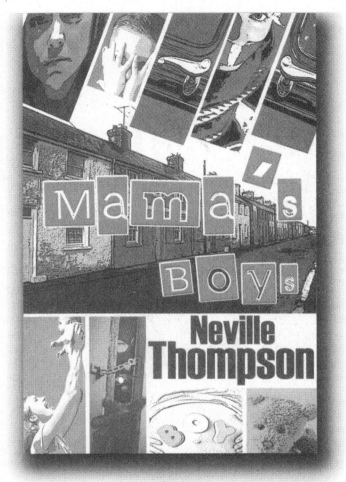

PRAISE FOR NEVILLE THOMPSON

The dialogue snaps and crackles with black humour
Evening Herald

Realism so gritty it's like the concrete of Ballyfermot between your teeth.
RTE Guide

Strong cinematic characteristics with definite shades of Tarantino.
U Magazine

ISBN: 1905706030

Also published by Killynon House Books

Three times nominee for the Nobel Peace Prize
Shay Cullen
Passion and Power
The emotional journey of an Irish Missionary Priest

"Father Shay is a very powerfull inspiration"
- Martin Sheen

"Father Shay is a very powerfull inspiration"
- Martin Sheen

Fr. Shay Cullen is an Irish Columban Missionary who has been nominated three times for the Nobel Peace Prize. In his own words, he describes how he set out to free children and women from dehumanizing and slave-like conditions in the Philippines. He also led a campaign to successfully close the US bases and championed child protection laws and pioneered poverty alleviation through Fair Trade . Fr Shay is a founding member of PREDA (People's Recovery Empowerment Development Assistance Foundation), which is an internationally know organisation.

Available from November 2006

ISBN: 1-905706-05-7